COMMON GROUND IN A LIQUID CITY

Essays in Defense of an Urban Future

•••

By Matt Hern

AK PRESS PUBLISHING & DISTRIBUTION

Common Ground in a Liquid City:
Essays in Defense of an Urban Future
By Matt Hern

ISBN 13: 978-1849350105
Library of Congress Control Number: 2009940727

AK Press
674-A 23rd Street
Oakland, CA 94612
USA
www.akpress.org
akpress@akpress.org

AK Press UK
PO Box 12766
Edinburgh EH8 9YE
Scotland
www.akuk.com
ak@akdin.demon.co.uk

The above addresses would be delighted to provide you with the latest AK Press distribution catalog, which features several thousand books, pamphlets, zines, audio and video recordings, and gear, all published or distributed by AK Press. Alternately, visit our websites to browse the catalog and find out the latest news from the world of anarchist publishing:
www.akpress.org | www.akuk.com
revolutionbythebook.akpress.org

Printed in Canada on 100% recycled, acid-free paper with union labor.

Cover design by John Yates | www.stealworks.com
Interior by Kate Khatib | www.manifestor.org/design

Table of Contents

For Sale
604 662 3000
SOLD
• Redevelopment Site
• Contact Agent for Details
David Ho
CBRE

Acknowledgements

I owe much gratitude to the good folks at AK Press, especially Kate Khatib, who have made this book happen and been so generous in their support. Chuck Morse was a terrific editor, again, and his friendship, articulate incisiveness, and brains were vital. Their enthusiasm for this project has been so appreciated.

Parts of this book have appeared in other publications in article form. Much thanks to *re:place*, the *Vancouver Review* (twice), the *Review of Education Pedagogy and Curriculum Studies*, the *Defenestrator*, and *Rain* for running pieces, editing them well, and helping me think through my ideas.

There are many people in each of the places that I write from—pals, collaborators, schemers—who were kind and hospitable to me this time round, hosting me while I was writing these chapters: Stavros, Fani, Kristos, Kostas, Elizabeth, Eylem, Emre, Tayfun, other Eylem, Metin, Yasin, Tuna, Barbara, Gabe, Ivan, Janet, Muriel, Frank, Lawrence, Ron, Dolly, Michel, Pastor Lance, all the Fort Good Hope kids who showed us what was what, Mark D., Terrance, Scott, Adelphi, Zoobomb, Ayten, Gaye, Ceren, Mariana, everybody at Kamer, Dirk, Shaveen, Richard, Brooke, Danno, Katrin, Amanda, John … and many, many more. Really, there are so many generous folks who have housed and cooked for me, shared drinks and meals, introduced me to friends, answered my questions and showed me around. Very literally this book would not have been possible with out you guys—I hope you hear some of yourselves in here.

Over the past three years I have interviewed something like seventy or eighty people here in Vancouver, trying to figure out what I wanted to say. It involved a lot of tea, coffee, beer, and bourbon, and a lot of people being real patient with my questions. There are a couple dozen folks whom I ended up quoting at length in here and I am so grateful to all of them—but also to the many, many folks who took time to talk to me but didn't end up in the book. I remain totally in all their debt and I look forward to hearing what you all think of this.

And, despite all those interviews, I still feel slightly embarrassed about all the people I really should have talked to but just didn't. If you're not in here but should be, please accept my humble apologies. There are a lot of you.

Huge thanks are due to Diana Hart for stepping up and taking these great photos (with support from Sarah Lum). Others who contributed pictures: Selena Couture, Barbara Trottier, Billy Collins, Mark Douglas, and Amanda Marchand.

Of course, much love to my Island family: Adele, Riley, Gan, Sean, Kelly, Kyra, Sam, David, Thirell, Riley and Fraser, Michele, Dave, Bronwyn, and Sean. Finally, and more than anything, this book is something like a love letter to East Van and my family here: Selena, Sadie and Daisy, Diana, Sarah and Mica, Ashley, Keith, OZAM, Stu, Pennie and Hamish, Goo, Mark and Levi, the gone but hardly forgotten Dan, Sarah and Layla, the whole Thistle and CFVD crews, our good neighbors, and all the lovely friends who make this our home.

Our tools are better than we are, and grow better faster than we do. They suffice to crack the atom, to command the tides. But they do not suffice for the oldest task in human history: to live on a piece of land without spoiling it.

—Aldo Leopold

EAST VANCOUVER, BRITISH COLUMBIA

PHOTO BY DIANA HART

HOMEBOY

East Vancouver, British Columbia

It's funny how people tend to describe Canada: fish, timber, prairies, empty beaches, crashing waves, lonely farmers, isolated small towns. That picture is a romantically attractive one but distorting. The reality is that Canada is an urban country. More than eighty percent of Canada's population lives in urban centers, half the country lives in Vancouver, Montreal, or southern Ontario, and virtually all the population is crowded tightly along the border.

That's a good thing. With a world population closing in on seven billion and not expected to stabilize until nine or ten billion, people are increasingly concentrating in cities all over the world. And thank goodness for that.

The only chance the world has for an ecological future is for the vast bulk of us to live in cities. If we want to preserve what's still left of the natural world, we need to stop using so much of it. We need to start sharing the resources and land bases we do have, to stop spreading out so much, and focus our transportation and energy resources carefully. It may sound counter-intuitive, but there can be no doubt that an ecological future has to be organized around cities—which kind of ironically is also our only route to protecting our non-urban areas. If we love and want to protect our small towns, rural, and farming areas then we had better start living compactly, stop sprawling all over them, and turning all of it into one faceless, concrete mess. That's the first core contention of this book.

The second is that cities have to be made solid. In a liquid era when people, goods, and capital are sloshing all over the globe we have to turn cities into comprehensible places that everyday people can actively inhabit. Vancouver has a particularly liquid quality and not just because I'm being metaphorically cute, but because so many people and so much capital wants to flow through the city. I'm fully in favor of migration and mobility but I'm searching for the kinds of attachments that turn "urban areas" into *cities* and "urban space" into common places.

I'm not interested in turning cities into villages or collections of villages—I think that's exactly the wrong way to imagine a city—but cities need to be full of solid, distinct, and comprehensible places. You can have the magic and possibilities of a city while building it around local vitality, self-governance, and neighborhoods. Those things are not antagonistic.

The third core contention this book is that city-building leadership cannot fall to experts, bureaucrats, or planners. People have to make cities by accretion: bit-by-bit, rejecting master plans, and letting the place unfold. Whether it's our safety, governance, or urban planning, it's everyday people who can make the best decisions. But for this to be possible, cities need engaged citizens: people who are willing and able to participate in common life—and governance structures that actively encourage them.

In lots of ways what I am calling for has to be an unambiguous leap: a straight-up call for a city organized for a very different kind of social milieu, rooted in an alternative vision of ethics and economic life. It is a vision that will require a certain amount of work, creativity, and antagonism, one that just won't accept neo-liberalism or global capitalism as de facto arbiters of who gets access to the good life. But it's up to us to contest and offer alternatives to the market as the allocator of land, housing, and resources in our society. I think there are clear routes to a better future, lots of them existing, some latent, and parts we are just going to have to make up.

•••

When urbanists all over the world talk about what a good city should look like an increasing number of them want to talk about Vancouver. This place routinely tops "most liveable city" lists and is widely admired all over the globe but, as my friend Marcus once said after reading the *Economist's* "Liveable Cities" list, "Vancouver? Geneva? Vienna? Why are world's 'most liveable' cities the world's most boring cities? It's like a list of the dullest cities in the world." And he's right. Those lists are inevitably put together by businesses like *Mercer* or *MasterCard*, whose ideological agendas, aesthetic sensibilities and cultural predilections are decidedly suspect.

I live here for lots of good reasons, and there are many things about Vancouver, especially East Vancouver, that I really admire but there is a whole lot to critique too. This is no urban utopia and being smug about our successes doesn't help. But I do think that Vancouver has a chance—because of its locale, its wealth, its climate, and its youth—to transform itself into the kind of city that supports, not plunders, the social and natural worlds.

There is surprisingly little written about Vancouver beyond guidebooks and some very good historical writing, which is part of my motivation here. I'm hoping to contribute to the literature about a city that is very dear to my heart, and one that is increasingly important to global conversations about what a good city could and should look like. Even more than that, I am writing about Vancouver because we have to think imaginatively about how to live together in cities. Mostly though, I want to talk about Vancouver because it's my home.

East Vancouver flavors all of these stories for sure. I don't have an East Van cross[1] tattooed on me, but I might as well have one, and I might still get it done. I am all bound up with my neighborhood, and I am occasionally ambivalent or straight up antagonistic (and sometimes kind of embarrassingly xenophobic, actually) about other parts of the city. But that's not all of it and at least partially affectation. There is plenty about Vancouver that genuinely pisses me off, but I love it here.

So, that's this book: considering and evaluating contemporary urbanism using Vancouver as a kind of Petri dish, as a place full of possibility, to think radically and realistically about what a viable and libratory city might look like. Following are nine separate chapters, each written from another part of the world that considers a particular aspect of cities and Vancouver specifically. The chapters bleed into one another significantly, but each stands on its own and it should work to read individual essays out of order. At the same time, there is a flow, so the book (with any luck) is a coherent argument for a new kind of urbanism and better city.

•••

I have traveled quite a bit over the past couple of decades and I have noticed that I always tend to think more clearly about cities in general and Vancouver specifically when I'm somewhere else. I'd guess that it is a fairly common experience. You know the feeling: walking around another city and wondering how it has developed, admiring a street, comparing neighborhoods, trying to make sense of certain designs, and thinking about back home.

These essays are drawn together by East Van, but also by my politics and by my visceral understanding of what a good city feels like. I spent one of the great years of my life, just before I moved here, in New York City living on the Lower Eastside, and when I think of what a city should look like my mind often turns to NYC first. But I also think of Istanbul, Montreal, Miami, and parts of many more. Generally speaking, I am in favor of unpredictability, serendipity, messiness, and walkable, dense cities with their histories visible. I am in favor of vernacular and organic planning, an absolute minimum of car traffic, small neighborhoods, street life, street vendors, street music, and street food. I want a self-governed city that can rise beyond disciplinary institutions and governmentality—a city run by citizens, not experts.

It's more than that, though, and let's not be too polite about it: the vast bulk of contemporary cities are built primarily by and for greed. When I think of a great city, it definitely doesn't include huge numbers of very poor, disenfranchised and/or homeless folks. But what city can you think of that doesn't include a grotesquerie of poverty? Havana maybe? I've never been there, and I've never been in a city that doesn't have way, way too many really poor folks.

When I am dreaming of an egalitarian city, I'm not imagining a place where everyone has exactly the same amount of money or privilege. But I'm definitely dreaming of a city that actively undermines inequity, one that doesn't reify massive capital accumulation, doesn't allow some people to get fantastically rich on the backs of others. We have to believe in the possibility of a city where the wealthiest only earn and control a small amount more than what the poorest citizens do—not scores and hundreds of times like they do now. The gap between rich and poor has to be kept as absolutely minimal as possible or the fabric of citizenship that binds a city together becomes a facade that can only be maintained with police control.

Right now the wealth gap in Canada generally[2] and Vancouver specifically is enormous. In this city "the bottom 10 percent had an average income of $8,700 and the top 10 percent had $205,200 on average. The lowest 10 percent therefore had one dollar to every $23.50 the highest ten percent had"[3] and, in 2006, 19 percent of the city was living in poverty.[4] The most obvious place to witness this is on Hastings Street, maybe at the corner of Cambie. Look east and you can see the poorest urban area in Canada, the Downtown Eastside: people all over the streets, shooting up openly, huge lines in front of soup kitchens, lots of people running very low on hope. Turn 180 degrees and look west up Hastings and you see gleaming towers, parking lots full of expensive cars, million-dollar, one-bedroom apartments, streets full of hedge-funders, and lots of people running very low on ethics.

This kind of incredible disparity is one of the features of what Manual Castells, Saskia Sassen, and others have called the new "Dual City," an urban formation precipitated by the new, globalized information economies. Cities have always had different

COZY APARTMENTS
GENERAL MOTORS PLACE

REACH
Community Health Centre

classes living in relative proximity, but in neo-liberal informational economies something more akin to two entirely separate categories emerge. One is composed of people who are hooked into what Castells calls the "space of flows," new digitally-based ways of living and generating employment and capital, free-flowing around local constraints and able to move with the same liquidity as their investment portfolios.

At the same time, there is another economic category of people who are stuck in a Castellsian "space of places," who do not have the knowledge or skills to profit from digital economics, and these folks are increasingly shut out of the opportunities that neo-liberalism provides. Traditional class formulations have always assumed a certain amount of mobility, that is there is always an opportunity (however slim) for people to move up (or down) the class ladder. In the dual city however, there are separate worlds living right beside each other, occupying the same space but living in isolated realities.

Right now, Vancouver exhibits all the classic signs of developing into a dual city—a housing affordability crisis festering beside endless condos that no one we know can reasonably afford, people carrying huge amounts of debt, highways packed with people driving because they have to travel an hour from where they work, developers propelling city policy. We need to actively resist this kind of city: we need new strategies and the political will to alter the trajectory that is creating one city for the very liquid rich and another for everyone else. But poverty is not an accident: The very rich and the poor have a contingent relationship. Our way of life demands serious inequality.

Talking about resisting inequality often makes people think of a very tightly controlled, uptight city, a city where overbearing governments restrict and tax people aggressively in the name of providing services and amenities. I think it is a mythology that a city striving toward egalitarianism must be an excessively regulated, boring city. It's just not true that a vibrant, living city is necessarily one where the market is god and capital accumulation is what drives innovation and culture. Why can't cities restrict unfettered greed in favor of local culture? Why can't we have a funky city without rolling over and showing our soft bellies to the market?

•••

I think the real issue is how to create an organic, unfolding city—what Christopher Alexander calls a living city; one that isn't run by bureaucratic planning or rampaging developers but is allowed to unfold, driven by a million decisions made by people on the ground. A city should be the best of humanity: an ethical union of citizens drawn together by mutual aid and shared resources. I know that sounds a little flaky but think of libraries, parks, public transit, movie theaters, patios, coffees shops, bars, beaches, plazas, festivals—everything that makes a city great. All of that is about sharing resources so we don't have to be walled off by ourselves buying and hoarding our own books and DVDs, hiking on our own property, drinking by ourselves, driving our own cars, isolated, and atomized.

And that sharing means public space or, better yet, *common space*. And that's my definition of urban vitality: constantly running into people who aren't like you, who don't think, look, or act like you, people who have fundamentally different values and backgrounds. And in that mix there is always the possibility to reimagine and remake yourself—a world of possibility that is driven by public life and space, that at its best turns into common places and neighborhoods. That's what makes a great city, not the shopping opportunities.

It's more than that too. Cities are the key to any ecologically sustainable future, a reality that most environmentalists are just coming around to. There's just no way seven billion people can spread out across the globe. Living densely, shortening the distances we have to travel, reducing our physical footprint, sharing resources, sharing energy is the only way that this thing is possibly going to work ecologically. To make that happen this city—and cities in general—have to become *more* urban, not less.

Looking at cities all over the world today though, it's pretty fucking hard to imagine them as radical generators of sustainability, diversity, and vitality. Globalization, colonialism, and corporate expansionism have rendered the cores of most cities virtually indistinguishable from one another. Downtowns everywhere have the same Mickey Ds and Burger Kings, the same Gap, Prada, Benetton, and Zaras, the same gleaming towers, the same parking lots, the same rhythms.

And it's not just downtowns. The Western world's rush for the suburbs is being replicated all over the globe as urban regions are reconfigured for massive private-car use. Cities are being replaced by massive, megalopolitan stretches of faceless urbanization where it's impossible to tell where one place ends and the next starts and traditional cities are surrounded by endless expanses of freeways, movie multiplexes, Wal-Marts, industrial parks, gated communities, malls, mini-malls, and mega-malls.

But you know all this.

The point of these essays is to give Vancouver and our conceptions of the urban future a hard shot in another direction. Even in the face of the Olympics, the Gateway Project, and an increasingly brazen corporate governance structure—I think we have still have a real chance to remake this city using some compelling, radical urban traditions and examples.

But that [illegible] is going to require commitment and discipline. Right now Vancouver, like so many other cities, has imagined itself almost entirely as a vehicle for capital accumulation. The city continues to pour its resources and energy into attracting investment, courting high-end tourists, building infrastructure for developers and international trade and doing anything and everything to pimp ourselves out to the highest bidders. But that strategy is unsustainable by definition.

I'm not much for futurism and Nostradamus, the Aztecs and Tupac notwithstanding; almost all predictions for the future tend to look pretty foolish. That said, I feel very confident suggesting that an economy based on massive and constant supplies of fossil fuels, huge infusions of capital, and a world-view based on the perpetual growth of consumerism is a losing proposition. We have to reject that juvenile economic and cultural logic and build meaningful ways to live on this land without destroying it. That has to mean reimagining this city as self-reliant and constructing a thoughtful re-localization of pretty much everything. That's not to confuse re-localizing with parochialism, but it is true that it will mean a constriction of the economy. To my mind, that offers up huge possibilities for alleviating inequity: The logic of neo-liberal growth is what has got us into this spot, and it's not getting us out. It's high time to act on the old "another world is possible" line.

Every city always has the opportunity to re-image itself, and these essays are reflections on what a *good city* could look like, what *this* city might look like: trying to articulate what an emerging, democratic, and living city might look and feel like.

•••

An ecological and an ethical city is one and the same thing—we can't have a "green" city without reimagining our social institutions. And that can't be made to happen by relying on politicians or planners or developers. They can't lead, they have to get out of the way and allow the neighborhoods, communities, public spaces, and common spaces that make a great city to become the ongoing expression of a constant series of choices made by everyday citizens.

That's what holds these essays together. They are written from disparate places, thinking about Vancouver as an exploration of how to make this place more alive, more democratic, more participatory, and more egalitarian. These cities are enigmatically chosen and are hardly representative of global urbanism—there is nothing from Africa, Latin America, South or East Asia, for example: they are just places I happened to be for a variety of reasons. I am not trying to say much about these other cities—I don't know enough about any of these places—but I am using them as a route to talk about Vancouver and our collective urban future.

Lots of the book is critical of Vancouver while much is laudatory and supportive. Some chapters have very clear and specific policy suggestions; other areas are a little more theoretical. I spent almost three years meeting with most anyone who would sit down and talk with me about the future of this city. Most are people I really admire, many I consider friends, others are probably less than fond of me, others are people I had never met before, some are people who have an important role in shaping the city but whom I may not agree with on all that much.

All of it adds up to an investigation into how Vancouver—and cities in general—can imagine themselves beyond greed, shopping, capital accumulation, and vulgar self-interest. This city has every opportunity to re-imagine itself as an ethical, ecological place that nurtures a generous and vibrant citizenry that can afford to live here. We have every capacity to start building that city right now.

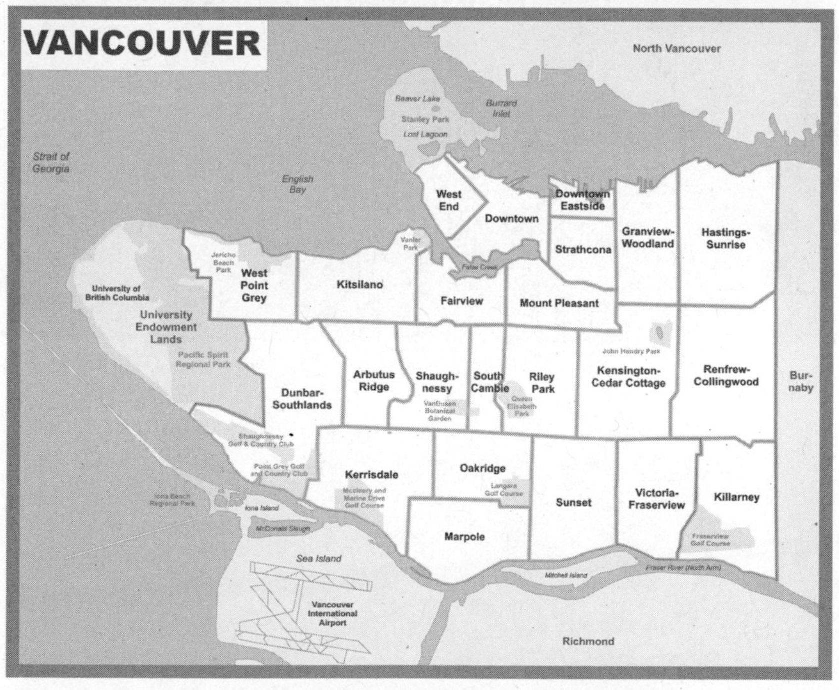
VANCOUVER
North Vancouver
Beaver Lake
Burrard Inlet
Stanley Park
Lost Lagoon
Strait of Georgia
English Bay
West End
Downtown
Downtown Eastside
Granview-Woodland
Hastings-Sunrise
Strathcona
Vanier Park
Jericho Beach Park
West Point Grey
Kitsilano
False Creek
Fairview
Mount Pleasant
University of British Columbia
University Endowment Lands
Pacific Spirit Regional Park
John Hendry Park
Dunbar-Southlands
Arbutus Ridge
Shaugh-nessy
South Cambie
Riley Park
Kensington-Cedar Cottage
Renfrew-Collingwood
Bur-naby
VanDusen Botanical Garden
Queen Elizabeth Park
Shaughnessy Golf & Country Club
Point Grey Golf and Country Club
Kerrisdale
Oakridge
Langara Golf Course
Sunset
Victoria-Fraserview
Killarney
McCleery and Marine Drive Golf Course
Iona Beach Regional Park
Iona Island
McDonald Slough
Marpole
Fraserview Golf Course
Sea Island
Mitchell Island
Fraser River (North Arm)
Vancouver International Airport
Richmond

THESSALONIKI, GREECE

PHOTO BY SELENA COUTURE

KEEPING IT REAL

Thessaloniki, Greece

I'm walking down the hill from the Old Town with Kristos, Stavros, and Kostas. We're looking for a bar that is somewhere downtown, near the water. We pass a smallish city block that is lazily fenced off, dropping down into what looks like a construction site. I stop and look down. There are a few brick piles of rubble, a few half-built walls here and there, a short dirt road winding around, some more fencing that seems to be fencing off nothing, a truck, and not much else. I ask what it is. The boys look at each other, "Just some Roman ruins."

I look around more closely and come across a little wooden box zap-strapped to a chain-link fence. The box holds pamphlets describing the area as the remains of a Roman agora, built in the fourth century. What the hell? There is almost no fanfare, no promotion, just a cheap fence and a box of damp brochures. There is virtually nothing to prevent people from wandering down there. Cars are parked densely right up against the fence, roads jammed in tight on all four sides, just short of obvious disrespect for these historic ruins.

It's kind of staggering for me, coming from the city of Vancouver where history is presumed to have started in the 1870s. Aren't these the kind of monuments people travel across the world to gape at?

The guys who brought me here are anarchists and social ecologists, so they are appropriately sneering at the remains of empire, and I'm good with that, but c'mon, these are freaking *Roman ruins.* Shouldn't they be celebrated a least a little? Shouldn't there be a big sign up, a tour guide, a kiosk to sell tickets, and audio tour headsets for rent? We have historical markers around Vancouver for shit that happened in the 1950s.

•••

I try to engage my friends on this point. I tell them that in Canada we learn extensively about Greek and Roman cultures in grade school and that people know vastly more about Athenian history than local history. Pretty much everyone I know has a sophisticated understanding of ancient Greek myths but knows virtually nothing of local Native mythology, myself included. Stavros looks at me and shrugs.

There are a few mitigating factors. West Coast indigenous cultures didn't really build in stone or cement and Vancouver's relentless climate and precipitation doesn't let wood structures last long. North American First Nations have also never been written cultures, relying dominantly on oral traditions, leaving more discrete historical trails. Still, though, the lack of knowledge and the lack of interest in preservation of the history of this region are pronounced: Vancouverites know virtually nothing of the history of this place beyond 150 years ago and for the most part do not care much.

There are some grasping attempts at honoring the past here but they tend to come off as reflexive and obligatory. Check out the official tourism Vancouver website (tourismvancouver.com): it takes a little hunting around, but there is a page over in the "About Vancouver" section called "Vancouver's History." There is a paragraph about 16,000–11,000 BCE talking about Native people arriving and settling here, including nuggets like "*And they liked the forests teeming with wildlife*" (I didn't make that up). Then the story leaps forward twelve-and-a-half thousand years to 1592–1774, when Spaniards start dropping by. The website then carefully documents each critical step of the establishment of the city from Captain Vancouver's arrival through Gassy Jack to the Canadian Pacific Railway to the opening of the first shopping mall to the opening of the Ford Centre to the first polar bear swim. Natives are not mentioned after the opening paragraph.

By comparison, the first thing that jumps out on any of the major Thessaloniki websites is that the city was founded in 315 BCE by Cassander, King of Macedonia, and was named after his wife, Thessalonike, Alexander the Great's sister. In 50 CE Paul first spoke of Christianity there, Demetrios was martyred in the city in 303 CE becoming the patron saint of the city, and Salonica (as it was then called) was the second most important Byzantine city after Constantinople. I knew all this after like fifteen minutes of the most vapid kind of browsing. Virtually all of the tourist material about the city prominently features old city walls, the White Tower, ancient churches, Roman baths, and markets. You think about Thessaloniki and you just have to think about its past, both near and very far.

Kostas is patient while I try to articulate this difference. He makes it clear that others are welcome to celebrate these ruins, but for him they are just a reminder of an imperial past that has long since passed, a history that is as much a burden as a source of pride. Thessaloniki is a city where the weight of the past is everywhere: spend half a day wandering the city core and without trying you will bump into at least a score of major historical sites. You couldn't avoid the past if you tried.

The best book I know of on the city is called *Salonica: City of Ghosts.* Mark Mazower writes:

> [Thessaloniki] is a densely thriving human settlement whose urban character has never been in question, a city whose history reached forward from classical antiquity uninterruptedly through the intervening centuries to our own time.[5]

But Mazower also makes clear that Salonica has gone through some catastrophic upheavals through the centuries. From the falls of the Roman, Byzantine, and Ottoman empires to the forced relocations of Muslims to Turkey in 1923 and the Jews to Auschwitz in WWII, the city has seen a long stream of bloodshed.

> Can one shape an account of this city's past which manages to reconcile the continuities in its shape and fabric with the radical discontinuities—the deportations, evictions, forced resettlements, and genocide—which it has also experienced? Nearly a century ago, a local historian attempted this: at a time when Salonica's ultimate fate was uncertain, the city struck him as a "museum of idioms, of disparate cultures and religions." Since then what he called its "hybrid spirit" has been severely battered by two world wars and everything they brought with them. I think it worth trying again.[6]

It strikes me that that is exactly the project Vancouver needs to undertake: to collectively describe its past in a way that does not laminate or soft-sell genocide, but effects a creative reconciliation with the collection of stories that make up the city's history, especially the substantially ignored indigenous history of this place. Once we learn to acknowledge and speak about this territory's roots and memory, maybe we will be able to shape a hybrid urban identity in a place where those "radical discontinuities" have been vastly more prevalent than any continuities.

Maybe the best historian of British Columbia is the geographer Cole Harris, who wrote in *The Resettlement of British Columbia*:

> [This is] an immigrant society [that] has hardly come to terms with where it is in the world, this Pacific corner of North America that just over 200 years ago no outsiders knew anything about, and that

since has become a crossroad of colonialism and the modern world. Brought into outside focus so recently and then changed so rapidly, it is not an easy place to know.

In these circumstances, immigrant British Columbians fall back on simple categories of knowing and the exclusions they entail. They assume that British Columbia was wilderness and that they are the bearers of civilization. Living within this imaginative geography, they associate colonialism with other places and other lives—a racially segregated South Africa, Joseph Conrad's fear-ridden Congo—where they can easily condemn its brutalities, yet are largely oblivious to its effects here. They turn the Fraser Canyon into a gold rush trail, a place where rugged land and sturdy miners met; a gondola gives them scenery and a touch of "gold pan Pete." The equation is simple and powerful, but leaves out thousands of human years and lives. The Fraser Canyon was not empty when miners arrived; it had as dense an early-contact, non-agricultural population as anywhere in the Western Hemisphere. The ancestors of these people had been there for thousands of years.[7]

Vancouver's official and vernacular disinterest in its past has a whole different tone than Salonica's: Likely a colonialist requisite, there is some kind of quasi-psychological reflex to rewrite the memory of a place and deny that there was ever anything else of real importance here. Vancouver wants to relentlessly look forward, ignoring what was once here even while the ancestors of conquest are still all around us.

What city isn't built on slaughter? Even though ours is so recent, there has to be a way to speak of fractured continuities, constant change, and an emerging city. In a lot of ways, Vancouver's signature naïve energy and headlong optimism is attractive. It's energizing to live in a place that believes that its best days are ahead of it, and I certainly feel and revel in that. But without reconciling with the real history of this place and developing a genuine understanding of what we are building on—and who we are standing beside—that optimism and energy is going to be facile and hollow.

I'm not interested in a sentimental approach to all of this. All culture involves forgetting and suppression, and sometimes (maybe even often) it is an excellent idea. It is a good thing, for instance, that the Confederate flag is not flying from the state house in Georgia. The issue is: who is remembering what, in what ways, and why? If we are going to build a real city, we have to get our ideas about our place—both within history and the natural world—clarified. Right now, the dominant narratives about both are pretty weird.

•••

These dislocations were particularly naked in conversations that took place after a powerful windstorm ripped through the city and tore the shit out of Stanley Park in December 2006. There was massive damage to the park: the wind virtually clear cutting huge swaths, knocking down thousands of trees, caving in long sections of the seawall, and setting off landslides.

The damage really was remarkable and humbling, but the outrage was equally colossal. Vancouver's genteel public was horrified that the "crown jewel of the city," our "heart and soul" could be so tarnished. A keen lament for the park echoed throughout the media, bathed in dismay that "Mother Nature" could be so capricious and unfair. Massive funds were immediately established; schools groups and volunteers scrambled over themselves to help clean up. It was estimated that $9 million was needed for "first-level restoration," and solemn promises were made to restore the park to its "original" state.

But of course neither the Vancouver nor the touristic public has any interest at all in seeing the park in its "original" state, and much less interest in its state of indigenous habitation. What is being "restored" is a simulacrum of a natural state, a clean and tidy version of "nature" that doesn't include fallen-down trees, collapsed roadways, reduced access, messy windstorms, or any lack of bathrooms or cappuccino stands.

Cleanup will take at least a year, according to head groundskeeper Dennis Dooley, who is leading the crew clearing the roads and trails through the park. The trails that crisscross the park are impassable.

About 20 percent of the park's trees were wiped out, Dooley said, damage that will take "generations" to heal.

"For the first couple of days the staff were devastated; a lot of them were just walking around with tears in their eyes," he said.[8]

I'm sure that's all true, and the deep feelings people have for the trees and the park in general are kind of touching, but there's something profoundly obnoxious about claiming the park will take "generations to heal." The suggestion that anyone has any interest in the park returning to anything like its "natural state" (whatever that might be) is absurd: Stanley Park is as much a construction as the concrete and glass buildings downtown.

In the fall of 2008, the Vancouver Museum opened a terrific exhibit exploring our paradoxical notions of the park called The Unnatural History of Stanley Park. I was impressed (in no small part because its sentiments echoed much of my previous writing) and talked to its curator, Joan Seidl.

> When I arrived at the Vancouver Museum in 1992, there was a proposal on the table to do an exhibit called Stanley Park: A Love Affair. I did not want to do that exhibit. Of course we love Stanley Park; who would dispute that? But I am more interested in exploring the degree to which the park has been shaped by people. We've had our hands all over that park. We expound lovely rhetoric about the park as primeval and ancient, but meanwhile we are tap-tapping away, fixing nature—pruning a tree here, planting others there. I think that nature is in the cultural realm—I don't know how we can have a relationship with all that stuff out there that isn't cultural—even the word "nature" is cultural. I would like people to think about the meaning of nature in general, but especially what it means for an urban park like Stanley Park in a city like Vancouver.
>
> We need to acknowledge that what we are managing is a largely human construction. Language like "the restoration of Stanley Park" seems to purposefully obscure the long history of human residence and park-making on the peninsula. Stanley Park would not necessarily be improved by "cleaning it up" and certainly not by tidying nature's mess, but also not by eliminating the hodgepodge of accumulated, contradictory activities and events in the park. I am entertained by a park that contains Saturday night renegade bike courier races at Prospect Point and Sunday afternoon cricket on Brockton Oval. I like the paradox that we seek to commune with nature by walking on the seawall (a project that would never pass an environmental review today).
>
> The old polar bear pit, now overgrown with blackberry bushes, wasn't removed when the zoo was closed. Now it stands as a relic of the days when we had a different relationship with animals when it was okay to put animals in cages and stare at them for pleasure. I am glad that its concrete presence will not allow us to pretend that we weren't those people.

But of course we were—and largely are—*those people*. And I'll submit to you that getting honest about our urban relationships with nature is a prerequisite for constructing a real city—here or anywhere else.

•••

Stanley Park is almost always one of the very first things visitors and residents alike speak of when they catalog what's good about Vancouver. It was established in 1888, right at the city's inception, and is one thousand acres of forest, gardens, trails, beaches, seawall, playgrounds, restaurants, and an aquarium in the heart of Vancouver, making it the third largest urban core park in North America. The park hosts more than eight million visitors annually, and occupies a central role in marketing the city.

Vancouver focuses much of its identity, branding, and advertising around its natural beauty, its proximity to the ocean and mountains, and its overall wholesome healthfulness. Stanley Park is a vital player in that effort, and reifying its "naturalness" and "untouched" splendor is critical both for Vancouverites and tourists in constructing an ideological space for the park. As an early city paper wrote in 1939:

> A city that has been carved out of the forest should maintain somewhere within its boundaries evidence of what it once was, and so long as Stanley Park remains unspoiled that testimony to the giant trees which occupied the site of Vancouver in former days will remain.[9]

It is clear that from the very earliest days of both the park and the city that maintaining this "unspoiled" character has been a critical (if absurd) project, which begins to explain the outpouring of very public hand-wringing and emotional sentiment about the trees. Notably, however, that interest has hardly extended to the Native people who occupied the park for millennia and were almost literally paved over in Stanley Park's creation. The city's 1985 *Stanley Park Master Plan* acknowledged that "[b]efore 1840, the peninsula was used by several thousand coast Indians" but failed to mention that Natives continued to inhabit the area for many more decades.[10]

In the 1880s, as Stanley Park was being established, Natives used sites all over the peninsula for a variety of uses and there were at least seven Native settlements in the park area, the biggest being

Xwayxway (Whai-Whai)—near Lumberman's Arch where eleven families lived:

> You know the Lumberman's Arch (Whoi-Whoi) in Stanley Park. Well, the big house was about 200 feet long, and 60 feet wide.... That was the "real" pow-wow house. The name of it was "Stah-hay"; no meaning, just name, and six families lived in it.
>
> Then to the west of it, was a smaller house, about 24 by 16 feet deep; one family lived in that, and on the extreme west was another pow-wow house—it was measured once—and I think the measurement was 94 feet front by about 40 feet deep; the front was about 20 feet high; the back was about 12 feet. Here two families lived. All these houses stood in a row above the beach, facing the water; all were cedar slabs and big posts; all built by the Indians long ago.[11]

The settlement was razed for Park Road. The eagerness to create the park meant that communities and homes were just in the way. Road workers chopped away part of an occupied Native house that was impeding the surveyors at the village of Chaythoos near Prospect Point. City of Vancouver historian J.S. Matthews interviewed August Jack Khatsahlano, who was a child in the house at the time.

> "We was inside this house when the surveyors come along and they chop the corner of our house when we was eating inside," Khatsahlano said in that 1934 conversation at city hall.
>
> "We all get up and go outside see what was the matter. My sister Louise, she was only one talk a little English; she goes out ask whiteman what's he doing that for. The man say, 'We're surveying the road.'
>
> "My sister ask him, 'Whose road? Is it whiteman's?'
>
> "Whiteman says, 'Someday you'll find good road around, it's going around.' Of course whiteman did not say park; they did not call it park then." [12]

Most of the Native inhabitants at Chaythoos left and went to live on the reserve at Kitsilano Point, which was later transferred by the province into the posession of the federal government and eventually sold.[13]

RICHARDS

•••

It's not entirely true to say that Vancouver's colonialist effort has attempted to erase Native peoples from this territory, but we want only very specific, very limited renditions of Native life to remain. There is now, for example, a tasteful little brass plaque at the site where the Chaytoos settlement once stood.

Some of the most iconic symbols of Stanley Park are the totem poles, which are prominently profiled in endless tourist publications and grace the cover of books and thousands of postcards. The Brockton Point totems are now the "most visited tourist attraction in all of British Columbia"[14] and are intended to symbolize and "honor" the area's indigenous population. But the Coast Salish did not traditionally carve totems and the poles that now inhabit the park were imported from all over the Northwest Coast, brought in from Alert Bay, Haida Gwai'i, Skeena River, and elsewhere.

The poles are a replacement for what was originally planned as a full-scale "Indian Village" tourist attraction, which was proposed to be built by the Vancouver Arts, Historical and Scientific Society who presented a plan to the Park Board.

> They proposed a "model Indian village" that would "suitably house and preserve historic relics and curios relating to the Indians." The idea was to purchase "some old, deserted village," transplant it to the proposed site, and reassemble it there. The Board gave vigorous assent to the proposal.[15]

The plan was also to transplant some Native folks who would "make permanent quarters there, carrying on their Native life."[16] The Society then began purchasing totem poles from various parts of British Columbia and erecting them in the park. In 1925, the Squamish Indian Council objected to the whole plan because neither the planned "village" nor the poles had much to do with local Native culture or peoples. The Society, concerned about controversy, quickly turned the whole project over to the Park Board who reluctantly abandoned the village project, but the totems stayed.

The Park Board has just now been taking some first steps to ameliorate this weird situation. In June of 2008, Susan Point, an excellent and renowned Musqueum artist, installed three traditional House Posts—often called portals or gateways—titled *People Amongst the People*, that now sit alongside the existing totems and are the Coast Salish people's welcome to visitors of Stanley Park. At the opening ceremony, Larry Grant welcomed people to the unceded land of the Halkomelem-speaking people. "We are finally being acknowledged as the Salish people of this territory. The rain you see coming down is very much like the tears of our ancestors who inhabited this land many years ago prior to the city making this into a park."[17] I spoke to Susan about six months after the installation:

> I was granted the commission in May 2005. It took over two and a half years to complete these three "gateway" sculptures, and I have to say that this project was the most challenging of all projects I've done and encountered as a Coast Salish artist over the last three decades. I wanted to ensure that the end result would make my people proud. It's something that I hope will always be recognized and appreciated for what it is: Coast Salish art. When my artwork is located in public spaces, it is my hope that the artwork will both reaffirm the Salish "footprint" upon the land, and most importantly, that it will speak to the viewer in a universal language.
>
> These art pieces are a gift to our grandchildren, from my elder's teachings and their ancestors that taught them. I am only the messenger and I did my best. I only hope that I did justice to the legacy of my ancestors. I wanted to honor them, and to create artwork which represented both traditional and contemporary Coast Salish art, reflecting our past and the living culture of our people.

Telling more honest stories about Stanley Park's past also suggests something about what it might look like in the future. To get some ideas I went and talked to Cease Whyss who is a local artist, herbalist, and healer.

> There was a village at Whai Whai which is now Lumberman's Arch. That whole flatland area of the park was where people lived and people would take canoes back and forth from the village in North Van where I'm from, Eslahan, across from Crab Park. Now my mother lives at Homalchasin which is right across from Stanley Park. It's really easy to see how easily our ancestors would travel back forth.
>
> Many of my relatives lived at Coal Harbour and at Whai Whai and I feel that sense when I go to Stanley Park: I feel like I have had a centuries-old dialogue with the landscape there. My earliest memories as a child are of going to the park at Whai Whai and because my aunts and uncles knew it used to be a village site we'd

have huge picnics there, practically every week, hanging out with all my cousins.

I think the visibility of our people there is really important. Every time I meet down there with young people or groups who want to learn about the plants, I always get out my drum and sing a song from a relative who lived there. No matter what other people are doing, I am going to stand there and drum. That's my inherent right and they can deal with it. I've never had a complaint, but people really do stop. It's a dialogue, an intervention in a public space, a tool I have a great sense of pride in my ongoing dialogue with that space: it's not a park to me, its part of my traditional territory

There's Haida art all over the city, all kinds of Northwest Coast art, but very little Coast Salish art. Most people couldn't tell you what Coast Salish art looks like, which is part of why we've done projects raising the visibility of Coast Salish people. We erected three stumps down near Science World—three stumps that represent the three amalgamated tribes: Musqueum, T'seilwatuth, and Squamish and each figure is bearing salmon, representing the people coming together.

We have to mark things. But we have to do a lot more than put a sign up and mark a spot. That's a start. If we can put our language up, then I'm all about the signs. But I'm not willing to stop there. Signs point you in a direction. We all know that signs are a message telling us something. But the last thing you want to do is follow that sign and find nothing. It has to point to something real, to something happening.

I'd like to see a longhouse at Whai Whai. I'd love to see an interpretive dialogue going on there all the time. We're tired of misconceptions of what we do. Our people don't make totem poles—we make welcome figures. We're starting to see a little bit of visibility, with Susan Point doing some work in the park, and that's a great, positive step, but we need more. It's hardly like we're not willing to share—we have shared so much already.

There's no reason why we can't have space in the park and a presence there all the time. I'd like to see an actual reconstructed village in the park at the old site. I'd like us to set up a longhouse and an actual village that we used. I'm not talking about a tourist attraction,

> but something we actually use. And when the longhouse isn't in use, people can come and visit and learn about our culture. It could enhance both our presence and our pride as protectors of the longhouse and the area. The historical markers tell people that we used to be there, but not why we were forced out, why we were made homeless, how we were all made homeless in our own land.
>
> We need to restore Stanley Park, but not to what it was like before this windstorm—colonialism was the real windstorm, and really it hasn't stopped blowing. We are all going to be sharing that park; it's a space that everybody loves no matter how long your families have been here. We're willing to steward that place back to what it once was, what it was meant to be. It has always been a vision of ours.

•••

Like history, constructions of nature are always cultural questions, and all too often Natives just get folded into "nature": one more piece of the landscape to be moved around and reconstructed as "we" see fit. We want authentic experiences, but only in very certain, specific, and secure ways that keep our engagement with the natural world very controlled and limited. We then develop a relationship with that rendition, sometimes even a deep one, and recast it as tear-jerking, quasi-ecological virtue, or deep aesthetic appreciation of totems or trees.

For Vancouver—or any city—to recast itself ecologically, it has to have an honest narrative about its place. That can't happen until we stop with the faux-spiritual renditions of nature and recognize that we have changed the landscape permanently. We have constructed this place and the responsibility is ours to make it right.

When Vancouverites speak effusively and very publicly about "healing the park," when there are multi-million-dollar fundraising campaigns plastered across the region promising to return the park to its "full glory," when a storm of journalists report on the "devastation" in the park, they are very explicitly not interested in talking about indigenous folks, and not much nature, either. What they really want is the park in an edifying, useful, and accessible state, a place to "improve" people in.

We want "nature" but not all messy and troublesome. We trim the treetops, we build roads and seawalls and pathways and restaurants—but want the "splendor" of "unspoiled" nature. We want rose gardens and swans and grand lawns but not too much native flora and fauna. No cougars and not too many fallen cedars.

We want the tourist-friendly multiculturalism of imported totem poles and decorative plaques, but definitely no Natives living there, and even more definitely no land claims.

The park is a manufactured space, with nothing particularly natural about it anymore. And that's just fine, but people should be honest about the quasi-spiritual status they ascribe to it: they are deifying scenery at the expense of people who had an everyday living relationship with that place. As University of British Columbia sociology professor Renisa Mawani, who has written some great stuff about the park, put it:

> Our understandings of the city and of Stanley Park are inextricably linked to one another. I think what is particularly interesting is how these identities have changed over time. The impetus for creating the park was to create an urban green space where citizens of the newly incorporated city could enjoy recreational activities while creating a distinct identity for what was to become a bustling port city. This, of course, required the removal of the Coast Salish. The imagining of Vancouver as a British Settler city was certainly accomplished through the forced removal of the Squamish, Musqueam, and Tsleil-Watuth. But these aspirations were also carried out through processes of emplacement—through the placement of monuments, buildings, recreational sites (cricket pitch), and gardens (rose garden, etc). In the 1920s, we see a changing vision of Vancouver, one which is trying to capitalize on aboriginality as an important "heritage" of the city, one that is materialized through the placement of totem poles and other Native artifacts.
>
> For me, the recent windstorm raised a lot of possibilities to talk about the displacement of Aboriginal people, and the possibilities for a more democratic ownership of the park. This was a time when the media was reporting a great deal about the types of histories that were unknown (I was asked to comment in the mainstream media several times, as were other academics). And members of the Squamish, Tsleil-Watuth, and Musqueum also seized this as an opportunity to speak of their claims to the land. To me, it seems that "reconstruction" offers a great number of possibilities: to think of what types of injustices our love for nature has allowed—thinking of Stanley Park as "unnatural"—offers more opportunities for social justice.

Neither Vancouver nor Stanley Park is going anywhere any time soon, but neither are Native folks. We have to embark upon a creative reconciliation that honestly engages with our past and current cultural constructions. And part of that package is the fact that there are still five unresolved and competing land claims covering much of what is now Vancouver and the Lower Mainland, plus a host of similar contentions and tensions throughout the region.

Vancouver is toying with new hybrid city and "global city" pretensions, and widely trumpets its multicultural sensibilities, but a democratic culture has to include people, not write them out. Reconciliations have to be a lot more than just putting Native stuff in museums, importing totems, or erecting historical markers—it's about truly remembering what we stand on and also acknowledging whom we stand beside as an ethical choice.

There is every reason, including incredible prosperity, to think that Vancouver could develop a genuine reconciliation with its Native past that begins to give substance to democratic, inclusive claims. That will come a lot easier if we stop being so creepy about pretending that our parks are "nature" and get down to the business of building a good city.

•••

The next day Kristos and I walk along the harbor to the White Tower, the symbol of Thessaloniki. It's more dirty grey than white now but still has a stirring quality, sitting kind of regally at one end of the bay. When we get there it is closed, seemingly randomly. There is some kind of construction work going on around the tower, but what is up is not exactly clear. Kristos says they have been fixing it up for years now.

Later that night I said goodbye to Thessaloniki, half-drunk, rushing to the bus station in the middle of the night for a fourteen-hour ride back to Istanbul. It was actually really touching, with a whole carload of lads there to see me off, all crowding around, checking the ticket, hugging, buying food for the trip, making sure the driver kept an eye on me at the border. My hosts offered the obligatory invitations to please come back, but they didn't really sound like they expected ever to see me there again. They don't get a ton of visitors, and those that do come only want to look at the ruins. On the other hand, everyone seems to want to come to Vancouver. This is a young city, imagining that we have made something out of nothing, full of a naïveté that, combined with massive infusions of capital and pretty scenery, makes this an attractive place.

The world is constantly in transition, never faster than now, and what exists now is not what was here before. There is no possibility of "going back," undoing wrongs, or returning Stanley Park to its "natural" state or anything like that. And that's fine. We need to acknowledge that Vancouver is a city with a colonialist past and in making a commitment to make things right with indigenous inhabitants we can perhaps find a route to a creative reconciliation with the natural world as well. We have disrespected and misrepresented what was here before the city—Native culture and the natural world—and it is wholly possible that we can do both with justice. As Cease puts it:

> I am very hopeful. Native or non-Native, we have to live with an open mind. That's how we have survived colonialism over the past 150 years—we have had to come to terms with new realities.
>
> We want peace but we can't be expected to give anything more up. Reciprocity works if what you give, you get back. That's how our people have operated for an eternity. Especially in hard times things come back to you and now it's Vancouver's turn to give back.

That seems foundational as the city moves forward: rooting our future in historical honesty. Vancouver needs to ditch its naïve pose that we are ahistorical—that we are making something out of nothing.

Let's make peace with the fact that this is a city, it's not "nature," and build on that. I think places like Thessaloniki and Istanbul, which have unapologetic urban histories measured in centuries, can provide some working ideas about how a real, or even great, city emerges, here and elsewhere.

ISTANBUL, TURKEY

PHOTO BY SELENA COUTURE

THE END OF LAWNS AS WE KNOW THEM

Istanbul, Turkey

Even before he won the Nobel Prize, Orhan Pamuk was the best internationally-known writer from Istanbul and famed for his work on the city. He has written a series of novels with a style that is so capable as to occasionally come off as clinical, almost cold in its technical fluidity. It is a tone he doesn't entirely abandon in his memoir, *Istanbul: Memories and the City*, but it is obvious right away that his complex relationship with the city pushes him into a different kind of emotional territory.

Pamuk roots the book in Istanbul's sense of *huzun*, a very particular kind of melancholy he perceives as infused and endemic to the city as a whole and all its inhabitants. More than just melancholy, *huzun* has a spiritual root appearing in the Koran as a mystical grief or emptiness about never being able to be close enough to, or do enough to honor, Allah. Even that description is inadequate:

> To understand the central importance of *huzun* as a cultural concept conveying worldly failure, listlessness and spiritual suffering, it is not enough to grasp the history of the word and the honor we attach to it....
>
> The *huzun* of Istanbul is not just the mood evoked by its people and its poetry, it is a way of looking at life that implicates us all, not only a spiritual state but a state of mind that is ultimately as life-affirming as it is negative.[18]

Pamuk points to a new tinge in modern Istanbul, an end-of-empire wistfulness, a collective realization that the city's best days are behind it. The opulent palaces and mosques and museums and mansions that dominate the city's architecture are constant reminders that it was once one of the greatest cities in the world, the center of empire, the home of wealth and power.

> Gustave Flaubert, who visited Istanbul 102 years before my birth, was struck by the variety of life in its teeming streets; in one of his letters he predicted that in a century's time it would be the capital of the world. The reverse came true: After the Ottoman Empire collapsed, the world almost forgot that Istanbul existed. The city into

> which I was born was poorer, shabbier, and more isolated than it had ever been before in its two-thousand-year history. For me it has always been a city of ruins and of end-of-empire melancholy. I've spent my life either battling with this melancholy or (like all *Istanbullus*) making it my own.

I can't imagine saying much that is less true of Vancouver right now. Every part of Pamuk's description finds it's opposite here in Vancouver: This is a young city of ebullient and energetic ascension, with all the attendant naïveté and optimism. This is a city with almost no urban past, and one that seems to believe that every day is going to be sunnier and more profitable than the next.

•••

It is surely true that Istanbul is not what it once was, and equally true that the city has exploded in population over the past hundred years: a city that at the dawn of the twentieth century had something like three-quarters of a million residents now has more than fourteen million. The overwhelming bulk of that growth is poor villagers, mostly from eastern Anatolia, crowding the urban edges in sprawling unregulated settlements. They come to alleviate their rural poverty while (ironically and predictably) contributing mightily to the economic woes of Istanbul.

Pamuk is not being melodramatic: there is no question that Turkey in general and Istanbul in specific is struggling more than maybe ever before, with little obvious relief in sight.

> To see the city in black and white, to see the haze that sits over it and breathe in the melancholy its inhabitants have embraced as their common fate, you need only to fly in from a rich western city and head straight to the crowded streets; if its winter every man on the Galata Bridge will be wearing the same pale, drab, shadowy clothes. The *Istanbullus* of my era have shunned the vibrant reds, greens, and oranges of their rich, proud ancestors; to foreign visitors, it looks as if they have done so deliberately, to make a moral point. They have not—but there is in their dense gloom a suggestion of modesty. This is how you dress in a black-and-white city, they seem to be saying; this is how you grieve for a city that has been in decline for a hundred and fifty years.[19]

But that's exactly what I've done: it's winter and I have just flown in from a rich western city, and right now I don't see what the hell he's talking about. I am standing on the Galata Bridge looking at palaces and the sparkling, blue Golden Horn and a million boats and ferries and ships all looking like they have somewhere to go. There are shoulder-to-shoulder people fishing, it's a bright day in early December and I am in reverie. It's freaking Istanbul and it's ridiculously beautiful. The calls to prayer crackle from loudspeakers mounted on the mosques looming in the hills, there are people selling stuff everywhere, and beautiful *yalis*[20] crowd up tight on the Bosporus.

I don't see a pervasive melancholy. I'm a visitor and I fall stupidly in love with the city within days of arriving. The Galata Bridge becomes one of my favorite places in the world. The aesthetic Pamuk calls pale and drab I read as Euro-style. The whole place seems alive with an energy that I am unfamiliar with. Of course, I don't see Pamuk's *huzun*; Westerners like me rarely see it through the haze of orientalism.

But it is true; the inevitable, fatalistic decline of Istanbul is something that in time I hear spoken of very often. Many of my friends have a resigned, good-natured assumption of the city's slow freefall into oblivion. "You like it here? *Really?* Why?" People often speak of the size and chaos of the city as untenable, as impossible to really live in, the city as lost, beyond help, beyond repair, to be temporarily tolerated at best.

The easy shot would be to describe Istanbul and Vancouver as two cities going in opposite directions, one heading down, the other on its way up, waving as they go by. There's something there, and it does feel like Istanbul's fatalistic sense of decline is mirrored by Vancouver's ebullience, punctuated by British Columbia's cringe-worthy current marketing tagline: *The Best Place on Earth.*

But I'm not really sure that's it, or maybe that's just a part of it. That whole construct seems a little too facile, a little too temporary to sit with entirely. There is a lot to suggest that Vancouver is not really a city in the historical sense, but more akin to a boomtown, and comparing its fortunes to Istanbul is like comparing Las Vegas to London: right now, in any case, they are just two different categories of settlement.

Istanbul can be seen as an urban flow—it has been the capital of three different empires: Roman, Byzantine, and Ottoman, and has a collective urban memory measured in millennia—while it remains questionable if Vancouver is really even a real city yet. In all honesty, Vancouver is still a small city of a half million people with another one and a half million sprawled out in suburbs vomiting off to the east. It's definitely getting closer, but what will it take to make a real city here?

And what is "real" city anyway? I think many of us have a visceral idea: a liveliness, a vitality, a concentrated structural and cultural environment, a density. I asked Frances Bula, who writes about urban affairs for pretty much everywhere, what she thought about the question:

> It is true that when I come back to Vancouver from New York or Toronto it often feels like Winnipeg in the middle of winter here. There's just so little action. It's not just the size of the city, it's the volume and diversity of things to do and look at—it's really *diversity* that a dense population brings. You have to have a critical mass of people living within a defined boundary. You just can't have a real city without density. While the downtown is very dense, single-family dwellings dominate the city and we have to find ways to build the liveliness and bustle of downtown in other neighborhoods. There is that feel in some places, but we really need a lot more. It doesn't have to be miles and miles of super-density, but concentrated high streets, pockets of real density, to focus neighborhoods.

That density or lack thereof has long been the subject of much hand-wringing in Vancouver, but over the last couple of decades that has changed dramatically, at least in the downtown core, and the city has been able to densify downtown in a reversal that has caught the eye of urbanists and planners across the globe.

Did you know that Vancouver has more high-rises per capita than any other city in North America? It's true, although those skyscrapers don't really scrape all that much of the sky. The city is considered to have a "mid-rise" skyline and most big buildings in the downtown only have a height of around 90 to 130 meters (295 to 426 feet), with the highest being the newly complete Shangri-La[21] at 197 meters (646 feet) tall or sixty-one stories.

In large part, these subdued heights are a product of strict guidelines that maintain view corridors in the downtown. The height limits are part of trying to protect sightlines both within and below the high-rises of the surrounding ocean and mountains. Those guidelines allow special sites to exceed the guidelines to add some diversity, but the desire to maintain the views has kept the heights down, even while the actual buildings multiply like bunnies.

That skyline—and the residential density it has ushered in—is the subject of much admiration and what many observers point to first when they talk about why Vancouver is "getting it right." Vancouver's now-celebrated urbanism is built around the idea of convincing people to move in from the suburbs, to stop sprawling, and to come live on the downtown peninsula. The strategy is called Living First and is perhaps the signature accomplishment of Vancouver's contemporary urbanism; it stimulated one local journalist enough to call it, "the greatest urban experiment to take place in Canada in half a century, one that has made Vancouver the envy of city planners across the continent."[22]

The towers that all those people are moving into overwhelmingly take a very particular form: tall, slim, view-preserving glass towers sitting on a podium of two or three-story townhouses that are specifically designed to be welcoming to families. This form, with slight variations, dominates huge swaths of the city core. "There were exactly six of them in downtown Vancouver a decade ago; now there are more than one thousand."[23]

They may be popular but they are not pretty: wall after wall of sterile, glassy towers with upscale, faux-brick townhouse bases on the bottom. Those towers may not be much to look at, but they are a very convenient model for mass replication that keeps everybody happy. The small footprints and number of units ensure high profit margins, the townhouses lure some families back downtown, and the whole thing is designed for density. Very tidy.

It is definitely true that Vancouver's downtown density has jumped up remarkably, to the point where it is often claimed to have the highest downtown residential density in North America, including Manhattan. That may be a little deceiving, however, because Vancouver's rate of residential growth is not even keeping pace with the Metro region:

> The GVRD [Greater Vancouver Regional District, now Metro] grew by about 13 percent over the past decade, while the city of Vancouver grew by about 8 percent, which means that Vancouver is actually losing its share of growth within the region. Or put another way, the surrounding suburban municipalities are growing faster than Vancouver is.[24]

But it is true that while the suburbs are booming, the downtown has also been taking on huge volumes of people, which is a major achievement when compared to virtually any other North American city. And the goal of building density in the inner city is a worthy one.

Living First was largely conceived and popularized by Vancouver's former co-director of planning, Larry Beasley, and his staff who were looking to create "an urban lifestyle that will bring people back from their 50-year romance with the suburbs."[25] The idea is to radically encourage downtown density by altering zoning laws to support condominiums, encourage pedestrian and bike access over automobiles, and to leverage developers for public amenities and subsidized housing in exchange for sweet profit margins.

> This collaborative process—offering developers density in return for public amenities and good streetscape design—would become Vancouver's modus operandi for the entire city core. In 1991, Beasley's department rezoned much of the commercial core to allow residential development where once only offices, small commercial, small industrial and parking lots were permitted. This "Living First" strategy gave the core a shot of adrenaline. Developers snapped up empty lots, underutilized office buildings and warehouses, converting them all to condos and other residential units. Real estate became a high-energy sport.[26]

Larry described his thinking like this, after I asked him whether or not Living First and the condo-ization of the downtown core has created a developer's profit-friendly city where the grail of density has exacerbated a housing crisis and urban inequality:

> It's a peculiar proposition to wish that developers would make less money. That's like wishing I was the handsomest man in the world or something. We can wish it, but it's not going to happen. I've taken another view. I'm perfectly happy to see developers make money. What I want to see is a significant amount of that created wealth come back to the commonwealth of the city.
>
> So, there is a quid pro quo in this city which is relatively unique in North America saying that it is a privilege to develop in our city and you will make contributions back. Real contributions. *Hundreds of millions of dollars* worth of contributions. And this is not just amenities. A lot of the housing we have built for low-income people has been built through leveraging wealth and land from developers. It's not just about creating a park—that's part of it because our theory is that the only way you're going to entice people to come back to the city and create the vitality you're talking about is to give them something they're going to want to come to in a free society.

> We live in a system where profitability is a driver, and whether I like that or not is beside the point. My point is to say, "let's take some of that profitability back." But don't kid yourself. In Istanbul, in Paris, in Shanghai, in Taiwan, in every city in the world, developers are getting rich. They are exploiting every city in the world, and they are exploiting Istanbul just as much as here. The difference is: in Istanbul they are not putting a nickel back in. They're telling the government: you manage it. Which is why cities like Istanbul are falling apart, because it's impossible to manage.
>
> So, don't look at the choreography of the street as an indication of what's going on. You have to look at the flow of money. The flow of power. Taking the drive for profit and using it to benefit the commonwealth is just not being done in most cities, and it is one way to augment the very limited sources of funds that cities have.

It's an interesting answer and Beasley is articulating an innovative approach that in many ways has clearly worked: Vancouver's downtown has changed radically over the past twenty years and is alive now in ways that it most certainly was not in even recent history. More than 20 percent[27] of Vancouver residents now live downtown,[28] the core is full of people with cash to burn, construction is seemingly non-stop, and it has a very peculiar but vibrant feel.

The strategy is widely viewed as brilliant and its successes are being replicated in many spots around the globe, in no small part due to Beasley's energetic proselytizing. But it so happens that Vancouver and Living First are turning the traditional idea of a downtown on its head, with some interesting repercussions. Most obviously, while condo building continues full-force, commercial development lags far behind. The number of jobs downtown has remained stagnant, and there are very few office or commercial projects being built. The logic is obvious: a developer can turn five times the profit on a condo as compared to an office tower, and the buyers just keep coming, so why the hell would they ever want to stop?

But more (perhaps) unintended consequences are emerging. Right now, Vancouver has a downtown that is increasingly looking and feeling like a resort town, full of tourists, language students, occasional residents, and those visiting their investment properties. And, in an ironic twist, Vancouver now has a huge number of reverse-commuters, people who live in the city but work in the burbs, and it doesn't appear that trend will slow any time soon. As Trevor Boddy wrote in 2005:

> We may once have dreamed of taking our place in the list of the world's great cities, but unless something is changed soon, to preserve and promote our downtown as a place to work, we will instead join Waikiki and Miami Beach on the list of resorts filling up with aging baby boomers lounging around their over-priced condos.[19]

The core of the city is dominated (and increasingly so) by condos, a huge number of them owned by people who do not live here full-time. Property has become another commodity for the global elite to invest in, to buy and flip, especially in hot cities like Vancouver and Dubai and Shanghai, and even in new, recessionary economic climates property is the investment that people tend to cling to. As David Beers, editor of the *Tyee* said to me:

> I totally buy the argument that we badly need density here, but how do you get density without a high-priced sterility? And that's what's been built here. I don't mind that there are some parts of town like that, but I really don't want every part of town like that. The needle-like towers are able to command a high price because of the view, which then turns them into a global commodity. Now you've got to compete with everyone in the globe who wants a view of the North Shore Mountains.

Thus, people with little attachment and few civic bonds to the city increasingly populate downtown: global consumers rather than citizens who care about the place as more than an investment or temporary stopping point. Along with that development pattern comes an avalanche of low-paid service economy jobs to service that economy: retail, restaurant, security, and tourism jobs with wages that ensure that workers cannot live near where they work. This, as every Vancouverite knows, is perhaps the biggest danger to the city: the incredible housing prices and lack of reasonably priced shelter, sending everyday people scattering. And what happens when oil prices start to rise, air travel drops, and the tourists and condo buyers start to stay home? As I am writing this in mid-2009, the ripple effects from 2008 are still being felt across the globe as luxury condo prices collapse. No one really cares much if a few yuppies lose their shirts, but what happens to the rest of us if/when it turns into a full-fledged rout?

BEER
$5
$10
BEER
$5

THE GRAND

The repercussive effects of the Living First strategy are hardly obscure; they are being debated long and hard, and as a model it has much going for it. Part of the root issue of its development is the urgent desire to see Vancouver remade as a "real" city. What is being contested is Vancouver's inherent "city-ness": are we or aren't we? And *what* are we? There is a palpable desire for this to be a great city, a world-class city, and not just among civic boosters or tourism hacks, but also from everyone who likes urbanity.

And that is really what underlies much of the conversation—what makes for a great city? The Living First strategy replicates the cockiness of Vancouver's current mood: we want a real city, and we can make it happen right now with energy and money. It is a boomtownish, reverse mirror image of Istanbul's *huzun*. As Larry Beasley has said over and over, "You don't have to wait for lightning to strike. You can choreograph this."[30] I asked Larry about Seaside, the infamous and tepidly bourgeois enclave that is often called the first New Urbanist development. I wanted to press him on the idea that vitality can be choreographed.

> The problem with places like Seaside is that the formulas are all wrong—it's a middle-class housing formula. What we've been trying to do—and I'm not saying we've successfully done it—is get the formula for urbanism right. Urbanism is about mixed use, it's about lining the streets with activities that generate activity, it's about making people feel safe and comfortable in the public realm.
>
> I use the word choreography because unfortunately, leaving the three-dimensional reality of the city to the spontaneous development impetus of the development community, under the conditions we have now, leads to a removal of the public realm. We have one group of people creating the private realm and one group creating the public realm, and the ones building the private realm are *those with the wealth*. And the people creating the public realm never have what's needed to do the job.
>
> Take some of the places you and I love. Look back in history and you'll almost always find that there was one creator. There wasn't the division between the public and the private realms; there was a kind of holistic attitude that brought attention to the public interest.
>
> Now, you gotta do this. I was in Sacramento, outside the tiny, struggling downtown and in the absolute effect of private development

> forces in control. There is *no* public realm; there is *no* commonwealth, there is nothing. It is austere to the point of anguish. And it is unbelievably banal. That's what modern society gives you. That's what the production process gives you because of where wealth is and where power is.
>
> That's what you've got to realize. You've got to look at a city like Vancouver in contrast to that and ask yourself are we putting the mechanisms in place to lead us where we want to go? And I will tell you that takes great choreography. That took me and all my staff working every single day on project after project, trying to bring as many people as possible to the table.

In some ways, it is a brilliant response to a city metastasizing in leaps and bounds in population and investment, and it's a hell of a lot better than letting the city sprawl even more. The city and Beasley have proved that it is possible, given certain conditions, to induce a lot of people to move downtown, something that a decade ago few people in North America thought possible. But is that enough? Is density the holy grail of contemporary urbanity?

•••

The simple (and highly qualified) answer is pretty much "yes." The basic formulation suggests that if you can densify, all good things will flow from there: There will be enough population to support public transport, more people will walk and fewer will drive, you'll get concentrations of services, and urbanity will flourish. If you give people reason to spend time on the street they will. Like Witold Rybczynski, who is an architect, urbanist, and now University of Pennsylvania professor, once said to me, "it has to do with density, above all. This puts a lot of people together in one place, keeps walking distance relatively small, and makes walking interesting."

It's not just simple consumer-choice logic; there are all kinds of advantages to densification that may appear ancillary but are really part of the package. More than anything, living compactly necessarily reduces everyone's footprint. Density means fewer resources required across the board: sharing is caring. In a great essay published in 2004 in the *New Yorker*, David Owen described living in a "utopian environmentalist community" where he and his wife lived austerely, without a lawn, shopped on foot, and bought few consumer items, in part because they had nowhere to store stuff. The community was Manhattan.

> Most Americans, including most New Yorkers, think of New York City as an ecological nightmare, a wasteland of concrete and garbage and diesel fumes and traffic jams, but in comparison with the rest of America it's a model of environmental responsibility. By the most significant measures, New York is the greenest community in the United States, and one of the greenest cities in the world. The most devastating damage humans have done to the environment has arisen from the heedless burning of fossil fuels, a category in which New Yorkers are practically prehistoric. The average Manhattanite consumes gasoline at a rate that the country as a whole hasn't matched since the mid-nineteen-twenties, when the most widely owned car in the United States was the Ford Model T. Eighty-two percent of Manhattan residents travel to work by public transit, by bicycle, or on foot. That's ten times the rate for Americans in general, and eight times the rate for residents of Los Angeles County. New York City is more populous than all but eleven states; if it were granted statehood, it would rank 51st in per-capita energy use....
>
> The key to New York's relative environmental benignity is its extreme compactness. Manhattan's population density is more than eight hundred times that of the nation as a whole. Placing one and a half million people on a twenty-three-square-mile island sharply reduces their opportunities to be wasteful, and forces the majority to live in some of the most inherently energy efficient residential structures in the world: apartment buildings.[31]

There's not really any way to think about our urban future, either in global or Vancouver-specific terms, without recognizing the need for density. If all of twentieth century, Western urban planning can be thought of as attempt to disperse and decongest Dickensian, Victorian cities, then twenty-first century city building has to be about the reverse: getting people to live more compactly, inducing them to stop sprawling and to stop gobbling up land with highways, 4,500 square foot houses, cul-de-sacs, and their freaking lawns.

The ecological imperative is the stick, but the carrot is cities that are potentially alive, vibrant, complex, and cosmopolitan. That carrot is not a given, however: Blind densification can also mean brutal squadrons of apartment blocks, faceless crowding, or sterile rows of glassy towers. Make no mistake; densification is going to mean lots of people giving a certain amount up—space, lawns that look like putting greens, cars, purchasing power, and lots else—but boo-fucking-hoo. Frankly, density is necessarily the future of this city, and every other one too.

I know that's a little rough, and probably should be tempered a little. I'm not talking about turning the whole city into Manhattan (as if that were even imaginable within the next century or two). It's tempting to brand everyone who resists density as NIMBY BANANAs,[32] quasi-pastoralist relics, or just plain selfish,[33] but that's no good. It is important to understand that density has to be nuanced, that there has to be a wide range of different kinds of spaces in the city, some more dense than others, and that not everyone wants urban vitality and bustle and liveliness. As Frances cautioned me:

> Certain people, from both sides of town and all kinds of political persuasions, really oppose density: they want a quieter, less-busy place. This has always been a growing city and will continue to be, so you'd think that people would recognize that and ask, "how should we deal with it, how do we want to shape that?" rather than opposing growth and density itself. Lots of people really love that liveliness, but others really don't. They find the crowded urban life depressing and scary. We need to find a way to accommodate those people too.
>
> And you need the variation of densities. You need places where you can go to get respite from the noise. You need quiet streets, places that feel restful. Even in New York the traffic is all on the arterials and some of the side streets are very quiet—and that's important. We want liveliness, but we can't be assaulted by the city. Even in Shanghai, which is incredibly dense, there are streets and areas that are very quiet. When I lived there, I would ride my bike downtown through some really peaceful neighborhoods with beautiful old houses and it was a restful commute.

And she's right, of course. The city has to contain all kinds of different spaces if all kinds of people are going to thrive here. All of us want (need) quiet places without traffic, without people rushing around, and protecting those spaces is contingent on our willingness to densify, especially high streets. But, sort of counterintuitively, it is sprawl, both within and beyond city limits that destroys the capacity to retain those peaceful areas. Endless single-family housing sprawl through the city brings traffic into every nook and cranny, just as suburban sprawl erodes our agricultural base and the character of rural areas.

When Larry talks about ending people's romance with the burbs, I'm right there and I applaud (for real) the significant progress this city has made in densifying. But there is a sterile, manufactured quality to the density that I am calling into question, and I think it reflects the quality of civic engagement and participation that Vancouver has nurtured.

Part of what I am poking at is the actual form. Glassy towers are just not a big part of my vision of convivial city life, for all the obvious reasons, some of them aesthetic, some practical. And they are not at all necessary for a dense city. As James Howard Kunstler said to me once: "Skyscrapers don't equal rich cosmopolitan life—Paris has lowish rise, but is very dense." Towers give you a peculiar kind of density, and not necessarily a convivial one. Often densely vibrant neighborhoods are entirely three or four stories high—think of Brooklyn or London, for example. There are almost no skyscrapers in Istanbul and it is as dense as I can imagine a city ever wanting to be.

As Berelowitz wrote: "Architecturally speaking, it [the podium tower] is a one-liner.... I am more interested in how we use the city than necessarily how it looks. It's packaged: look but don't touch. It's very much about a sanitized vision of the city."[34] Beasley doesn't dispute this per se, but argues that the vitality will come in time.

> This is something I have struggled with all my career. I travel all the time, I am always visiting new cities, and I love their public spaces, filled with people—and I often asked myself why aren't the public spaces here like that? And you've got to realize that part of this is a difference in culture.
>
> In northern cities all over the world, the public realm is not where you hang out because of the weather, and in this culture people are often socializing in other circumstances, not the street or plazas. What I've tried to do, contrary to what is happening in many North American cities, is to design the public realm so it *can be* repopulated, it can be rediscovered. My hope is, and I don't think this will happen overnight but over generations, that Vancouverites will rediscover how to use the space.
>
> I always tell the story of False Creek North—we designed the whole thing with the Seawall, parks; everything linked and five thousand people move in and there's no one on the street. And I go, "My God.

> What have I done wrong? There's no one on the street. I want street life!" Then a little food store opens and all of a sudden there's people all over the street because up until then people had been taking the elevator down from their tower, getting in their car, driving to the suburbs where they used to shop, driving back to their tower. They were never outside. But that all changed as soon as local establishments opened.
>
> Right now, one of the criticisms of this city, and it's a good criticism that I buy and one I don't feel anxious about, is that it does feel packaged. But you know what? If you were in eighteenth century London, it would feel packaged too. When something is new, it's just been created—it feels new. And that's true of all cities, and then they get repopulated. The spaces that you and I love, say in Delhi, they were initially designed as great, government image-making things, and they weren't populated. But human beings have this way of learning how to use cities and how to take advantage of what's there. But our job is to make the infrastructure of the commonwealth of the city. In North America, that's a dead art.

•••

It's more useful if the question "Is it all about density?" is a little more nuanced. While a more compact city is critical, there are a lot of different kinds of densification, and the nature of that density is contingent on the processes that get us there. In Vancouver, we're getting a very particular kind of density: a developer-friendly, instant-mix version that is injecting huge swaths of the city with a concentrated, pre-planned density in an incredibly short period of time.

But density without community just sucks. Thousands and thousands of people jammed into faceless little boxes, trying to pay off exorbitant mortgages is not much of a city. The ostensibly public spaces in the new downtown are the opposite of common—they are filled with people rushing around through highly-manicured landscapes without a pause—mirroring the frenzied construction all around them. We really should be aspiring to density, but too often what we're getting here is a rendition that threatens to undermine the virtues that theoretically inhere in dense urban life.

Interestingly, many of the same things were being said twenty years ago about the West End. Critics claimed that it was being built too fast, that people were being herded into high-rise cages, that it was a faceless landscape of towers. But now, the West End proper is a terrific neighborhood in all kinds of ways, full of vibrant city life. Maybe in twenty years my critiques will seem equally unfounded.

Maybe. But I think there is something different going on right now. First, the building frenzy going on presently is on a whole other level of magnitude. The West End was built fast, but nothing like this. Second, the West End really has a remarkable diversity of building forms. The other day, Selena and I spent an afternoon walking around the neighborhood and there is really a surprising lack of repetition; there are huge numbers of buildings and they are mixed-up very nicely. And the scale is something else. The West End is one whole order of magnitude lower than what is being built now and is mostly made up of five and six story blocks, and that matters. Past a certain height, you necessarily lose conviviality and neighborliness, especially when it is so choreographed.

More than anything, though, density has to unfold, not sprout in a just-add-water boom. Christopher Alexander has often written about the need for incrementalism or accretive growth. His first rule of city building in *A New Theory of Urban Design* is: "Piecemeal growth as a necessary condition to wholeness." It's a principle that's getting its ass kicked here. It's possible that this is just the first blast to kick-start a new era of density, perhaps in time this will all settle down. It's not the speed per se that I am objecting to here, but rather the process of growth that is reflected on the street.

It's something that Vancouver environmental designer Erick Villagomez echoed when I asked about his thoughts on density:

> We need more nuance about the implications of densification. This city was founded by developers and that has remained the core of the city. Obviously developers love density—it makes them a lot of money, as we've seen downtown—and although the city has handled it in a relatively decent way in terms of urban design, our densification has been pretty simplistic. Yes, density is important toward reducing our ecological footprint and creating vitality, but it can't be that alone. If we are going to densify sustainably we have to connect it to many other factors.
>
> Coming from Toronto, it's incredible how uptight this city is. If you are going to densify toward an urban culture you have to have more faith in people. We have to look closely at the pockets of the city

> where density and vibrancy co-exit and examine how they thrive. I'm a big proponent of a more traditional city-building approach that looks closely at smaller spaces, of enlivening specific spaces, building from the bottom up, rather than these large scale "revitalizations." In the bureaucratic management of a large city we've lost a lot. Vancouver has always been a top-down city: we need to get to a grassroots, bottom-up style of small-scale local transformations that, in aggregate, will create a better public realm.

An excellent example that Erick uses is a laneway on Commercial Drive that the Vancouver Urban Design Forum worked on. Looking at the hidden value of residual spaces throughout the city and using donated materials and local labor, they changed a thin, half-block stretch of unkempt alley into a lovely little public place through simple means. They replaced the beat-up asphalt with a strip of grass bordered by two permeable paved driving edges and a local community group painted murals on the walls enclosing the space. It is a humble adjustment, but one which has changed that alley.

Predictably, the city fought them on it and asked that it be removed within days of its creation. Local people mobilized, backed them off, and that now-grassy lane remains a small, lovely example of two things: the city's signature intransigence, and people's capacity to build a city. It's not a huge deal, but it is precisely what Villagomez and Alexander point to: a grassroots unfolding of the city, small piece by small piece.

•••

The depth, diversity, and vitality of a city are contingent on its public space and common places: it is where we encounter strangers, debate, the unexpected, and the need for civic engagement. Parks, museums, playgrounds, sidewalks, city squares, outdoor cafes, libraries, markets, sports events, bars, bike paths, theaters: it is what is best about every city, and what makes urban life worthwhile.

More than that, though, the health of public space is closely tied to the health of democratic life: they require one another. A democratic culture requires citizens engaged in dialogue, exposed to new ideas, interacting with people not like them, and confronted by others. That much is obvious. But the relationship is not that simple—you cannot just provide public spaces and boom, you get democracy, nor is it true to say that if you have more democratic discourse you'll necessarily get more common places. It is closer to the truth to say that there are many different kinds and shades of public space and they inform the kind of political life that exists. We have to look at public space and ask the same questions we would ask of politics: who participates, what kind of activity is encouraged, is it equitably and equally distributed, are users in control?

Istanbul is sometimes described as one of the world's great cities and it is obvious right away what a densely public place it is. People are everywhere: selling stuff, talking, smoking, taking the ferries, drinking tea, fishing, and walking around. And most of the activity takes place in unofficial rhythms and colonizes space intended for something else: impromptu cafes on street corners, simit sellers in every alley, tea vendors on the sidewalk, fishing off the Galata Bridge.

But let's not get too romantic here. Part of the reason the streets of Istanbul are full of people is that lots of them have nowhere else to go. People are selling shit in every nook and cranny of the city because they are desperate for some cash. All those guys fishing on the bridge might make a great photo, but many of them are trying to get dinner. It's important not to aestheticize or exoticize people's harsh lives—all that vitality is probably a lot more enjoyable for a visitor.

But there are also lots of different kinds of poverty. Who's richer: the guy fishing on the bridge, smoking with his buddies, and walking home through Beyoglu to his extended family, or the guy who leaves his cubicle, jockeys his car onto the highway, stops at Superstore, buys a bunch of food, and hustles back to his suburban home to eat in front of the TV? There's lots unfair with that comparison, but the core of it is salient. The point is not to blindly replicate the dense public vitality of other cities, but to be able to recognize it, not as a consumer good but as an expression of something deeper.

Public life in Istanbul is a total mess—and beautifully so. Everyone I know there goes out constantly, almost every night, to drink tea or beer, shop, visit, do business, or just chill out. Public life happens everywhere. Some of it is clearly planned in the ways that I expect, but often it is in an apartment-turned-bar, or at a teahouse set up with some folding chairs in an alley, or a political club on the top floor of a housing block, or a café under a bridge. It is an ethic reflected in the traffic, both pedestrian and vehicular, which is predictably nuts and turns almost everywhere into fair game.

The awkwardness of Vancouver's public spaces, their regulated, organized, and planned character is so evident when you come back from Istanbul (or frankly almost any city outside North America). Our public realm seems to have an antiseptic quality and the only places where a healthy mess seems evident, even vestigially, is in immigrant neighborhoods like Commercial Drive, Chinatown, or Little India.

It's a tendency that Living First is exacerbating right now. One of the key platforms of the strategy is to extract commitments from developers to include public spaces when they build. It's the least they can ask for in return for a virtual guarantee of windfall condo profits. Throughout downtown there are little parks, playgrounds, seating areas, mini-squares and proto-promenades that have been built as a kind of graft to the city. Many of them are nice enough, but like so much of the rest of Vancouver's public realm, they taste pre-packaged, and are about as healthy as twenty-six-cent Ramen packs. And of course they tend to be under-used, or superficially used, because they didn't emerge from any kind of community need or local desire—they are just one more hoop for developers to jump through in return for those sweet views.

As Villagomez pointed out, one of the reasons much of downtown's new public spaces are mostly empty is that they are often hidden from whatever sun might be out, left in perpetual shade throughout the year. "More sensitive planning may have created a more varied built form that ensured public spaces receive the most sunlight (a key attribute of successful public spaces) throughout the day as possible. It seems the city has attempted to push all public spaces to the outer edges—especially the seawall—and away from all the real action."

It is difficult to resist reading Living First in straight-up Marxist terms: as an amelioratory governmental response to a crisis of capital.[35] Put less pompously, Vancouver has given the development business a near-free reign here as a way of covering up for the lack of other vitality and activity. The new planning and regulatory efforts have allowed new concentrations of capital and profit generation to emerge while designing in enough social provisions that citizens will accept (and possibly even welcome) the massive profits being reaped by elite developers. That's certainly part of the picture, but there's more color and nuance to be added in, more than simple capital-labor contestation. There is a shared cultural response to the challenge and value of public space, and in some ways Living First has morphed into another subtle variant on enclosure, delicately displacing the power of public space into private hands.

•••

All too often, and explicitly in Living First dogma, the creation of new public spaces is being driven by developers working in "partnership" with the planning department, which might explain why so much of the space in this city feels hollow and over-planned. The instrumentalization of public space is antagonistic to non-managed, non-official uses of urban territory: planners want the spaces they design to be used in the ways they have imagined. But a democratic culture relies on non-commodified, genuinely common places. As Lance Berelowitz writes:

> A society that allows its true public spaces to be turned into benign venues of consumption and leisure … is in danger of losing the will and the ability to appropriate those spaces as theatres for vital, legitimate political expression. And the role of public space in the metropolitan city's history is essential to the democratic impulse.… Every society and every city needs its public spaces for the exercise of democracy.[36]

This speaks to the fundamental difference between public spaces and common places, and this is one of the core themes of this book: how can a city, *this city*, become a city of common places. Public space, and lots of it, is crucial but we have to realize that we need more than that. People move through public space—but common space is where they stop, what they learn to inhabit, and make their own.

The re-energizing of downtown with residents, pedestrians, and bikes and the commitment to public space is critical, but there's just no way to master-plan a great city nor can you make it happen just by throwing money at it. But you can prevent one from emerging by insisting on instrumentalizing public spaces and marionetting their uses.

Great cities are built bit by enigmatic bit by a huge number of actors, not by planners or developers, whatever they might want to believe. Great cities have to be inherently democratic projects built in ways that can never be planned or predicted, as products of a vibrant everyday life. I frankly really like and respect Beasley, and think Living First has done plenty of good. As much success as Larry and his colleagues have had, and it is real success, there is a threshold of control that is very easy to cross and in many cases I think this city has leapt it. The contemporary rendition of urban growth is being played out a little differently here in Vancouver, but massive capital accumulation is hardly fettered, it's just being asked to kick a little into the kitty.

Living First is a thoughtful, powerful approach, but you can't manufacture vitality or it has all the heart of a laugh track: Density has to come incrementally, and the process has to be driven by citizens and communities. Planners can set the conditions for density, and they can act as a firewall from greed and capital accumulation monsters, but when they try too hard to orchestrate development, when they extend too far, it tends to homogeneity, singularity of vision, and an insistently disciplinary mentality. The scope of planning has to be very clearly defined and aggressively limited.

But it's important not to be naïve here. Planners have been in the thrall of global capitalism for a long time and there are very real conflicts of interest. Planners, like pretty much everyone else, are not interested in relinquishing power, nor are they going to epiphanically change course. It is not an accident or an oversight that this city has emerged as a playground for developers and global elites while working people are an accoutrement or afterthought. Planners are more than complicit in the construction of this social order. There are certainly some worthy ideas in play in this Vancouver, but there are core issues and real antagonisms that cannot be wished or cajoled away.

There are many different kinds and shades of densification and public space and they all inform the kind of political life that exists. We have to ask the same questions we would ask of any development: who is benefiting, in what ways, who is participating, what kind of activity is being encouraged, is it equitably distributed? Right now the answers to those fundamental questions in Vancouver are interesting, but not overwhelmingly positive.

•••

Sitting on the Galata Bridge, drinking tea, and eating simit, I can feel—almost see—what's missing in Vancouver. All our city's optimism and energy is terrific, but we have to build a city that generates commonality not profit. We have to build a city that unfolds, one that people can really inhabit and live in, not just liquidly move through. Public space in itself is not nearly enough, and density is only a start. So, how is it that those common spaces emerge? How does a city get that dense urban vitality, that flavor that is so obviously wanting here? How can a city nurture its own unfolding? Looking to Montreal is a good start.

MONTREAL, QUEBEC
PHOTO BY BARBARA TROTTIER

NO RECIPE FOR URBAN FUNK

Montreal, Quebec

The park across the street from my house was closed for pretty much all of 2007. They tore the shit out of the place: surrounded it with blue construction fence, huge machines rolled in and ate up the field, the playground was taken down, the bocce ball runs disappeared, and the benches were piled in a corner.

It has always been a great park. It's only a single square block, but it is used actively by families, kids, teenagers, dogs and dog-people, packs of Italian guys, people drinking, Latino guys singing and playing soccer, and lots else. So there was a certain amount of Eastside cynicism when the backhoes rolled in and then stayed for months and months: maybe it was some kind of quasi-gentrification scheme that was being needlessly extended so all the drinkers and kids would find somewhere else to hang out and never come back. The city workers' strike extended the project by a couple of months.

But the park reopened right at the end of 2007 and you know what? They did a really nice job. The whole thing is well designed, in large part because of a solid public consultation process. The new playground, bocce area, the paths, the little bit of landscaping; everything is tasteful and well used already. And, with any luck, the new drainage will keep it from turning into the grassless mud-pit that has been its traditional spring fate.

There's something new about it, though, that seems emblematic of this Vancouver. Scattered all through the park, ringing the grassy area, and posted at every entrance are eleven separate signs detailing exactly how you are required to behave. Pick up after your dog (maximum $2,000 fine). Leash your dog—leash maximum: 2.5 meters (maximum $2,000 fine). Park closed from 10:00 PM to 6:00 AM. The bocce courts are for everyone to share (this sign comes in English and Italian). Dogs must be kept a minimum of 15 meters away from the playground at all times (max. $2,000 fine). *What*? Good Lord, why are they talking about *15 meters away from the playground*? Is someone going to come out and measure?

Bocce Ball Park (Victoria Park on the map) is definitely what some might call "contested space." It's pretty small and a lot of different people use it, which sometimes means conflict: People singing too loud at night; dogs shitting in the playground; hipsters pretending they know how to play bocce and getting in the way of the old Italians who want to gamble; people drinking; teenagers sounding intimidating; people passed out face-down, etc. Lots of this can be a drag and any complex, multiple-user space has to have some way of mediating conflict. But ever-more-precise regulation is heading in precisely the wrong direction.

These specific rules are on top of all the other rules that you can probably guess apply to a small urban park: no guns, no golf, no Chainsaws, no 4 x 4-ing, etc. But there is also a registry of other by-laws that apply to all the Vancouver parks that you are probably less aware of. And all of them are "punishable on conviction by a fine of not less than $50.00 and not more than $2,000.00 for each offence." Here's just a quick, selected sampling, lifted directly from the Parks Control By-Laws document:[37]

> 3. (a) No person shall climb, walk, or sit upon any wall, fence or other structure, except play apparatus or seating specifically provided for such use, in or upon any park.
>
> 7. No person shall play at any game whatsoever in or on any portion of any park except upon or in such portions thereof as may be especially allotted, designed and provided, respectively, for any purpose, and under such rules and regulations and at such times as shall be prescribed by the Board.
>
> 8. (a) No person shall take part in any procession, drill, march, performance, ceremony, concert, gathering or meeting in or on any park or driveway unless with the written permission of the General Manager first had and obtained.
>
> (b) No person shall make a public address or demonstration or do any other thing likely to cause a public gathering or attract public attention in any park without the written permission of the General Manager first had and obtained.
>
> (g) No person shall sing, play a musical instrument, or otherwise perform or provide entertainment in any area of a park which has been designated by the General Manager as an area in which entertainment is not allowed.
>
> 9. (a) No person as owner or having the control of any animal or fowl shall suffer or permit such animal or fowl to run at large or

feed upon any park except that a dog which is in the custody of a competent person is permitted:

(i) Any area, except where the General Manager has posted the notice referred to in subsection (aa) if it is on a leash not exceeding 2 and ½ metres in length; and

(ii) to be off a leash in an area designated in Schedule 1of this By-law within the time limits established by the General Manager and posted within the area.

19. No tournament, series of games or competition shall be played in any park or on any court, green, grounds, lawn, golf course, pitch and putt facility or putting green by any person, group of persons, organization or club without the written permission of the General Manager.

I've just picked out a few especially dorky ones, on top of about a million other provisions and sub-sections detailing possible encumbering, hindering, interrupting, removing, obstructing, occupying, interfering, traveling, conducting, offending, selling, painting, posting, affixing, riding, breaking, lighting, displacing, replacing, contravening, and many, many other possible behaviors.

OK, I'm reading from by-laws, which always sound stupid and lawyered, but did you know that you're not allowed to sit on a retaining wall, kayak, play guitar, gather in groups, address the public, sing, or play football except in designated areas unless you have written permission from the General Manager? And you could be fined up to two grand? Did you know that no park except Queen Elizabeth is designated as a Frisbee- throwing area? It's true.

In a 2007 *Vancouver Sun* article, Joyce Courtney, a Parks and Recreation spokeswoman, said that "bylaws are to educate people about how they use public space.... We're not the police.... Bylaws are, by and large, rules of conduct. It's to educate, inform and change their behavior."[38]

So, the rules are there, but they aren't going to be enforced? Or they are just exercises in governmentality, ready to be used when necessary? How creepy is that? Have you ever heard people reflexively talk about Singapore as a crypto-fascist city where you're not allowed to chew gum? How's that feel coming from a city where you ostensibly can't gather in groups, play football, or sing in a park without permission? Nice place you got there, buddy.

To get some clarity, I called the (then) Parks Board Commissioner, Spencer Herbert, who is a good guy:

> Some of these regulations puzzle me more than anything. They don't really bug me because they are not really enforced, and the public don't know they're there so it's not really hampering their freedom. But, as they are not all really enforced, it puzzles me why some of them are there....
>
> Some rules and regulations for protecting public space are absolutely necessary, but rules about not playing Frisbee anywhere unless you have the written consent of our general manager are pretty draconian. I think rules and regulations that, for example, make it unlawful for someone to set up a private business in a public space for private benefit are crucial—otherwise public space starts very quickly to become private space. Some private companies very desperately want to invade what public space we have. The government must ensure public space is for public benefit.
>
> Some other rules seem pretty ridiculous. They seem to be an overzealous application of trying to make sure we use our parks responsibly. I like things when they're a little more specific rather than blanket rules that cover everything. The trick is knowing when rules go too far, and when maybe allowing people to use their common sense might be the better way to go.
>
> For the record, in my years as a Parks Commissioner, I have never heard one complaint about our by-laws being too restrictive, or not restrictive enough, though I have heard complaints that they must be more strongly enforced.

So, is all this regulation anything more than post-modern weirdness? Is it just the kind of regulatory absurdity that we are so familiar with? There's an argument that this is just what is required in a diverse and dense urban environment where lots of people have to share space: we need complex packages of rules to induce civility. But I just don't buy it.

The neurotic signage all over one little park is symptomatic of how so much of the Western world, and Vancouver in particular, is micro-managing its public space, fixating on controlling, mandating, and governing the conduct of people (and dogs). The result is not just sanitized public space but a social milieu that is so tightly clutched by bureaucrats that it can't breathe. A lot gets lost when there's nowhere to throw a ball for your dog. Mary Brookes, who owns Sophie's Pet Palace ("Where a Bitch is the Boss") just around the corner from the park, said it perfectly:

> What's this world coming to, luv?
>
> These by-law officers, they'll target a park and then police it repeatedly: check that dogs are all registered, that they have the right length leashes, that they have correct tags on, that they are not running free, that they've had all their shots. It's crazy.
>
> It has been proven time and again that a neighborhood is better and safer when there are people out walking their dogs, hanging around in the park watching their dogs run round. You meet each other, you chat, you notice people, you notice strangers, and you pay attention to the neighborhood.
>
> It's a healthy community when people can be outside together and relax in the park without worrying about some by-law or getting fined for something ridiculous.

The over regulation of Vancouver's parks is one thing, but it points to bigger, more pervasive, and more troubling trajectories that are determining what kind of city this is going to be and how its development will be governed.

•••

The real question I want to ask here sits near the intersection where aesthetic and political arguments meet: How can Vancouver develop some funk, some flavor? How can we densify without being sterile and choreographed?

It's something I think about every time I am in Montreal. There's a vibe there, a rhythm, a sensibility that somehow feels so much more urban and alive than Vancouver. Have you noticed how pretty much everyone who visits Montreal comes back and says, "Now, *that's* a great city. That's what a city is supposed to feel like"? Its architecture for sure, streets that were designed before the car, a Euro influence, a Francophone pace and style, people dressing well,[39] and a density of culture. But it's a lot more than just aesthetics; it's about a rich, cosmopolitan urban experience that is simply lacking in so much of Vancouver.

That's not much insight, frankly. This city just doesn't have an urban vibe like you find in Montreal, or even Toronto, let alone Paris or Buenos Aires, and that's no secret.[40] There is something missing or ignored here, and I don't think there's a simple answer, but a confluence of a bunch of factors, all of which are entwined, reinforcing, and rationalizing each other.

The tight control over public space, the growing income gap, the spiraling housing market, by-law and permitting red-tape, a fixation on what tourists will encounter: all these are factors in constricting public life, but they are hardly unique to Vancouver. There are more artists per capita in Vancouver than any other city in Canada, there is a fantastic diversity of immigrant cultures here, and there is a real network of defined, largely walkable communities, a dense and densifying downtown core. So, what is it? What's missing? How can this city get some flavor that doesn't taste prepackaged? Can we plan for funk? I checked with one of my oldest friends, Marcus Youssef, who is a playwright, theater luminary, and used to live in Montreal. I asked him if he felt the difference between the two cities as keenly as I do:

> My experience of living in Montreal (and not the sexxxy going out to shows and drinking 'til 4:00 AM part but the nuts and bolts, walking with the kids to the park going for a coffee part) is that everywhere is packed with people. There are just way too many people per square foot to ever feel like you actually own very much. What we call urban in Vancouver is deep suburbs in Montreal. When we moved back here, the hardest part was walking on my so-called urban street and there being nobody for blocks, just big, wide streets full of cars and a mostly hyper-organized division between residential and commercial activity. The flip side of that for me is the green space we have in Vancouver. Much as I will always love Montreal, the sad little park I drove to in order to run with my dog made me pine constantly for the density of natural spaces that is so deep a part of Vancouver's cultural fabric.
>
> In Vancouver, we face a city planning bureaucracy that is so risk-averse that it actually seems openly hostile to the idea that alternative artists might be natural creators of funky, accessible space. It strikes me that some of the "trouble" that zealous city planning seeks to mitigate—people coming and going, noise, the coexistence of work and leisure—is the sort of activity that levels out neighborhoods in the right way, makes them more penetrable, porous, and accidentally

> democratic. When there's a bunch of different kinds of people in an area for events it necessarily forces different sorts of people into social relationships with each other and has a healthy, negative affect on property values. Like many new North American cities, we fetishize comfort and become addicted to an idea that where we live should always have ease and convenience as its primary focus. I think Vancouver's planning practices, at least as far as culture is concerned, reflect that.

In some ways it's a question that's endemic to North American urbanism. A century of freeways and highways and parkways and fast food and strip malls and suburbs and parking garages and drive-thrus have left most of our (newer especially) cities bereft of most anything compellingly urban. It's a condition that many people think we can design our way out of. James Howard Kunstler says straight up that North American cities don't know how to do urban design properly. Andres Duany argues that planners just have to create appropriate building codes. Its pretty standard New Urbanism and progressive planning dogma to think that a generation or two of really good planning for communities with walkable streets, multi-use buildings, density, and compact neighborhoods will solve our problems.

And in a lot of ways that's good and true. Cities *can* be designed a lot better and vastly more ecologically. And Vancouver, as much as any city on the continent, has embraced some of the right kinds of planning priorities. In many ways, though, I think placing our faith in good design and master planning is exactly wrong. Maybe it's a place to start from, but really, that's it. We're dreaming if we believe that central planning and design is going to save us from urban sterility, car culture, and unfettered capital. Urban flavor is a lot more than "good" aesthetics.

A funky, vibrant city can only be made by everyday people. Planners have little capacity to nurture dense cosmopolitan life: the best they can do is set the stage. It has to be about a democratic and organic city with thousands and thousands of people making planning and design decisions, not just a professional few. The more rules, the more regulation, the more attempt to govern people's conduct—whether through park by-laws, design codes, zoning, or security culture—the less chance a city has of really emerging, both metaphorically and actually.

I'm not making an argument for allowing the market to run free: in fact, what I'm really getting at is sort of the opposite.

Simplistic deregulation in an era of profound inequity and hyper-capitalism will only allow developers, venture capitalists, and avaricious entrepreneurs dominate everything around us. The point is for planners to check themselves: to set up the conditions for development to become locally-generated, then stay out of the way, and prepare to be surprised. Our public space has to emphasize flexibility and agility—for everyday people not planners—with concrete and recognizable decisions that support very particular kinds of growth.

Red tape has its function, and its correct function is to establish guidelines for development to protect the character of neighborhoods, to keep heritage buildings from being destroyed, and to keep capital at bay. A city has to develop overtly politicized stances about the size, scale, and nature of development it wants. It's no magic: it's about building flexible formulas (even logarithmically) that favor local, anomalous, and flexible growth over profit-driven development.

Good planning can make a big difference and, in many senses, Vancouver is a model for developing walkable density and bringing people back to the city. But if planning over-reaches and tries too hard to mandate how people are going to behave, it falls over into social engineering and sucks the life out of the place. Marcus said it nicely:

> I do think that societies with an historical affinity for collective ownership (not just Montreal, but also Saskatchewan and Newfoundland, for example) do seem to create urban environments that reflect that accidental, unpredictable excitement, and funk you refer to. Moose Jaw is a city I love. St. John's, too. Like Montreal, they seem to actively expect people to be out, in person, walking around drinking, and seeking things and visiting. All three of those provinces also have long histories with labor and cooperative movements and importantly, perhaps, they are "have-not" provinces (at least historically and when compared to Canada's industrial and financial centers), and it's pretty common for places less fixated on wealth creation to be way more fun and interesting to hang out in.
>
> At some point it's important to balance questions of responsibility and safety and appropriateness against a basic trust that if people are left to their own devices, they will make cool things happen. That's something I think we can learn from Montreal.

NOW SELLING!
Beasley
THEBEASLEY.COM

No Dogs
Allowed

•••

I was thinking about exactly this walking up St. Laurent in Montreal, passing out of the Plateau and working into Mile End. I had spent most of the afternoon wandering back and forth, along side streets on either side of the St. Laurent, consistently running into little surprises: a corner bar tucked into a neighborhood with no other commercial activity on either block; a pocket park the size of one house-lot—just a little grass, a few benches and a swing set; a tiny restaurant in a line of row-houses; the pedestrian zone along Prince Arthur; and then the cobblestones at Rachel.

In so much of Montreal, and not just the little Plateau/Mile End area where I tend to stay, dense, anomalous activity seems to thrive. There are unexpected cafés and bars, buildings that have clearly been transformed from one use to another over the years, businesses that seem beautifully out of place. There's also a flexibility and so much mixed-use everywhere: small manufacturing, residential, commercial, parks all in close proximity, etc. It looks and feels like the city has been layered and rebuilt on top of itself over and over again.

I asked Witold Rybczynski about this. He has written some great books that often reference Montreal, where he lived for twenty-five years.[41] He said:

> The key factor is age. Montreal grew mostly before 1950, hence mostly before formal city planning, zoning, modern architecture, etc. The great advantage that Montreal has over a new city like Vancouver is that heritage of Victorian and Edwardian building. The Art Deco period is also a great help. That was when architects knew how to build in a city. The newish architecture of Montreal is not any better than in Vancouver, but there is so much less of it, in relation to the old city. My impression of Vancouver is of changing architectural styles, the 1950s, 1960s, and so on, but without that great ballast of the Edwardian architecture.

Is that it? Vancouver is a startlingly young city, perhaps still growing into its intellectual and urban culture, still fixated on the frontierist ethics that continue to build the place. And it's definitely not fair to critique a city for not being older. The city is not only young but it is also faced with enormous pressures of growth, which in many ways is a great compliment. Vancouver is growing at an incredible rate, not just in population but also in physical terms: it seems like you can't look in any direction without seeing a half-dozen cranes working away. So, rather than getting a layering and evolution of the city, we're getting a vast, steroidal expansion.

It's a growth fuelled by monster investment and mega developments in ever-less-subtle, public-private "partnerships" all designed to pimp the place for profit: the Olympics, the bridges, the convention center, port expansion, the Skytrain extensions, the literally hundreds of enormous condo projects, and new hotels. It is the polar opposite of what Christopher Alexander calls "generated complexity"[42]—the process of building in small, accretive increments, with design unfolding and emerging. "Accretive processes of creation are spread out in time and place, and are initiated independently by many different people," says Alexander.[43] As David Beers suggested to me:

> It's always hard when you try to design things all at once. It's really hard to design any kind of organic funkiness on a drawing board. But as Peter Calthorpe used to tell me, "But it's better than suburban sprawl," and it's hard to argue with that. But architects and landscape architects and planners are working from a grid, they're looking down at the paper, they're not at street level. And from that perspective, how do you plan for serendipity?

This is very much what I am after here: how a city gets some flavor, some funk, or, in Alexander's terms, the "process of creating life." Part of the answer is the separation of process from ends in Vancouver right now. A participatory city—where all kinds of people are out creating the city socially, culturally, and physically—is the unfolding of the city as the project of thousands and thousands of people. You can't get that result by master-planning—the process has to be in sync with the outcome—the city has to unfold itself unpredictably, incrementally, and anomalously. Processes are much more critical than the "design":

> The mechanistic view of architecture we have learned to accept in our era is crippled by this overly-simple, goal-oriented approach. In the mechanistic view of architecture we think mainly of *design* as the desired end-state of a building and far too little of the *way* or *process* of making a building as inherently beautiful in itself.... As a conception of the world, it roundly fails to describe things as they are. It exerts a crippling effect on our view of architecture and planning because it fails to be true to ordinary, everyday fact. For in fact, everything is constantly changing, growing, evolving.... Buildings and streets and

> gardens are modified constantly while they are inhabited, sometimes improved, sometimes destroyed. Towns are created as a cooperative flow caused by hundreds, even millions of people over time.[44]

A rich cultural, architectural, or social urbanism just can't be mandated. If you try to force it, if you try to closely prescribe and monitor how people ought to behave, what their buildings and communities have to look like, you get bland sterility.

You know this from your own house—it takes a long time to get it right, to move the bed from one side of the room to the other, to mess around in the garden, to paint some trim, to throw some crap out, to take down a wall, to install a trapeze, to build a fence, to tear down a fence, to build a fire pit, etc. It's a process of accretion: it takes time for a house to stew, to build up some flavor—and the best parts of your house are imbued with layers of memory and innumerable small decisions.

This is why those cheesy condos with the "distressed" wood, the faux-industrial floors, and the stainless steel look so pathetic. There's no authenticity there—no matter how hard hipsters and yuppies try to buy some legitimacy—it just doesn't fly. Those places don't feel anything like the funk they are so nakedly grasping at. They feel hollow.

The process of city building has to be the same—freed from simplistic and rigid zoning and regulatory attempts to marionette conduct. A vibrant city takes time to emerge and we have to be prepared for surprises, for development to happen in unexpected patterns, for its character to reflect diversity and unpredictability, and always with user-control as the bottom line.

•••

There are great places all over Vancouver where city life has been allowed to unfold, where it obviously hasn't been choreographed. You see it in the West End when you walk by a condo, a flower shop, and a car-repair place all tight together. How about Finn Slough in Richmond, where someone must have been a little creative with the building codes. Not surprisingly, much of it is older neighborhoods like Chinatown and Strathcona: it's the click of mah-jong tiles from inside a house with a tiny "social club" sign out front. The mess of live-seafood tubs on Pender Street. The crazy sculpture on the roof of a converted garage. The houses built off the laneways in backyards. The gardens spilling out into laneways and boulevards. The beautiful clan-association buildings.

One of my very favorite places in the city is the Strathcona Community Gardens. For millennia the entire area all the way east to where Clark Drive is now was tidal flats, and for years after the Canadian Pacific Railway reached the coast, the flats were used to dump industrial waste.[45] During the First World War, False Creek was blocked off at Main Street and filled in by the Great Northern Railway and Canadian Northern Pacific Railway to create new land for their yards and terminal. The area between the rail lines and Prior St. remained swampy and unstable and the rail company dumped waste and Strathcona residents threw their garbage in there.

Then, in the 1930s, a hobo squatter settlement grew up on the flats, in part because it was near the terminus of the rail lines where unemployed people riding the rails looking for work ran out of options. The city eventually destroyed the squatter village and began to turn it into recreational park area. When WWII broke out, the area was taken over as a military training field and dumping ground.

After the war, the city started filling in the still partially soggy area with alternating layers of garbage and soil. Then Hawks Avenue bisected the park, and by the late 1950s it was being used as a city works yard and, in the 1970s, a fire station was built, taking over part of the west side of the park. Finally, after Eastside activists fought off the proposed freeway, which would have blasted right through the area, a community garden was established by a number of residents and community groups. In the early 1990s, the original gardens overflowed and Cottonwood Gardens was established just adjacent and perpendicular to the original.[46]

The combined community gardens now sprawl across seven acres, with scores of individual allotments of various sizes, school plots, raised wheelchair accessible beds, and a huge youth garden. There are also herb gardens, picnic areas, children's play spaces, ponds, an espaliered heritage apple orchard, a traditional orchard, bee keeping, a kiwi orchard, a massive composting program, and so much more. There's a memorial to murdered Downtown Eastside women, a community nursery, a beautiful small building that is ecologically built with solar power, a composting toilet and grey water system, and several brick and glass greenhouses. That's what I can describe just off the top of my head and I don't know the half of it.

In lots of ways, I think the gardens are a great example of what a city can be at its best. There's so much that's right about the place, but there's no way you can make places like Strathcona and Cottonwood quickly. You couldn't have planned it. No planner, no matter how visionary, could have imagined how it has emerged. It is incredibly dense, complex, and constantly shifting. I am there all the time and there is always something new to see. The whole is a creation of thousands, all building their plots and doing their thing, with no supervision and an absolute minimum of regulation.

•••

Just like the manufactured "heritage-style" cabinets at the back of Home Depot, so much of New Urbanism comes off flat, in large part because it tries to interpret "public space" as primarily an aesthetic question. Even with obvious "good" design, New Urbanist creations tend toward sterile, middle-class homogeneity. Granville Island is a good example: it should be perfect. It's designed beautifully with a perfect mix of uses, is car-restricted, has some great architecture, is humanly and pedestrian-scaled, but it largely it feels contrived, consumerist, and middle-class dull. The best of New Urbanism is a step forward in rebuilding urban neighborhoods as walkable and transit-friendly, and Vancouver in many instances has done very well to rearticulate urban patterns while wringing public amenities out of developers, but right now too much of it feels facile.

Municipal governments have to ensure that housing, development, and public space are not simply abandoned to the mercy of the market, and that should be interpreted as creating specific guidelines to allow complexity to happen—social, architectural, and urban complexity. I'm not making an argument for formal or informal structure or design per se, but calling for an unfolding, or emergent growth strategy that is largely driven by people who don't have training or professional expertise.

That has to mean real community planning, with very local guidelines developed for growth, a maximum of flexibility, and a very high tolerance for messiness and public process. Here too, there are big parts of this kind of development that Vancouver has done well, especially when compared with other Canadian cities. The City Plan and Community Visions programs are really sincere and honest attempts to engage wide swaths of specific neighborhoods, and they have produced some excellent work that has gone beyond simple consultation.

That process has to be both deepened and broadened, but also made more agile. Sherry Arnstein's Ladder of Participation is well worn, but it remains a good touchstone: is the public participation process tending toward manipulation, consultation, actual partnership, delegation, or—ideally—citizen power? There is a real danger that local power may descend into NIMBYism, and that's a legitimate concern, but that's a factor regardless. Rather than neighborhoods informing the city, which then attempts to mediate competing needs and demands, the equation has to be turned on its ass, with local neighborhoods building enigmatic character, constrained by needs of the larger whole.

But that's another argument. The point is that public space cannot be orchestrated: It has to be built by people, not regulation. Planning can be the armature, in both the protective and supportive senses, but it really has to know its place.

•••

Lots of what I am talking about here requires time, both longitudinally and latitudinally. A city where people want to be in public, want to get out of the house and off the Internet, and want to participate in social decisions requires people who not only *want* to talk and hang out and get involved, but also have the time to do so. It is both a cultural and an economic thing. It's one of the things Rybzcynski said to me:

> I think that there is such a thing as an urban culture, and Montreal has it. People like to eat out, for example, so restaurants and bars have a clientele. People like to see and be seen. Arguably this is a Latin thing (Miami has it too, so did New Orleans, once). Perhaps it is also tied to the nature of the housing stock. As in Paris and London, Montreal urban housing is small and minimal, so people like to get out and about. (Montreal also has a MUCH higher proportion of tenants than other cities in Canada.) When people have large comfortable houses, as in LA or Houston, they tend to stay home.

He's right. Montreal has pretty much always had the highest percentage of renters among major Canadian cities by far; right now just a titch below 50 percent. Vancouver's percentage is far less at 39 percent, a proportion that still places it third in Canada, well ahead of Calgary (29 percent), Edmonton (34 percent) and Toronto (37 percent).[47] Montreal is also currently ranked the most affordable urban center in Canada to rent in, while Vancouver is second worst, just behind Toronto (but T-Dot is actually improving its rental affordability, while Vancouver is staying stable).[48]

By virtually every major statistical measure, let alone everyday evidence, housing affordability across the board is a major issue in Vancouver (duh), and significantly less so in Montreal.

So, its not just a cultural predilection for chilling out in public, but an economic reality—Vancouverites might well want to go to a community design meeting, have a beer on a patio, wander around in the park, or redo their garden, but they're hustling to pay the rent. The project of getting people seriously engaged in planning and building a city gets punched in the mouth by the ole time and money problem here.

I often think about this when I'm crossing a busy street in Vancouver. I tend to feel pretty safe and presume that I'm not going to get hit by a car. I assume that people are going to try hard not to hit me. But it's not me they're worried about. They just don't have time to deal with getting in an accident. Drivers are much more worried about having to stop, figure out the paperwork, waste hours standing around, and miss appointments: "It would just waste so much fucking time to hit this guy. I'd better brake." You know I'm right, too.

You ever notice that when you ask people how they're doing the answer is always: "crazy busy," "stupid busy," "busy, busy busy," and they often say it as they're moving away from you. I do it all the time too. Hopefully a little less now that I realized how much it pisses me off. Are people really that busy or do they just say that shit to emphasize their quasi-importance? I know that's why I used to say it. Or maybe it's true. Maybe people are really hustling like crazy to pay their bills and *don't* have time to stop.

I used to think that Vancouver's lack of flavor was because everyone was outside hiking or parasailing or rock climbing or some shit. That's definitely part of it, but now I wonder whether it's just because people are too busy doing something else. Or maybe it will just take time, as in many years.

Maybe Larry Beasley is right that all the places we love for their public spaces—Montreal or Paris or Havana or Delhi or wherever—were all stiff and awkward at one time too. Maybe people just need time to learn how to use them best. Maybe that's right, but I do know that a lot of adjustments were made along the way and the cores of those places were all designed before the car and modern zoning and codification. And maybe that's right, maybe Vancouver doesn't just need time for people to "learn" how to use their new built environment; maybe the city itself needs time to rise and fall a few times. David Beers put it nicely to me once.

He said he was looking for serendipity in a city, the surprise, the unexpected joys that are often so hard to find here.

> In some ways, a recession could be good for this city. As Jane Jacobs wrote so insightfully, cities are constantly dying and being reborn, all at the same time. But in the past several decades in Vancouver, so little has had the time to decay gracefully because we keep sweeping away the old for something shinier. I think we need a little scruffy decay around the edges to nurture those serendipitous experiences. Right now the life has just been squeezed out by this real estate boom, leaving certain neighborhoods—like Main Street where I live—feeling fragile and precious.

It only takes a few minutes in Bocce Ball Park to understand that Vancouver's got it only half-right in our rush for the shiny. Our public spaces need less grasping governmentality, a lot fewer mega-projects, and more emergent and incremental growth, more flexibility and a lot more room for a real democratic urban tradition to grow. There's just no funk in endless glass towers and sanitized parks. There has to be room for people to create culture. You can't manufacture it. The flavor has to stew: let it come and let people build the city.

•••

So, stew it we did. As soon Bocce Ball Park opened, we decided to start having neighborhood potlucks there. For several years now, spurred on by our friends Steve and Jen, our family, and a pile of our pals have spent our New Years Days cooking food and then giving it away on the Downtown Eastside. On the first day of 2009, for example, we gave away several hundred meals in less than five minutes. The experience is so startling—just the sheer number of people grateful to have a nice plate of food handed to them—that we decided to hold regular events in our neighborhood park.

The idea is to host a huge potluck picnic lunch in the park, with seventy or eighty people bringing food, and invite as many homeless and broke people as possible from the neighborhood to come join us. This way we can all eat together, it is a little less charitable, and we get to know each other: middle-class homeowner families sharing a meal with the tattoo-faced kids sleeping on the street.

We email people, knock on doors around the park, and hassle friends to come out and put up posters around the park with an open invitation. Then, in the morning, the kids and I walk up and down the streets and alleys, inviting every homeless person we can find, drop in at the mental-health center and hand out flyers advertising a free meal for anyone who is hungry, encouraging them to bring food too, if they can swing it. Finally, we put out a few tables and a couple of ten-by-ten tents, bring a bunch of paper plates and plastic forks, and that's about it: hardly any work at all.

And they go beautifully. A couple hundred people come and the whole park is filled with people eating, drinking tea, playing music, throwing footballs and climbing in the playground. Maybe a little more than half the people bring food, and the homeless folks eat or pack away every last carrot stick and cookie that is left. After a couple of hours we fold the tents up, do a sweep for stray garbage, and carry the tables back home. *C'est ca.*

It's really not an original idea in any sense. Food Not Bombs, community kitchens, churches, temples, soup kitchens, and all kinds of others have been doing this kind of thing forever. These neighborhood potlucks are just one small and limited project, both fun and sort of problematic in their own way, but I think they are one step toward reconfiguring our park. We're not allowing it to be reduced to a regulated, constricted public space; instead we're remaking it as common space where we can get to know folks in a complex, fluid neighborhood, and doing it in the face of every sign and attempt to officially choreograph what happens there.

FORT GOOD HOPE, SAHTU, NWT

PHOTO BY MARK DOUGLAS

WHERE THE RAPIDS ARE

Fort Good Hope, Sahtu, Northwest Territories

"Alright. I want everybody to do up your seatbelts nice and tight. Wouldn't want your body to fly too far from the wreckage. Don't want yer mamas to have to search too far and wide."

The pilot leaned back and leered at us with a wide, gap-toothed grin. The co-pilot turned and slid a big metal lunch box down in our direction:

"There's a bunch of chocolate bars and chips in there if yer hungry."

We were crammed into a ten-seater leaving Norman Wells, aiming for Fort Good Hope: half of us in this plane, half in another just behind. Obviously southerners. So obviously.

We had flown via Edmonton and Yellowknife then the Wells, each plane decreasing in size and bureaucracy. By the time we boarded the final Twin Otter, the security and baggage checks and official officiousness were long forgotten. The pilot and co-pilot eyeballed each traveler, then our bags, counting weight on their fingers and adding it up in their heads.

"How much do you weigh? 190? OK, and then the bag."

He lifts it.

"That's about 40 pounds I'd say. So that's 230. And you, 140? Sure. That pack, say, 25. So, what's that come to?"

Together they assessed and tabulated as each kid stepped onto the plane, tossing their bags into a pile at the back of the cabin. As the last kid ducked through the door, the two pilots looked at each other.

"What did you get?"

Their counts were pretty close to each others' and they nodded.

"We should be all good."

Then they looked at me, as if I had the final say or something. I just shrugged.

"If you think so. You guys are da men here."

"OK. Let's roll."

•••

Fort Good Hope is a settlement of 550 people right on the Mackenzie, 750 km (That's 466 miles for you Yanks) northwest of Yellowknife, 20 km (12.5 miles) shy of the Arctic Circle. There are no permanent roads in, only boat, plane and winter ice-road access.

The Northwest Company established it in 1805, and it's the oldest settlement in the Lower Mackenzie River Valley. The community slowly concentrated dispersed groups of semi-nomadic Dene, who have lived in the area for millennia. At the turn of the twentieth century, the population of Good Hope was estimated at 1,000. Cycles of disease left the community at 98 by the early 1930s but the population recovered to about 300–350 by the late 1950s and has continued to grow since then.

Our trips up there are part of a youth exchange project that we run. The basic model is a familiar one: match up sets of kids, put them into counterpart pairs and have them stay in each other's houses. Our exchanges are a little different because they are specifically designed to get Native and non-Native kids to hang out. The idea is to move past the "Just-Say-No-To-Racism" buttons and the dogma of tolerance that kids are so energetically fed and toward some kind of comprehension, friendship, and hospitality. We get two groups of kids together: non-Native, low-income kids from East Van and Native (Dene and Métis) kids from Good Hope, to travel, work, and live together for a few weeks and see what happens.

The Native/Settler conversation is the core of the project, but it's hardly the only cleavage between these two places, which are about as different as you can get in Canada. One is a small, homogenous, isolated Northern town; the other is a diverse, booming, wannabe "global city" in southern Canada. My trips to the North are always disorienting—even reflecting on the fact that they are disorienting is weirdly disorienting in itself. Being in Good Hope makes things seem really immediate, more in-your-face, starker, and in a not-unpleasant way really makes me wonder what it is exactly that I believe in and why I live where I do.

•••

Currently 30 percent of Good Hope's population is under the age of eighteen and the town is overwhelmingly Dene, with a Métis minority, and a few Whites, who are mostly service and government workers. By virtually every social and economic indicator, Good Hope is poorer and worse-off than averages across the Northwest Territories, and fares even more poorly in comparisons with the rest of Canada.

We started organizing the first exchange in 2002 when a long-time friend of the Thistle,[49] Mark Douglas, told me about Good Hope, a town he had spent part of his youth in. He had just returned from a visit with childhood friends there, among them the chief and the mayor, who was interested in developing some kind of cross-cultural program for local youth. Drug and alcohol abuse is a real problem in Good Hope, school attendance is extremely minimal (of the one-hundred-and-twenty youth in town between the ages of fifteen and twenty-four, one hundred have not earned a high-school degree) and, even though there are only one-hundred-and-sixty-five youth total,[50] there are at least two rival, and active, gangs.

The violent crime rate in Fort Good Hope is well more than double the rate for the North West Territories as a whole (4 per 100), which itself is approximately five times higher than British Columbia's rate (1.2 per 100)[51] and the youth crime rate is stratospheric. Violence in Good Hope is always personalized: the small population magnifies every incident; everyone knows the victim, perpetrator, and circumstances. Tragedy seems to be right there in everyone's lives. People talk about losing children, cousins, friends in ways that are too painful to talk about, too painful not to.

Perhaps death is so evident because the town is very small and everyone knows everyone else, but that ain't all of it. Suicide is two to three times more common among Aboriginal people than non-Aboriginals in Canada. It is also five to six times more prevalent among Aboriginal youth than non-Aboriginal youth.[52] It is something you think about and encounter a lot there. Three Good Hope kids from our first two exchanges in 2002 and 2003 are now resting in peace.

Looking over what I just wrote makes me a little uncomfortable. Everything is true but that only tells a very slim part of the story and as always the statistics are obscuring. Reciting numbers seems to exoticize our relationship in a weird way. It is undoubtedly true that Good Hope is struggling in lots of ways—no one denies that—but it's a place full of joy and strength. There's lots that needs to change in Good Hope, but there is so much goodness that is impossible to miss. Part of that strength is a cultural strength and solidity. People know where they live, know the place they inhabit, and trust the land. The Sahtu Dene have thrived in the North for millennia and they will continue to be there forever. It couldn't be more different in East Vancouver, a decidedly emergent and hybrid-city environment where people come from all over the world, revel in and rely on their constant mobility and are surrounded by people with whom they share very little.

This exchange project happens entirely within the borders of Canada although it is really an international exchange between the Sahtu Dene nation and East Vancouver and, as much as anything, it's about getting city kids and rural kids together. One of the first things that I notice when I am in Good Hope is the homogeneity, although it took me a few days to be able to name it. Aside from colonialist incursions and a certain amount of historic inter-nation movement in the North, there has been virtually no immigration to Fort Good Hope. Statistics Canada divides its most recent immigration data for Fort Good Hope into three categories: before 1991, 1991–2000, and 2001–2006. All three categories identify the number of immigrants as "0." The number of "visible minorities" (not including Aboriginal people) is listed at "0."[53] Contrast that with Vancouver, where 98 percent of us are very recent, non-Native Settlers.

There is so much that is so different from Vancouver in Good Hope, in ways both predictable and not. The obvious differences are, well, obvious, but there's lots more too. Most everything is a little less saccharine and more visceral in ways I am not used to. It's how you've got to pay attention to wolves that occasionally cruise through town. Or the cold that drops below minus forty-five Fahrenheit for big stretches of the winter. Or how different freshly hunted meat tastes.

Going to the North is often considered one of the requisite travel destinations for the contemporary traveler. In an age of cheap flights, ubiquitous roaming, and "adventure" tourism, visiting "untouched" destinations is a certain kind of Holy Grail, and going to an isolated northern community has a particular kind of cachet. As one of the participants' parents said to me, "Now you guys can check 'the Arctic' off your lists!" This is exactly the kind of relationship we are hoping to avoid but one that is all too common: southern travelers stopping at an isolated settlement, sampling local culture, and leaving, never to be heard from again. It is a voyeuristic traveling that reduces Native life to props in travelers' theater, takes much away, and contributes very little except corrosion.

Good Hope stands at a particularly sharp historical juncture. Their culture and traditions as a people are millennia-old and rooted in the experience of their foremothers and fathers. On the other hand, the twenty-first century is pouring in everywhere via new media and technologies. The digital world is as attractive and alluring to kids in Good Hope as it is to all of us, and maybe even more so in such an isolated place. TV, movies, and the Internet allow a connection to global economic and cultural flows in ways that alleviate some of that isolation. But digital life is also dangerously undermining traditional ways of life, corroding younger generations' bush skills and the willingness of youth to weather the hardships of life on the land.

Fort Good Hope is just one small town in one small territory in one small country. But in a lot of ways the experience of Good Hope and our relationships there exemplify a great deal about the conundrums facing traditional communities all over the world and highlight the antagonisms between cities and rural communities.

•••

A deep-rooted historical antagonism to the city has been a thread throughout Western culture[54] and is frequently voiced in small towns and rural communities all over the world: the idea that cities are full of vice, depravity, degradation, and alienation. That suspicion is often evident in Good Hope, but that antagonism is being displaced quickly by a widely held and near-total global valorization of urbanity. All across the world, rural areas and small towns are emptying out as people flee for urban concentration. The world is urbanizing at an incredible clip as whole generations abandon catatonic villages, dreary small towns, and the drudgery of rural work.

The lure of the city with its speed and possibilities is totally dangerous for traditional areas everywhere. It doesn't take long watching MTV, playing Grand Theft Auto, or listening to Fiddy to realize that there are incredible parties full of hotties happening *right now*—and you ain't invited. Actually, you are four thousand miles away and will *never* get invited. Most everything about pop culture reinforces the banality of small towns, and garishly invites the brightest and most energetic to leave as soon as possible. Everything the digital world pumps out is hostile to the patience, temperance, and stoicism required to flourish in the North.

The conversation about how to respond to those lures is on though, and Fort Good Hope is handling it. Not perfectly, maybe no more successfully than anywhere else, but the conversation is there. The hope of course is that some kind of reconciliation is possible, that one worldview doesn't necessarily have to emerge as hegemonic, that somehow traditional Dene life and (post-) modernity can co-exist. And after surviving contact, colonialism, the Hudson's Bay company, disease, the Indian Act, the Catholic

Church, residential schools, and so much else, there is every reason to assume that the Sahtu Dene's resilience will hold. It's their cultural solidity that anchors them: the innumerable generations of life in the Sahtu, a surety of purpose and commonality.

Traditional life and culture are the foundation for native flourishing, but those ways of existing are not static: they evolve, take in new perspectives, add some pieces, and reject others and make choices. The problem, of course, is that colonialism has never been much into sharing—it's an ideology of domination—and First Nations have hardly been afforded much real choice in how to react to Settlers, nor asked to participate in conversations about what kinds of co-existence might be possible. Still, though, in the face of genocide, Natives are still here, and in many senses emerging stronger. As writer and activist Winona LaDuke put it:

> That is the challenge.... This conceptual framework between one worldview and another worldview, indigenous and industrial, or land-based and predator. That's what we call it sometimes—the predator. The predator worldview. It is, in fact, manifest in how we live here. And every ecological crisis that we have today is a direct consequence of that—and the human crises that we have as well. Our communities have seen that and we are still here. We survive.[55]

They are not just surviving, but thriving, and I see that in such evidence in Good Hope. It makes me wonder what can people have trust and faith in, what can they rely on in a diverse, fluid, and globalized city like Vancouver? That's so much less clear to me.

Part of what I am interested in here is what makes for a resilient city or community. What makes a community strong, able to respond to threats, mobilize, take care of each other, and talk to one another? What are the essential components of a strong community? It strikes me that Good Hope has survived unbelievable trauma, gone through so much, and yet is still there and in lots of ways still remains vibrant in large respect because of a shared trust in a cultural solidity. In a globalized, urbanizing world, those kinds of traditionally constituted communities are dispersing with alarming speed, and urban neighborhoods are increasingly liquid and insubstantial.

A world where people, goods, words, and money are sloshing all over the world fits nicely with the neo-liberal fantasy of a totalizing, individualist ethic: everyone on their own, reduced to individual consumer units, competing in the same globalized market, constantly mobile. But even that constant mobility is a ruse: goods and capital are allowed virtual unfettered movement, whereas people are sorely restricted, and immigration is state-selected so that migration is governed as another mechanism of social reproduction.

In this kind of world, people are often only bound together by their families, their Blackberries, Twitter, and Facebook. It is a world that is "free" in some senses, but hollows out ideals like community and neighborhood, solidarity, and commonality. It is a vision that is well worth resisting, but how can we imagine commonality and neighborhood in such a relentlessly liquid world?

And what does a place like Fort Good Hope suggest for hybrid, cosmopolitan cities like Vancouver that are evolving, growing, and morphing in constant motion? Of course, Good Hope has hardly been static; it too has seen movement and shifts, new ideas and changes, but is there something in its resilience and solidity that urbanites can learn from?

•••

In the last couple of decades, the idea of *social capital* has become very popular for thinking about and assessing community, and certainly Good Hope has an unmistakable surfeit of it. I remain fairly ambivalent (and often straight-up antagonistic, actually) about the formulation but maybe it might be a useful route for thinking about Vancouver and cities in general.

The evolution of the idea of social capital has been pretty well documented. Its origins are often traced to 1916 when L. J. Hanifan, a young educator working in West Virginia, used the term to help describe the corrosion of community social life. The phrase poked its head up occasionally over the next couple of decades, but its modern incarnation is typically traced to French sociologist Pierre Bourdieu who, through the 1960s and 1970s, mapped various kinds of capital, predominantly economic and cultural capital, but also included social capital as a poor sister to the first two, describing it as a "multiplier of other forms": a distinct and independent form, but subservient, especially to economic capital.

The idea was further developed in the late 1970s by American sociologist James Coleman, who looked at the relationships between educational achievement, social inequality, and advancement. He defined social capital as the "set of resources" built by family and social organization that support a person's development, and act as a prime source of educational advantage. Coleman described social capital as accruing unintentionally, as a by-product of other activities, and extended the scope to include people of all classes, not just the elites that Bourdieu focused on. Coleman is criticized often for placing primary emphasis on "primordial" or family-based sources of social capital rather than social on "constructed" generators, but his analysis began to congeal the idea into something much more tangible.

Now, more than anyone, Robert Putnam is associated with the idea of social capital. A long-time Harvard political scientist, Putnam's 1993 book *Making Democracy Work* and especially *Bowling Alone: The Decline of Social Capital in America* (2000) has had an immense impact across disciplines and ideological lines. The book documented the collapse of civic engagement in America over the past generation, in terms of formal and informal networks, association and interactions, and points to a wide variety of culprits including TV, personal mobility, changes in family structure, time, and economic pressures. Putnam describes social capital as "social networks and norms of reciprocity" that create value:

> The basic idea of social capital is that a person's family, friends and associates constitute an important asset, one that can be called upon in a crisis, enjoyed for its own sake, and leveraged for material gain. What is true for individuals, moreover, also holds true for groups. Those communities endowed with a diverse stock of social networks and civic associations are in a stronger position to confront poverty and vulnerability, resolve disputes, and take advantage of new opportunities.[56]

This basic formulation has been leapt on by all sorts of people, for all kinds of reasons: in 2007, for example, Putnam was enthusiastically received at a Vancouver event hosted by the Dalai Lama Centre for Peace and Education and sponsored by the Vancouver Board of Trade(!).[57] There is enough malleability in the concept to have kept Putnam and a small army of quasi-acolytes busy revising and clarifying it since the mid-1990s.

One of the key early critiques was that social capital is ambiguously neutral, so that the Mafia or the Klan are two organizations that spring to mind as built on high levels of social capital. Putnam responded by delineating between bonding (linking similar people) and bridging capital (connections between heterogeneous folks), acknowledging that there is a potential "dark side" to social networks, but arguing forcefully that social capital should be seen as a complement, not an alternative, to egalitarian politics.

There are other salient critiques and basic issues at play that I have not really seen social capital theorists resolve, including immediate reservations about the attempt to quantitatively assess qualitative relationships: what kind of survey could you design to accurately assess levels of trust or love? And, deeper than that, the formulation of "neighborhood" and "friendships" as assessable in terms of "capital" points to an instrumentality, and perhaps an inherent parochialism. As East Van author and activist Francisco Ibáñez-Carrasco puts it:

> I am old fashioned this way. I think that the old notion of social capital that creates leverage in social standing, when getting jobs or credit, still exists and is predicated on a bit of favoritism, a bit of xenophobia, a bit of discretion, and a bit of unfairness. Well, if we want to talk about "capital" then we talk about investment and return, greed and fear, and we are not talking about the most ethical or the most benign of human endeavors but not monstrous either.

Despite my critiques, I appreciate social capital theory for what it points to: wealth beyond money. There are more radical formulations—like the idea of a gift economy—but for my purposes here, social capital is a useful tool for thinking about how people thrive. I am interested in how everyday people can construct a good and vibrant life beyond careerism, privilege, or a fixation on monetary accumulation. The answer really comes down to community and neighborhood, and social capital is one limited but useful way to concretize that desire.

As you might imagine, there is an avalanche of publications and conversations about social capital, some of it pretty interesting, but the point I want to leverage here is a relatively recent twist. In 2000, Putnam and colleagues launched a massive study of forty-one U.S. communities, the results of which apparently demonstrated a clear *negative* correlation between "diversity"[58] and social capital: that trust in neighbors, confidence in local government, volunteering, expectations of reciprocity, and much else declined in neighborhoods where there was more ethnic diversity, and especially, immigration.

The study was perhaps the biggest to ever examine social capital specifically and was pretty rigorous. Not only did it demonstrate that neighborhoods with high levels of diversity had a marked deterioration in "bridging capital," but also "bonding capital," meaning that people became less trustful, less open, and less engaged with other kinds of people and even among those like themselves. The study found that in diverse communities people are extremely prone to "hunker down" and withdraw from all kinds of civic engagement, both formal and informal.

Putnam hung on the data for some time, speaking very little on the study for obvious reasons: his results were entirely disquieting for liberals, including him. Putnam told the *Financial Times* in 2006 that he delayed publishing his research until he could develop proposals to compensate for the negative effects of diversity, because it "would have been irresponsible to publish without that."[59] Clearly the data plays to the arguments of anti-immigration activists, bigots, and xenophobes of all kinds, especially volatile in contemporary American political and cultural life. Putnam was trying to figure out how to frame the study and answer it.

Finally, in 2007, Putnam published a major description of the research and his response as *E Pluribus Unum: Diversity and Community in the Twenty-first Century*. His argument acknowledges the findings and suggests three core, interlinked points:

> • Ethnic diversity will increase substantially in virtually all modern societies over the next several decades, in part because of immigration. Increased immigration and diversity are not only inevitable, but over the long run they are also desirable....
>
> • In the short to medium run, however, immigration and ethnic diversity challenge social solidarity and inhibit social capital....
>
> • In the medium to long run, on the other hand, successful immigrant societies create new forms of social solidarity and dampen the negative effects of diversity by constructing new, more encompassing identities.
>
> Thus, the central challenge for modern, diversifying societies is to create a new, broader sense of "we."[60]

Essentially Putnam says that it is true, that immigration and diversity do constrict social capital and cause people to withdraw in all kinds of ways, but he argues for patience. He asserts that given time, space, and successes, people tend to become accepting and embrace diversity, particularly the wide creativity it brings, and construct new ways of thinking about identity.

Putnam's research has caused a flurry of hand wringing and supplementary research because the results fuck with widely held liberal notions of multiculturalism and diversity, and I think his responses to the data are sort of okay, but revealing in their limitations. Immigration is managed and controlled by the state and only very particular kinds of migration are allowed, with people slotted into particular roles and permitted certain kinds of participation. In Canada, for example, there are over thirteen-thousand deportations every year. Putnam doesn't contextualize who is allowed to immigrate, where and why. Immigration is a vital tool of social reproduction and notions of "diversity" and "multiculturalism" are overwhelmingly instrumentalized as tools to support existing power and social relations.

It's better to examine exactly what kinds of diversity are being allowed and propagated and exactly what new forms of social relations are created. Contemporary immigration is conducted specifically to support neo-liberalism and to undermine actual pluralities or value shifts. There are all kinds of ways to think about and work with the sorts of questions Putnam has raised, and their complexity shouldn't be a reason to retreat into liberal platitudes. But it's also a challenge to rethink the reality of urban neighborhoods, re-imagine our notions of community, and recognize that perhaps simplistic assimilationist ideals around diversity are not very useful.

More than anything, perhaps what Putnam is misidentifying is the fragile and insufficient character of our conceptions of community and belonging. It may be that what he calls the decline of social capital is not a cause, but a symptom of a larger malaise: a cultural and political undermining of the ideals of community, in part via deeply embedded Othering and marginalization which this research betrays. I asked South Asian activist and Vancouver resident Harsha Walia about this:

> Given the degree of hostility and marginalization that refugees and recent immigrants face, the onus is hardly on them to build diverse community with others (another way of saying "they better integrate"). For these reasons, it is not surprising that "immigration inhibits social capital" because of the racism and anti-immigrant sentiment embedded in Canadian society that ghettoizes, marginalizes, and isolates these communities.

•••

Vancouver has a fluid population with few shared cultural traditions. Globally there are approximately two hundred million international migrants every year; this means that approximately 3 percent of the world population migrates annually, a population that would make it the world's fifth biggest country if it congregated in one place. Those folks are also sending huge amounts of cash around the world, most of it being sent back home via remittances. In 2007, worldwide remittance flows were estimated at $337 billion (US), the vast bulk of it to "developing" countries.[61] In many ways Vancouver is a city of immigrants, a kind of poster-child for a new form of liquid city. But is it really that new? As Ibáñez-Carrasco says:

> Vancouver has pockets of homogeneity and stability but one has to accept new parameters of those words. We have pockets in which a group of citizens are homogeneous, they may be virtual or material, and we "feel" stable in them. We have accelerated the travel back and forth, the zigzagging between homogeneous and stable pockets and one can be at ease or in danger virtually or materially, in public, or alone, in a matter of seconds. However, this is not new, it is faster. I recall Santiago de Chile where I lived until I was twenty-two and how one could go from a very affluent neighborhood and walk into a shantytown; before gentrification took hold, the feeling and the actual danger were similar. I am a bit wearying of romanticizing one place, its people, and its circumstances over another.

The 2006 Canadian Census identified 46 percent of Vancouver's population as "immigrants" and almost 8 percent as "new immigrants" who had arrived within the last five years, the vast bulk of both from Asia.[62] This indicated the existence of a plurality that is very real and very welcome and, after growing up on Vancouver Island with seriously limited exposure to non-WASP culture, living in this vibrant milieu feels like a cool drink of water on a hot day. But if it is so obvious that the core strength of Good Hope is a set of shared cultural traditions and shared experiences that generates a deep kind of trust, then what does that suggest about Vancouver, about my neighborhood? What kinds of shared understandings can this place rely on if even literally talking to each other is sometimes tough? How do diverse communities not become endlessly fractured, especially when 98 percent of us are Settlers?

Noor Jahan
604 301 9
Chicken Goat Lamb Veal Beef
Bangladeshi Fish
Grocery, Produce
حلال
NOORJAHAN
OPEN
Halal Meat
Chicken, Lamb
Goat, Sheep
Beef, Veal.
All slaughtered on Islamic way at wholesale price
Noor Jahan
حلال
Halal
Meat
BD Fish
Grocery
قصابة
نور
جاهان
دجاج خروف ماعز
بقر عجل غنم
كافة أنواع اللحوم مذبوحة
بالطريقة الاسلامية
وبأسعار الجملة

喜食品廠
DOUBLE HAPPINESS FOODS LTD.

50% off

What I am after here is a radical plurality of values in the context of community and neighborhood. It's more than just asking how people with different kinds of backgrounds can get along, but about how people with very different (and often clashing) values can share a place, co-exist, and genuinely appreciate one another. And I'm not talking about surface-level values, but really deeply held values about fundamental issues.

Values collide in millions of ways in any complex community. While some of those collisions have cultural roots, it's a terrible idea to assume that all (or even most) people of any similar geographical background share similar ideas. Obviously all people from one country, or one region, or one religious background, or even one street do not share values or politics or necessarily very much at all. The formulations of "us" versus "them," "their" values versus "ours"—I hear them sometimes on call-in radio shows and at family dinners—and how immigrants need to learn to "fit in" and get with "the way we do things here" and accept "Canadian values" are just tired and racist. So much of that dialogue is tied up with illogical racialization and crazy assumptions about what people coming from certain parts of the world "believe."

What I am considering here is something very specific: how is it possible that an urban community can flourish with a values plurality? Or, to put more directly, how can extremely diverse urban communities build the same kind of trust that I see in Good Hope, without losing the magic of the city and reducing themselves to the "village"? All too often that conversation gets obscured by renditions of community that are actually facades of exclusion. Whether it is intra-national migration from small towns or cross-border immigration is irrelevant, the questions and issues are the exact same: how to build solidarity, commonality, and trust. Cultures have always been fluid and permeable, always sharing ideas and people, always evolving; the imperative for us is to re-imagine our conceptions of "who belongs" in ways that simultaneously acknowledge the speed and agility of contemporary mobility, resist neo-liberal segregation, and rely on common trust. Harsha framed it nicely:

> In the context of the occupation of Turtle Island, any envisioning of community must be rooted in the recognition of Indigenous self-determination. We need to shift the debate from who has the entitlement to live where to what are you going to do in your life to sustain and live in harmony with the Earth, your neighbors, the

> whole world. For example, can someone like me only claim rights to use the land in a place where I was born [India] but where I currently do not live?
>
> It is possible to acknowledge the inherent claims to land and territory that Indigenous communities hold while maintaining an ethics of anti-segregation in which violent divisions between humans, nations, and territories can disappear and cultures are constantly re-founding themselves. We need to forge new ways of understanding the local and the global and fundamentally transform whom we see ourselves in struggle and community with. I would rather think of human interconnectedness rather than social isolation as foundational to building strong neighborhoods and communities. This requires us to think of our identities as a place of connection rather than exclusion, and to radically reconfigure our kinship and solidarities based on shared experiences and visions.
>
> As an Elder from the Kahniankehaka [a.k.a. Mohawk] community once told me, "Our assertion of Title to the land derives from our understanding and belonging to this land. It means we have a right to live here with dignity. It does not mean we own the land. Try owning the Earth, the sand, the waters, and it will run right through your fingers. No legal system can say you do not belong here. We are in no place to refuse anyone the gift of life and livelihood. We welcome you here with respect, and we expect the same from you."

I'm interested in a kind of resiliency that is both individual and collective, that is a distinctly different formulation than social capital. I'm really just talking about community, and a trust and faith in people around you. When you need help, will people be there for you? Whether its little things like needing childcare in a pinch or big stuff like what if you house caught fire or you found yourself broke—could you turn to your neighbors, your friends in the community? Are "community" and "neighborhood" ultimately losing ideals in a liquid world? Obviously I don't think so, but sometimes it's a tough argument to make.

It is being able to rely on the people around you at some kind of fundamental level, and its necessary corollary—reciprocity (that the trust rolls both ways)—that is what makes community. Conservatives have always argued that family has to be that bedrock, and while I am sort of amenable to that argument (as long as the definition of family is a highly flexible one), the ideal of community doesn't displace family, it deepens, emboldens, and enlarges it.

Family suggests a certain kind of stability: those people will always be your family and they will always have to take care of you and you them, no matter what. Community has a similar depth that necessarily infers a commitment to place, not to an Internet network, or professional affiliation,[63] but to a chunk of land. It's the kind of trust that you can't miss noticing in Good Hope. The Sahtu Dene have always lived there and always will and will always be welcomed home. It is something many of us feel in our communities here, not as powerfully or as completely (especially in a time of predatory real estate markets where many of us could easily be ejected by our landlords), but that feeling of trust and reciprocity is essential.

I have built most of my politics on faith in community: on the ideal that the most authentic arena for democracy to flourish and for an ecological economy to develop is at the community level. It is one that relies on trust both implicitly and explicitly as a political notion. There are all kinds of very cogent critiques of that approach, and rooting a politics in community has the potential to get really flaky for sure, but perhaps the most critical urbanist challenge is the simple freedom that mobility and fluidity offers.

On top of that, it is vital not to become naïve or pastorally dogmatic about notions of community because there are still layers of problems there. In many instances "community control" looks very ugly. "Everyday people" are sometimes vicious and reactionary, and "community control" can actually mean citizens taking responsibility for the repressive, disciplinary functions of the state (think of "neighborhood watch" campaigns, Astroturf posturing, or even worse, citizen militias burying weapons in the backyard and patrolling the Mexican border for "illegal" immigrants). Speaking about neighborhood has to be done alertly and politically, not just reduced to populism or lowest-common denominator pandering, and knowing that it's a lot more complex than just dropping sweet-sounding clichés about "the people" or "community."

The conundrums of neighborhood in a fluid world are sort of encapsulated by the story of Hogan's Alley—a small community of black people that flourished in Strathcona, Vancouver's oldest residential neighborhood, for almost six decades before being leveled in the early 1970s to make way for the Georgia Viaduct. The scattering of Vancouver's black community is kind of a microcosm of the dissolution of urban social capital and commonality.

I talked to an old pal, Wayde Compton, who is a founder of the Hogan's Alley Memorial Project:

> It's important not to romanticize the Alley too much because, in talking to many of the elders who lived there, some have said, "It was a slum. You should be grateful that you can live anywhere you want." That's true, and obviously I am grateful, but it is also true that in assimilation we lost a lot. I am not interested in re-segregation (who is?), but there used to be an all-black church, black dances; you could go to a café run by a black woman and meet other black folks there, and there were neighbors who you could talk to about dealing with racism or whatever. As a kid growing up as one of only a handful of black kids in my high school, I missed that. There was a social bonding and support structure that was inherent in having a neighborhood.
>
> So, the black community has traded a certain kind of social cohesion for a certain kind of freedom. There's not even a black community center to fill that absence. And when I think of such a center, I think of a place to hold archives and historical materials, but when I mentioned the idea of a black community center to one black Vancouverite elder, he said he'd just like a place to go where he knew his friends would be so they could meet and play cards. And it's kind of heartbreaking—what he was saying is that there is no place like that now for him.

But this conversation is not an isolated one: it's happening in the context of neo-liberal globalization. In a world that is shifting constantly and with governments increasingly overpowered by multinationals, cities are very often left to fend for themselves against incredibly powerful capital forces.[64] At the same time notions of place are increasingly liquid as many people are willing and (some are) able to move for better jobs, better housing, and less oppressive social milieus. Basing a politics on community is tough in a world where so much is running in the face of local power and epistemologies. Difficult, but I would say essential.

There is still another layer to this: lots of us have come to the city to escape stifling and dreary small towns. The city has to be a place of freedom, a place to get lost in, and a place to express individuality and divergent interests. Thinking about community power really needs to avoid the parochialism, small-mindedness, and local bullshit that drive us crazy about small towns. It's a trap to try to recreate small towns in the city, which is why it's a good idea to eschew pretty much all facile "urban village" language.

The city has to be a city; if you try to reduce it to a village, the magic of a city gets lost. If you want a small town, move to one. A city has what Jane Jacobs called an "innate extroversion," a sense of possibility, of difference that a town by definition just doesn't offer. Small towns, villages, rural areas, country living all offer other particular appeals and advantages, but trying to conflate them and have the best of all worlds turns the distinctions to mush and the world flattens.

> As a sentimental concept, "neighborhood" is harmful to city planning. It leads to attempts at warping city life into imitations of town or suburban life.... We shall have something solid to chew on if we think of city neighborhoods as mundane organs of self-government.... I am using self-government in its broadest sense, meaning both the informal and formal self-management of society.[65]

Jacobs goes on to describe thinking of a neighborhood as an inward-looking island as "silly and even harmful" and urban neighborhoods "cannot work at cross-purposes to thoroughgoing city mobility and fluidity of *use*. Without economically weakening the city of which they are part."[66] This, of course, is lovely and pretty much exactly right.

Marx once wrote that the "whole of economical history" is summed up by the "antithesis between town and country." I agree with that, in as much it's a loose-enough bumper-sticker phrase to be open to lots of meanings that I might want to attach to it. For this book, I think the history of urbanization can in some ways be summed up by the relationship between neighborhood and the larger city.

In her essay called *The Ideal of Community and the Politics of Difference*, Iris Young argued that "community" can and should not be the basis for a libratory or transformative politics because it is based on denying difference, creating coarse inside/outside distinctions, undermining creativity and diversity, and "makes it difficult [for community members] to respect those with whom they do not identify." She goes even further and writes that: "The desire for mutual understanding and reciprocity underlying the ideal of community is similar to the desire for identification that underlies racial and ethnic chauvinism." Young concludes that even if small-scale communities were desirable, they are impossible to conceive of in modern society and would require "a gargantuan physical overhaul of living space, work places, places of trade and commerce."[67]

I'm not going to answer all of those important and sentient challenges to community, but you very likely already have answered them yourself. Suffice to say, I think that facile and straw-mannish characterizations make it easy to equate community with chauvinism. I also believe that it is well within our theoretical and practical capacity to come to a creative understanding of community that provides cultural resilience and political coherence while retaining the flexibility and difference of the city. I know it's possible for urban neighborhoods to be nurturing and warm without negating the vibrancy and possibility of the city as a whole. Obviously.

I know this because it's my own experience. Every time I walk up and down the Drive I run into plenty of people whom I care about, trust, and love. And so does most everyone else. But I can go to any number of other areas of the city and be totally anonymous. I am pretty sure you have the same experience. It is hardly beyond our grasp to imagine "neighborhood" without losing the freedom of the city. But freedom when defined only as liberty is not much. We have to be willing to consider renditions of "freedom" as a social phenomenon, not just an individual proclivity. As is his want, Francisco put it sweetly:

> Freedom will come with the growing city. There are more places to hide or to hang out with only those we want to relate to by money, hobbies, work or other reasons, but freedom engenders loneliness and isolation; truly free people roam, they are not city rats. I choose the latter cause I want to be protected, fantastical as it may be, from complete freedom and loneliness. I leave that for the male heroes in movies.

I think it is a much more germane question to ask how we create community out of difference without fearing mobility or the city. Some of the answers are all simple and well-worn: good common space, a minimum of traffic, festivals, hockey games, bike rides, events, community kitchens and gardens, family centers, organizing, residents' councils, protests, farmers' markets, bands, picnics—all of this and tons more: everyday community life and more formal self-governance are all bound up with each other.

But that narrative twists significantly when immigration is managed by the state. It's not just anyone who can move to

Vancouver, it's people who are expected to fulfill very particular roles, whether it's as investors or nannies, but they are "welcome" as long as they fit the plan. If people were as legitimately fluid and mobile as capital, and immigration wasn't an overt exercise in social reproduction, then community and mobility are theoretically complementary. People have always moved and populations have always been fluid, technology is just speeding things up. A more honest and genuine diversity, a radical plurality might well be possible if we can embrace a genuine hospitality, not an assimilationist "multiculturalism."

■■■

The complexities of building community around a values plurality should not frighten us. Stability and commonality are clearly at the heart of Good Hope's resiliency. Vancouver and the rest of the urban world are immersed in a complex and shifting world. It is clear that a particular lack of diversity is a strength for Good Hope, and equally clear to me that Vancouver's diversity is equally a strength. I believe that not just because I am afraid to say anything else, but because we have to assume that communities all over the globe will just keep getting more heterogeneous, so either we can turn inward and claim our solitudes, turn hostile and try to barricade others out, or we can embrace the plurality and learn more community-building sophistication and be open to actual diversity. One of those positions seems a dead-end, the other full of possibility.

I think the answer, really the only answer, has to be to re-commit to ideals of urban community and insist that local control and epistemologies are at the center of what it means for a neighborhood to thrive. We have to re-examine our conceptions of community in a liquid world, without hollowing out the political impact of neighborhood. But that insistence has to come with a realistic and patient engagement with the challenges of pluralism of all kinds and an honest evaluation of the contexts.

I think it should also come with a reassessment of the ideal of tolerance. Contemporary Western multiculturalist urbanity, and Vancouver for certain, has long-trumpeted its commitment to a "tolerant" culture, which to my mind just invokes a hegemonic liberal notion of dominant society's capacity to absorb competing interests and groups without requiring any fundamental adaptation or restructuring. It depoliticizes existing power relations and allows inequity, domination, and oppression to escape critical inquiry under the "live and let live" presumptions of liberal orthodoxies.

Obviously I'm not arguing for *intolerance*, but instead for something more radical and more engaging, something that goes a lot further than simply tolerating difference. As Gustava Esteva put in 2006:

> Tolerance can never embrace. It suffers differences, instead of being hospitable to them. Though more gentle or discreet, tolerance is merely a different form of intolerance. "Toleration," Goethe observed, "ought in reality to be merely a transitory mood. It must lead to recognition. To tolerate is to insult." Hospitality, in contrast, embraces the radical pluralism of reality: the incommensurable otherness of the other. Hospitality means opening your arms and the doors of your heart to those who are radically different.

The key phrase that Esteva uses is "incommensurable otherness," which I read as lacking a common measure or aliquot quality that can be used for comparison. This otherness cannot and should not be collapsed into a tolerant multiculturalism, but requires an acknowledgment of, appreciation for, and trust in profoundly different ways of living and social organization. A city of immigrants has to learn to live together, but if it is going to thrive people have to learn to trust each other. Paradoxically, that trust cannot emerge without community, but community needs trust to develop. Perhaps hospitality and friendship are a partial way out of the chicken vs. egg thing here.

> I do not believe that friendship today can flower out of political life. I do believe that if there is something like a political life to remain for us, in this world of technology—then it begins with friendship....
>
> This goes beyond anything which people usually talk about, saying each one of you is responsible for the friendships he/she can develop, because society will only be as good as the political result of these friendships.
>
> I do think that if I had to choose one word to which hope can be tied it is hospitality. A practice of hospitality—recovering threshold, table, patience, listening, and from there generating seedbeds for virtue and friendship on the one hand—on the other hand radiating out for possible community, for rebirth of community. [68]

To my mind, the first steps come from hospitality and friendship. Vancouver and all our cities can (and should) only get more and more complex. We can admire the cultural solidity of places like Good Hope but that's not our urban future. We have to be reimagining and rethinking our cities as full of neighborhoods—in their social, physical, and cultural constructions—as places that nourish friendship: where hospitality can flourish.

I frankly don't think we have much choice. And thankfully there is plenty of work for us to do. In the act of remaking cities, as full of vernacular and unpredictable common places, the possibilities for sharing food and space, for practicing discipline and hospitality are opened.

LAS VEGAS, NEVADA

PHOTO BY SELENA COUTURE

SNAKE EYES

Las Vegas, Nevada

"Yeah, I've lived here all my life, bra. Gone and looked at other places, but nowhere's as good as here. You can get anything you want here. 24/7. Always available. It's a 24/7 city, bra. You want to party? You want to gamble? You want pussy? It's aaaall here. I don't party much no more. Don't hit the pussy like I used to. But if I wanted to it's right here. 24/7."

I looked over at dude as he was driving. His lips were really moist and he spoke wetly, panting slightly. He was probably three-fifty, four bills maybe, and filled his side of the truck pretty thoroughly.

Our car had broken down immediately upon arrival in Las Vegas: literally, the first time we stopped at a red light inside the city limits, the vehicle just refused to move forward anymore. Apparently it had more or less the same reaction as Selena did: shock and awe and revulsion. We had driven for a couple of days down from Vancouver and the car was perfect. We entered Vegas and it turned into a conscientious objector. So, we got the kids to the hotel then I came back and thumbed a ride with the last of our bags from this friendly and generous guy who was just passing by. Despite the ominous prospects of dealing with Vegas car mechanics, I still felt grateful to arrive.

Vegas is probably the worst place in world—or the best, depending on your perspective. Everything is wrong and evil. The omnipresent cheap porn, filth, brutal poverty, endemic racism, waste, environmental catastrophe, genuine vice, heartlessness, quasi-fascist urban planning, facile culture sold as "glamour," hysterical noise everywhere, cheap spectacle, the strong dismembering the weak, and total lack of compassion or civic virtue. And that's not all of it.

So, what am I doing in Vegas for New Year's? Why have I dragged my family down here with me? What possibly is there to like, let alone admire? Is there anything, at all, to be learned from Las Vegas?[69] It really is the worst place in the world, but I love it, in a certain very-fucked-up kind of way, and so apparently do hordes of others. Is it just some weird ironic pull, being attracted to spectacle just because it exists, or is there something that Vancouver can learn about what a city should look like? Is there anything that Vegas can show us about healthy urban neighborhoods, aside from what not to do?

•••

To begin to understand Las Vegas it's important to acknowledge that it's no longer a Mob show. There are still plenty of gangsters running around, it's still a freaking dangerous city (its was recently rated the fourth-most dangerous city in the United States[70]) and corruption and scams are always part of the deal, but the old days of Vegas as wholly owned by the Mafia have given way to a corporate playground, represented by the conceptual shift in branding from "gambling" to "gaming." Almost all the casinos are now owned by some of the biggest, blandest, and ostensibly cleanest corporate entities in America.

Kirk Kerkorian started things off in 1970 when he sold the Flamingo to the Hilton empire, and soon the profit opportunities were so apparent that everyone from Holiday Inn to Ramada was piling on.

> Things were so profitable, in fact, that in 1976, the Hilton corporation, which owned a total of 163 hotels worldwide, derived a whopping 43 percent of its gross revenues from just its two Vegas holdings....
>
> "In this climate, organized crime suddenly became financially obsolete," say Rothman. "In an instant, the passage of the revised Corporate Gaming Act redistributed power in Las Vegas away from the Teamsters and toward Wall Street...."
>
> The rum-running gunboats of the mob had been swamped and sunk by the veritable nuclear-missile cruisers of corporate capital. The world of the Five Families could hardly compete against the global muscle of the Big Board. [71]

If you try to untangle who owns what now in Vegas, you run into a ridiculously complex web of buyouts, mergers, takeovers, partnerships, subsidiaries, and holdings involving names like Harrah's,[72] Boyd Gaming Corporation, Accor, Transcontinental Corporation, Colony Capital, Tracinda Corp, MGM-Mirage, Inc., Wyndham Worldwide Corporation, Columbia Sussex, the Mandalay Resort Group, Wynn Resorts, and dozens more, everyone wanting a piece. If Las Vegas was once a glamorous and styling Rat Pack world, it ain't now. It's just another corporate hustle.

Every casino, every slot-manufacturer, every promotional team, every Ivy-League-educated mathematics consultant, every ad director is focused on creating thematic constructs to keep you occupied and keep you spending. And what they have found that works is apparently a freaking five-ring, five-sense circus.

If you haven't been to Vegas in, say, the last decade or so, be prepared for on onslaught of marketing that you probably aren't prepared for unless you spend most of your days in Times Square or downtown Tokyo. It's not really the hustle per se, it's the total assault of noise and flash and crassness and repetitiveness. It's the lines of little old Salvadoran ladies handing you XXX cards with names and numbers of Eastern European or Filipina ladies to call. It's the two-hundred-decibel Eminem ad on the fifty-foot jumbo screen rolling over and over every twenty seconds. It's the insane cacophony of the slots, everywhere, in every casino. It's the moving billboards on the backs of flatbeds truck rolling up and down the Strip all day and night promising "$85/hr to your door, Barely Legal College Girls." It's the absurd light and flash and rolling thunder shows of the fake volcano.

Part of the reason so many hipster observers and academics like to fetishize Vegas is that it really is the perfect post-modern storm. As a totality and within individual institutions, the place is profoundly disorienting: it is placeless, faceless, and timeless, with a very decisive prison-like quality. There are no windows and no clocks in the casinos, so you don't worry about what time it is, oxygen is pumped in to keep you moving, and casinos are designed like mazes so it is legitimately hard to find an exit.

The Strip is an epicenter of image collage: ahistoric, disconnected, and disorienting. Take a short stroll and you'll encounter Paris, New York, Venice, Treasure Island, ancient Rome, volcanoes, tigers, dolphins, talking statues, castles, pyramids, the Sphinx, canals, pirate ships, one after the other after the other. Every thing is simulation, nothing is real. Of course none of it makes sense, but don't worry about it. Just relax and enjoy.

A lot was made some years ago about Vegas re-branding itself as a family-friendly destination, and while there are still pockets of places that are marketed to kids, those days are pretty much over. Sin and vice are back,[73] front and center: "What happens in Vegas stays in Vegas," porn is *everywhere*, the XXX shows, the drugs-to-your-door sales pitches at every corner, the gallon-sized mai-tais first thing in the morning, the pints of Bloody Mary's in the elevators.

But the transition from old school, gangster-glam to theme park is still on. The dumbing down of Vegas is focused around the infantilization of adults, fetishizing and emboldening our basest desires for creature comfort, then making the whetting of those appetites always available, 24/7, bra. Slots play a huge role in this, wrapping players in a cocoon of low-ceiling, dim-lighted comfort where you don't have to interact with anyone else, don't have to worry, just keep playing. But the overall effect of Vegas is all about the theme park; everything is right here, you don't have worry, it's perfectly safe, you don't have to go anywhere foreign, don't have to risk anything. It's the opposite of adventure: the perfect destination for a culture that reviles real risk.

•••

So, what does any of this have to do with Vancouver? Could any two cities be more unlike one another? Can't we just say that Vegas is an absurd anomaly and that Vancouver is a real city and it, like most others, is struggling with affordability and liveability and sustainability? Can't we say that Vancouver and Vegas are two different breeds, two different categories of settlement, and just leave it at that?

That's fine, and fair enough in some ways. But there's something embedded there that should stop us from getting too smug. Vancouver is being built at a voracious clip. The 2010 Olympics have certainly accelerated things and, like Vegas, this is a city that has hitched its civic, economic wagon to large-scale development and mega-projects. It's a strategy that (especially pre-economic crash) was presumed to be the really only viable way for a city to generate income and attract capital. It is an approach that requires cities to act like corporations in the global marketplace and, as such, aggressively brand themselves.

It's one of the great urban conundrums of our era: as national support for urban infrastructure fades and cities become important actors in the global economy, how can municipal governments raise money? With a limited tax base and exploding populations, how can cities meet the new constellation of demands? Time and again, I have heard financiers argue that cities have to repackage themselves as commodities, that cities have to learn to market and package themselves just like every other corporation.

The argument is that in a neo-liberal, global marketplace, where capital can easily leap over tall borders, national governments are largely an economic anachronism. Cities have to disembed themselves from their national and regional binds and learn to act like businesses. They have to find ways to package their particular attributes and make themselves attractive to international investors, corporations, tourists, the "creative class"—to capital. Specifically, cities have to "brand" themselves so that they stand out; they have to create an image and a clearly defined appeal to attract investment. As Placebrands ("Places with Purpose"), a transnational branding corporation, puts it:

> In a globalised world, every place must compete with every other place for its share of the world's wealth, talent, and attention. Just like a famous company, a famous city, region or country finds it much easier to sell its products and services at a profit, recruit the best people, attract visitors, investment and events, move in the right circles, and play a prominent and useful part in world affairs....
>
> A place brand strategy determines the most realistic, most competitive and most compelling strategic vision for the city, region, or country, and ensures that this vision is supported, reinforced and enriched by every act of investment and communication between that place and the rest of the world. But unless every government department or agency consistently communicates and demonstrates the same carefully developed brand, people in other places will quickly become confused about what the place brand stands for.[74]

And, sure, from a certain vantage point in late capitalism, we're all just buying and selling something: if Vegas is selling sin and vice and flash, Vancouver is selling mountains and ocean and clean virtue. It's all just marketing strategy, all just competing for the same investment dollars, the same tourists, and the same globalized capital. Anything is fair game and cities have to do what it takes to compete on the world stage. If that means sustainability, so be it.

Turn your head another way and it's an incredibly cynical and depressing view that fundamentally reduces the city to another product moving in the great flow of commodity culture. People, animals, the air, the view of the ocean, sex, gambling, vice, virtue: whatever we can sell, we'll sell. Everything has a price and everything can be packaged, bought and sold, and the whole thing is a game of accumulation.

And Vancouver, in perfect neo-liberal fashion, has branded itself as a happy, healthy, and green location for global capital. Historically, the city's economy has hinged on British Columbia's resource sector: fish, mining, agriculture, and lumber, but over the last four decades that focus has shifted very dramatically. False Creek, right in the heart of the city, is a perfect metaphor: its shores were once crowded with sawmills, small port businesses, and railway operations. It was also filthy and polluted. Now the area has been totally transformed. Beginning in 1986 with the World Exposition (Expo 86), a massive redevelopment effort has crowded the shores of False Creek with high-end condos, a science museum, a casino, the new Olympic Athlete's Village,[75] and other amenities. The lights of the glassy high-rises sparkle on the (much cleaner) waters, joggers and bikers parade along the seawall, yachts lurk happily, and the area is tidy, immaculately choreographed, sculpted, and sanitized. And the promised social housing that was supposed to center a model mixed-use post-Olympics community has evaporated, the whole area is planned within an inch of its life, meets all kinds of green and LEED standards, fits the downtown steel-and-glass aesthetic milieu, and reeks of privilege.

The reconstruction of False Creek highlights the city's economic focus and the strategy is hardly subtle or difficult to read. The 2006 Census[76] documents the top-four job classifications in the Metro region: retail trade (12 percent), hospitality (11 percent), management and administration and support (10 percent), professional, scientific, and technical services (10 percent). Catalogued in a slightly different way (by the same Census), the two biggest "major occupation groups" in the city are sales and service occupations (26 percent) and business, finance, and administrative occupations (21 percent). Add in the third biggest category, management (12 percent), and you have 60 percent of the city's jobs. In that same document, "Occupations Unique to Primary Industry" are listed at less than 1 percent.[77] It is a transformation that has branded the city unmistakably and rendered it beautifully successful in some senses and tremendously vulnerable in others.

•••

In reducing the city to a product, many of the best and most important values of urban living get stripped. In lots of ways, Vegas is the king of this: relentless, cold-hearted competition, unadorned and unapologetic, which of course is the corporate ethic: a gangster ethic, cleaned up and made efficient. But Vancouver is no slouch either.

It's often argued that you can't evaluate Vegas using regular measures—that it's beside the point to compare it with other cities. It's a circus, a theme park, a Club Med, or something. Yeah, OK, but you know what? That's real water that's being sucked dry and the real natural world getting consumed. That *is* a real place with real people living, working, dying, and birthing. And it once set a certain standard of success that many cities, Vancouver among them, have implicitly (and explicitly) emulated. It is also now a standard for collapse in the face of the economic "downturn." Thirty percent of the labor force in Vegas is employed in "leisure and hospitality," so, as tourism declined drastically through 2008 and 2009, Vegas started coming down, like, well, a house of cards.[78] As of July 2009, unemployment was booming like the casinos used to: "the [July 2009 unemployment rate of] 13.1 percent compares to 12.3 percent in June and to 6.9 percent in July a year ago."[79] That's almost doubling the number of unemployed in a year (!), and of course that doesn't take into account the immense underground, non-official economy in Vegas for which jobless claims aren't counted.

The Vegas economy is like a Petri dish study of the fragility of an economy almost solely dependent on the liquidity of global capitalism and built as a monoculture. When tourists stop throwing away their cash, it's not just the dealers and laundry ladies and room-service waiters who get downsized, it's the 10 percent of workers in construction who aren't building new casino extensions, the limo and cab drivers not getting calls, everyone who has built their living around gaming slough-off. The casinos may be fantasyland, but those are real workers not getting paid and not making mortgage payments.[80]

•••

The same corporate ethic that has driven Las Vegas for the past thirty-plus years has infected Vancouver and cities all over the globe and while condos aren't casinos in terms of revenue-generation, they're not bad. This condo-frenzy has been more-than-well-documented and bemoaned by virtually everyone who lives here, and despite the recent "market-correction" prices remain vastly beyond reasonable. And its not just condos of course: housing/shelter costs in general continue to hamstring Vancouver's citizens with little sign of any real effort to ameliorate the situation and, in an atmosphere of overheated greed, it is little wonder that the housing needs of everyday people are of little interest to those with money to make.

When condos are moving out the door there is so much cash to be made that every two-bit developer who can throw together a proposal is working overtime and every hack with a real estate license gets breathless. In the rush, developers grab at every imaginable thematic hook, any possible angle to build an ad campaign around, in part to obscure the paper-thin architectural variation. The result is total absurdity, and theme-park marketing tactics with anything possible. A recent quick search generated these listed Vancouver properties: Allure, Camera, Envy, Compass, Zora, DWELL, Zone, Agenda Village, Tantalus, Pure, Aura, Axis, Silhouette, Symphony, COCO, Cadence, Bohemia, Donovan, Raffles, L'Hermitage en Ville, the Sapphire, Duke, Discover, Tapestry, Cinque Terre, Pomaria, Milano, L'Aria, Shangri-La, Bentley, Domus, Tribeca Lofts, and Choklit, etc.

There are hundreds[81] more of these things, all virtually indistinguishable from the next with scores of buildings already filled and off the market and god only knows how many more to come. All have multi-million dollar penthouses, advertise stunning views, full security, granite countertops, stainless steel appliances, and their own "unique" hook.

Pomaria has a whole apple-themed marketing scheme (the Apple = Temptation. Get it? Tempted?) How about *Camera—picture yourself living here*. Weird. Or *Espana*?[82] What possible connection is there? Oh, it's in the International Village. *Tribeca*? There is no triangle here, and no canal to be below. *Bohemia*? As fucking if. *Donovan*? God only knows why they're naming a Yaletown condo after an aging Scottish folksinger who was tepid at best.

These douches are just thumbing through their Thesauruses, pulling out anything, and seeing if it sticks. Nothing is impossible and the effect is pure Vegas. It's all disconnected from this place or time, all just image-collage, theme-park fun, and individual possibility. It doesn't matter, don't worry about trying to make sense of it, just enjoy.

When the thematic constructs are chosen so randomly, they are easy to shift on a dime, because they are not grounded in anything. It happens all the time in Vegas. *Treasure Island*, for example, turned into *TI* and mostly replaced the pirate theme with a more edgy Gen-X quasi-porn feel. The *Aladdin* turned into *Planet Hollywood*, the *Venetian* used to be the *Sands*, the *Dunes* was replaced by the *Bellagio, Wynn Las Vegas* is on the old *Desert Inn* spot, etc. It just doesn't matter, it's all marketing.

Apples. Paris. Bohemia. New York. Spain. Egypt. Pirates. Cameras. Sahara. Raffles. Venice. Donovan. Whatever sells. Whatever people will buy. Who gives a fuck? Just spend and enjoy.

Paris
GAIRWILLIAMSONARCHITECTS
ITC
Quality Counts
CONDOMINIUMS

•••

Learning From Las Vegas was in part a genuinely important book because it plainly and aggressively articulated a post-modern architectural appreciation, even veneration, of symbolic communication. There is something to it, of course, and this is a world of fractured symbolic association that these condos, like Vegas and Disneyland, are playing in. There's a certain amount of cultural value in mining and exploring the free-flowing interplay of images and associations, but on the ground, in the real world of cities, in the everyday lives of everyday people, the effect is to suck meaning out, leaving a hollow, facile urbanism.

In the wave of weird, disconnected references people just stop trying to make sense of it all. It just is what it is, and notions of citizenship get reduced to consumerist isolation. Don't worry about it, just enjoy. Michael Sorkin called it the Disneyzone:

> Disneyzone—Toon Town in real stucco and metal—is a cartoon utopia, an urbanism for the continuous transformation of what exists (a panoply of images drawn from life) into what doesn't (an ever-increasing number of weird juxtapositions). It's a genetic utopia, where every product is some sort of mutant; maimed kids in Kabul brought to you on the nightly news by Metamucil, Dumbo in Japan in Florida. The only way to consume the narrative is to keep moving, keep changing channels, keep walking, get on another jet, pass through another airport, stay in another Ramada Inn.[83]

The absurdity of Disneyland and Dubai and Las Vegas are fun to think about and, to a certain extent, visit, especially if you have degenerate notions of fun and an aversion to healthy habits. There really is something to learn from Vegas about elitist tendencies about not getting too tied up in high culture, but it's not something to emulate, and Vancouver like many other cities is toying around with that route, a little too perilously for my liking.

It's not just investors who are buying and flipping Vancouver property as commodities, it's the ethic of the frenzy itself. By severing any relationship to place, by throwing up random thematic condos one after the other, wherever permits will be granted with primary regard for profit, any notions of real community get butchered. The fractured, disassociated forest of Espana and Milano and Shangri-La and Bohemia and Tribeca just laughs at the uniqueness and frailty and resilience and enigmatic character of place—it doesn't matter where you are, it's all one big theme park.

Theme parks are fine if they're isolated and understood explicitly as, well, theme parks. But when they become models for urban development, look the hell out. Of course, developers all over the world want to emulate Disneyland and Vegas because there is so much cold cash to be made, but cities like Vancouver have to explicitly resist the temptation, reject the prospects of placelessness, and rely specifically on this place.

•••

Physical place is the basis for all community and all ecological thinking—acknowledging and comprehending the uniqueness of a place. Somewhere cannot be everywhere, but hyper-modernity threatens to reduce living places into liquid space, a constant, fragmented flow.

It's said that city air makes people free, but freedom can't be interpreted as simple liberty, and the faux-wild-west liberty of Vegas and Disneyland is no freedom at all. Real freedom can't be delivered on the backs of developers. We need to make this place better and more unique—less like the everywhereness of global marketing. The best of cities transcend individualist profiteering and rely on the magic of common space and common social life. Vancouver's a ways off from totally reducing itself to theme park, but the eerie Vegasesque qualities of the condo frenzy are pushing us quickly in the wrong direction.

The resistance has to come in the form of placemaking. If we don't want the city to be reduced to the disconnected space and random-association of condo-dominated life, then we better get off our asses and make places worthy of pause, worthy of living in. We need to be making neighborhoods, community centers, gardens, parks, public art, festivals, and commonality—and taking over and using those spots that already exist. And I'm not talking about waiting for the city to do something—its everyday people who have to be building this city—bureaucrats and politicians can't lead, they can only follow.

A big part of placemaking has to be rejecting car-culture. I'm not arguing for getting rid of all cars tomorrow, but we better bring this plane down quickly and perhaps we can avoid a crash-landing. There can hardly be any doubt that a sane future has to include massive reductions in SOV (single-occupancy vehicles) use, car-reliance, urban planning for the auto, and wanton use of fossil fuels. Maybe peak oil will do the trick for us and force changes, but let's not rely on that. Just a little visionary remaking of the urban landscape is right within our grasp and can make it way more possible for people to live in place.

When a city is built on image collage, it loses coherence and is reduced to a collection of disassociated sites: a city you *have* to drive around—moving from randomly-situated malls, movie theaters, entertainment facilities, condos, and Costcos. It's the city of highways, collector streets, arterials, and cloverleaves: all about intra-urban flow and mobility, a city run by engineers, traffic patterns, and constant road widening. It's also a city that eviscerates neighborhood.

There is an obvious and unambiguous reciprocal relationship between traffic and community. The more cars that flow through a neighborhood, the more disconnected people become from each other and their place. When there is too much traffic, kids can't play outside, people don't want to hang around on the sidewalk or their front porches, the streets are dangerous to navigate, and no one wants to walk anywhere. On the other hand, when traffic is kept to a minimum, people are more likely to relax in public space, meet their neighbors, and pedestrianism makes sense. This is hardly a secret—just look at the kinds of interactions that are possible standing beside a bustling six-lane city arterial compared to those on a chilled, traffic-calmed street.

People love their cars and the specific kinds of freedom they offer and I can understand that, for sure. Who doesn't love a road trip? But our reliance on private autos has come on the backs of unbelievable amounts of public subsidy and the malicious dismantling of this (and many other) city's public streetcar and transit systems. If we poured the same amount of money into public transportation, pedestrian access and bike infrastructure that we currently funnel into facilitating car travel, there's no question that people would be happy to change their patterns. Too many of us drive too much because there are too few viable alternatives. Surely we can construct a city so that people can viably live without owning a car.

But that city sure ain't Vegas. A couple of days into our holiday, my family was so tired of cheap buffet food that I was volunteered to go out and buy some groceries to eat in our room. It was mid-morning when I left our hotel (Circus Circus!) and figured it couldn't be too far to some kind of supermarket. I asked at the front desk but they looked at me like I was crazy. So I skipped outside and got directions from a cabbie. He too seemed skeptical, so I took one of his business cards in case I needed a ride back.

I did. It took me an hour and a half to find a Mexican *supermercado*, wandering through acre after acre of bleak subdivisions. I stopped three times and asked for directions and each time I was assured that I was going the right way but it was just really far. Finally, a nice guy offered to drive me (which was my second encounter with random generosity in Vegas!). He was sitting in his 10' x 10' front yard, totally encased in a chain-link fence, drinking Bud Light with the air-conditioner running on the picnic table. He pulled out his low-riding, tricked-out Mustang and we were there in ten minutes. He graciously waited, then helped me load my bags of corn chips and jicamas into the trunk and drove me back to the hotel. "It's just too far to walk, homes. Too hot. You'll be a puddle."

He was right. As far as I could tell, it is almost impossible to live in Vegas without a car. It would have been a real stretch for that guy to get to work, buy food, and go out anywhere without his (admittedly lovely) vehicle. But of course that is exactly the kind of urban space Vegas is: totally dislocated from its place, inculcating an individualist ethic where everyone is constantly uprooted, moving freely, and without pause. Vegas has created a kind of monument to this kind of lifestyle and politics, promising everything and nothing. If we want a city that's headed in different direction than Vegas, it's past the time when we need to start causing car culture a little trouble.

Fortunately, it's not that hard and we have lots of cities to emulate. Vancouver has a rep as a "green" city, but of course that's a joke. This is a city built on people flying in and out constantly, purchasing voraciously, and expecting a very high standard of consumerist living and energy gobbling. Our footprint is grotesque compared to pretty much any city in the Global South, and we are only making a dent in reducing that.

But what we *do* have is the privilege and money to make some structural changes in how we move around and to make them quickly. There are a ton of strategies, most of which you know and are just obvious. Pour money into public transportation, build compact neighborhoods, electrify wherever possible, look to rail and Light Rapid Transit, expand bus service, build bike lines, and calm neighborhood streets, etc. Those pieces are all good and well trod, so I'll spare you a recitation here. We know what has to be done. What's missing is energy and will; in its place are mostly tepid platitudes, but the animating force (as always) has to be everyday people: citizens. It's us. We are the ones who have to get out in front, drive the agenda, force change, and do what politicians and bureaucrats just can't do: lead.

Back in the day, when I lived in Kingston, we got pissed off at the cars speeding down our street, so one evening we went out and built speed bumps ourselves. We mixed up concrete in the back yard late then wheeled it out and laid down three or four ugly little mountain ranges across the road at intervals down the block. By morning they had set beautifully and it took the city two or three days to remove them, during which time traffic was effectively slowed, at least on our block. We repeated the process until the city got the message and put in speed bumps of their own.

I unapologetically encourage all kinds of similar activism. Are cars repeatedly speeding through your neighborhood? Drag logs out onto the road. Put up your own traffic-calming signs. Dig trenches, install speed bumps, stand outside with signs, play hockey in the road and don't move, whatever. Direct action works.

I'm old and fragile now, so a few years ago when I started to seriously think about reducing traffic here in this neighborhood, I thought of a festival. I was (and remain) well beyond infuriated about the Gateway Program,[84] wanted to push the neighborhood toward a more pedestrian future, and figured that a community celebration might be fun. So, I called a few pals, we got the necessary permits, and in 2005 put on the Car-Free Commercial Drive Festival. It was no work of genius; it was just like festivals all over the world that have been going on for millennia. We closed off about eight blocks to all vehicular traffic, businesses put tables out, we let some vendors sell crafts, social and environmental organizations had tables, we set up four or five stages with music, DJs and spoken word acts, and we had performers wandering through the crowds.

It was all pretty standard stuff, with two key additions. The first is that we politicized every part of the festivals with a car-free, bike-and-pedestrian message. Our back-of-the-shirt message is: Less cars = More community, More Community = Less Cars. The algorithm isn't obscure and people get the formulation easily. And they come out in force. The first year we had twenty-five-thousand people flood the streets and, in 2006, it jumped to fifty thousand, so we expanded the project into Car-Free Vancouver Day (CFVD).

It took me a year of hustling to get people on board, but by 2008 we had four major neighborhoods putting on car-free days simultaneously. Together the festivals brought one-hundred-twenty-five-thousand people into the streets, formed a patchwork that put a serious crimp in city traffic patterns, and forced car-free initiatives onto the city agenda in a powerful way. In 2009, we had our second Car-Free Vancouver Day that expanded existing sites and saw one-hundred-fifty-thousand people out. Now we have every civic party talking about "building on CFVD's success," the city is shutting down four neighborhood high streets for multiple Sundays, and we've begun to normalize the idea of car-resistance.

The other thing that should be noted about CFVD is our horizontality. Local folks autonomously organize each fest site, we have a collaborative forum that coordinates the whole project, and we make decisions together. Every fest is 100 percent volunteer run, everyone performs for free, the total cost for all four fests is well under forty grand (mostly city-mandated costs), and every fest we have ever put on has run a surplus.[85] It's a huge project that is shared so thoroughly that no one has to do an inordinate amount of work. I'm definitely bragging here, but the point is that it is eminently possible to push this and any other city away from car culture. If we want a city of neighborhoods that is built for people, it is blindingly obvious that we need fewer cars charging around, and that future is something we can build. If we don't, who will?

Despite this momentum, I am occasionally a little skeptical about the impact of our Car-Free Vancouver Day fests, so I asked a co-conspirator, Carmen Mills about whether she thought festivals and celebrations could really have repercussions beyond just a day of fun. She was characteristically enthusiastic:

> Absolutely! Festivals like CFVD give people a vision of possibility. Until we opened the street to people there was so much skepticism, but once people experience the freedom and see the reality with their own eyes, there's no looking back. Next thing you know people are demanding car-free festivals on a regular basis, and car-free streets, districts, cities. It all starts with one simple party, to open up the possibilities.
>
> More fundamental than just shifting people's transportation choices, is the dawning awareness that as the public commons has been paved over, citizens' fundamental right to share space and communicate—their fundamental freedom of assembly—has been slowly eroded away by car culture. Along with the pleasure and freedom of street openings comes a subtle current of outrage, and the realization

> of what has been denied to us by the repressive economic machine represented by the fossil fuel industry.
>
> What is more fundamental than the ecological impact of car-dependence is the social impact. Car culture has alienated and disempowered us, and we want our power back. As people stop driving, we will return to a more local way of living. Everything will change as people stop driving and, as they stop driving, everything will change. And that is a GOOD THING!

At a certain level, thinking about cars and traffic is really asking: what is a city for? That's also a question that keeps springing to mind when I think about Vegas or the forest of Disneyesque condos in downtown Vancouver. Is that kind of image collage just goofy or fundamentally antagonistic to the best ideas of what a city should be for?

The desperate attempt to forge Vancouver as a key hub in elite flows of real estate speculation and tourism definitely brought a ton of money into Vancouver and, in certain ways, many of us have benefited. But that development route is also undermining our relationships to this place, remaking the city as a space of flows, disconnection, and autonomous consumerism. At heart, resisting car-culture is not just about cars but also about rethinking the city.

I'd recommend going to Las Vegas. I think its something everyone should see. I'm glad Vegas exists, but it should really be isolated like smallpox. I'm afraid it's too late for that, but at the very least Vancouver should be thinking very hard when this place starts to resemble a theme park. It's worth looking to Vegas for what we don't want. We need a city that is driven by commonality and a commitment to place, not greed and cynicism. The random fractured weirdness of the casinos and slots and hustle of Vegas is all good in its own way and its populist sensibilities really are valuable, but how 'bout we just leave it there.

PORTLAND, OREGON

PHOTO BY BILLY COLLINS

SUSTAINING PRIVILEGE

Portland, Oregon

It's hard not to like Portland. With all its sincerity and dorky wholesomeness, it's kind of like the American antithesis of Las Vegas. For years now, Portland has been spoken of by progressive planners and local governance geeks as one of the cities that "gets it right"—exemplifying the promise of New Urbanism and developing sustainably, perhaps more than any other place in North America.[86] It's a mantle that has been only partially ripped by Vancouver.

It doesn't take much walking around to figure out what they are talking about. The place looks great at first, second, and third glances. The architecture all through the downtown core is lovely. There is brick everywhere, tons of old industrial spaces now occupied by funky bars, a couple of great bridges (highlighted by the beautiful Steel Bridge), and lots of the urban design features that are textbook-executed. Not far from downtown, it's easy to find neighborhoods that would be a pleasure to live in, many with a pastoral kind of charm; as Annie said while we were walking through Sunnyside just off of Hawthorne in the southeast, "God, it feels like the Shire in here. I keep waiting for a hobbit to run out of one of these houses."

Portland and Vancouver neatly match each other in all kinds of ways. They are almost exactly the same size in terms of population: in 2008, the city of Portland had 568,000 people and a metro regional population of 2,338,000, eerily close to Vancouver's population of 612,000 and 2,250,000. Despite the population similarities though, Portland looks a lot smaller. There is a strange paucity of high-rises, especially downtown, and the whole city is vastly more low-rise than Vancouver. It's a lack of density that is reflected across Portland's metro region.

The city of Portland alone sprawls across 145 square miles (376 km^2), while Vancouver sits on only 44 mi^2 (114 km^2). Or, to put it another way, Portland has only 14.1 people per hectare, while Vancouver's density dwarfs that at 48.3. That gap is reflected in some basic housing stats: Portland averages 6 units per hectare, while Vancouver has 20.9 u/ha, despite having almost the exact same people-per-housing-unit ratio.[87]

In some ways, Portland's comparative lack of density makes their greening accomplishments that much more impressive. When people talk about Portland and its successes, they are really talking about its transport and related land-use planning strategies. There definitely is a lot to be impressed about when you look at the work they have done reconfiguring how people get around.

There are beautiful Euro-style street cars that slide around quietly on a downtown continuous loop. The whole City Center and out to the Rose Garden is a Fareless Zone where public transit is free. The Max light rail extends out into the surrounding suburbs. There is a solid bus system supported with huge promo and outreach. And more than anything there, is a ton of biking. Portland is doing more than any city I know of in North America to get people riding bikes: clearly marked bike lanes and boulevards, dedicated lanes and bridges, aggressive infrastructure development, all kinds of promotional "pull" campaigns, covered bike parking, and lots more.

All of this is driven by some genuinely progressive work on land-use planning and transit-oriented development (TOD, sometimes called transit-proximate development). The regional governance body, or Metro, has a lot more capacity and authority to enforce regional, sustainable development goals than anything remotely available to Metro Vancouver, and the city and region appear to have a genuinely collaborative planning relationship.

One of the key architects of the new Portland is Metro Councilor Rex Burkholder. I asked him which pieces he thought were most essential to Portland's success:

> Number one would be a strong culture of direct citizen involvement in government decision-making. It is the first goal of the statewide land use planning program. There are hundreds of Advisory Committees at every level of government (government actually feels obligated to go out and recruit members!). Much of this is an outgrowth of government-sponsored disasters that began in closed rooms in the 1950s and 1960s: the interstate highway system, urban renewal, and the heavy pollution of rivers, land, and sky. A strong counter-culture demanded better, neighborhoods stood up for themselves, and they used the system to demand a place at the table. Like myself, many movement/grassroots leaders start small: in their neighborhoods or on their one issue, then see the connections and grow to meet the challenges. There is also a very healthy, collaborative third sector, focused not just on charity but on social change, that supports each other in their advocacy.

But there is something askew in Portland and it takes a while to figure out exactly what it is. I really do have a lot of admiration for Portland, but I think there are a series of interconnected and pretty fundamental issues that it, like Vancouver, is a very long way from resolving. The core of the problem is a conundrum that you are very familiar with: in making a compact, well-designed city core built on neighborhoods that are walkable and well-served by transit, Portland and Vancouver are pricing everyday people out. In some ways, Portland is far ahead of Vancouver in getting progressive policy on the ground, but in other ways neither city is doing nearly enough to honestly address these issues and is willfully ignoring their ramifications.

•••

Housing prices have skyrocketed all over North America in all kinds of cities and, even after 2008, this northwesterly rendition of New Urbanism is very clearly creating a new and specific dialectic of tidy unaffordability. It's a real dilemma: in making a city more attractive and liveable, "sustainability" is fast becoming just another commodity. Yuppies and speculators buy up all the downtown housing stock that is pedestrian, bike and transit friendly, while working-class people get forced out into burbs like Surrey or Coquitlam or Vancouver, Washington where they become ever-more car dependent—a shackle that is swiftly becoming more and more costly. The "smart growth" trajectories in Vancouver and Portland both point toward cities where privilege is accentuated by sustainability and marginalization is compounded by isolation.

Somewhat ironically, this tendency is the polar reverse of the abandonment of inner-city cores that began post-WWII but rapidly accelerated in the late-60s and early-70s all across North America. In fleeing cities that were perceived as dangerous and uncivilized, suburban living and values were valorized and embraced in ways that has radically altered contemporary conceptions of urbanity. Perhaps the core achievement of the current planning regimes in both Portland and Vancouver is in making urban living attractive and potentially sustainable, but that re-embrace of the city comes with the all-too-familiar displacement of working people, gentrification, and all the attendant consequences.

Among the most egregious mistakes that are being made is describing sustainable local communities as "urban lifestyle alternatives": this is an oft-used phrase that begins to explain how progressive planning and local community development can be reduced to commodified assets. It's the bun without the tofu. It's the aesthetics without the fundamental and antagonistic politics that are so essential to an actually radical urbanism. Building a better city just cannot willfully ignore the "who is it for?" questions while trumpeting its sustainable "smart growth."

All layers of people in Vancouver and Portland are acutely aware of the problem. At seemingly every gathering, formal and informal, talk relentlessly reverts to housing issues. People really want to talk about housing and affordability, and while lots of it is lip service, most of it is genuine. But there are all kinds of nuance when we're talking "affordability." As Gord Price, Director of Simon Fraser University's City Program, said to me:

> Affordability of housing is a personal measure: everyone can relate the value of their home, the cost of rent, the change in status, to their income. But it's hard to keep perspective. We tend not to adjust prices into "real" dollars, i.e. inflation-adjusted. And our expectations stay the same even as circumstances change. In particular, as land near the center goes up in value, we still see single-family housing on separate lots as the norm, even though multiple-family housing may be a "fairer" comparison.
>
> There is also the question of what constitutes "affordability" and it often falls into the politics of envy. Government assistance for non-market housing, providing access to those below a certain threshold, may be resented by lower middle-income renters who aren't eligible but will be taxed to fund such programs. Interest rates and liquidity, determined by forces beyond the boundaries in any city, have as much to do with affordability as local supply and demand. Likewise, housing that is "low-cost" may actually be more expensive if incomes are comparatively lower. Homes in Detroit don't cost much, but in fact may be more relatively expensive to those with very low or no income than expensive housing in a prosperous city.

As Gord cautions, it's easy for conversations around "affordability" to slip into personalized whining, but, while bearing that in mind, there is something very specific that is happening here and by almost any measure Vancouver, like Portland, is seeing shelter prices emerge as a fundamentally entrenched issue. And city planners are equally aware of the issues that they are faced with and, in many ways, have created. Much of the glossy literature tries to, well, gloss over affordability, claiming that Vancouver actually *has* dealt with it:

> Strategies that bring security to low-income people who have long resided in the inner core are vigorously pursued. By seamlessly meshing an array of household types, Vancouver's new neighborhoods have avoided the differentiated enclaves that appear in so many other cities.[88]

That's true to a certain extent but is mostly bullshit, and planners know it. Are you sure that there are no "differentiated enclaves" here? Really? You want to stand by that? You really think that low-income folks have housing security? As one city planner told me (way the hell off the record), "There's not much we can do. The nicer this city gets, the more people want to live here. The more people want to live here, the higher the prices. What are we supposed to do? Make it uglier? Honestly, we are kind of proud at how expensive housing is—it shows that we're doing a good job developing this as an attractive locale."

If that's the evaluative baseline, then the city must be doing a terrific job because even after a market crash and the still continuing volatility in the maret that has equaled a 12.5 percent drop in the average price for a detached home in Greater Vancouver, the current shelter prices in this city remain absurd. In early-summer 2009, the average cost of a single detached home across the region was $675,268 (CAN). In East Van, a section of the city that's ostensibly working-class and poor, it was a little less at $608,174 and a truly stupid $1,237,674 in Vancouver West.[89] In June 2009, according to the CMHC, Vancouver had the highest rents in the country, with an average two-bedroom setting you back $1,154 per month.[90]

That trajectory is difficult to address, given Canadian cities' limited range of tools, but political will is the most important requisite, including the backbone needed to confront certain sectors' reticence to give something up. As Gord put it:

> American cities typically have a larger range of tax tools and senior-government assistance than Canadian cities. But the most important tool is land-user controls, particularly density, and even those in favor of more affordability tend to be resistant to substantially increased densities. No one from City Hall goes into a neighborhood and says, "Hi, I'm here to change the character of your community in order to increase its affordability." When it comes down to it, no one really believes that government would deliberately introduce policies that would lower the value of existing housing in order to

address affordability—especially if it would lower the cost of housing below the value of mortgages on existing housing.

In talking to many of Vancouver's key power brokers over the past three years on and off the record, they, almost to a person, appear befuddled at best, as if the housing crisis is both independent of them and beyond their capacities to address—as if market forces were immutable and unassailable. It's conventional wisdom that despite everyone's best efforts, despite whatever progressive planning a city might adopt, the market will eventually set its own level, and given that Vancouver is such an attractive locale for so many reasons, people will inexorably drive prices up. As Larry Beasley told me in 2008:

> In the last two years, the situation has changed fairly dramatically, creating problems we can't ignore or sidestep. The main reason for that is the very popularity of the city we have designed. And this is very much a designed city. It's not by accident. So many people want to be here that prices are skyrocketing, very dramatically over the last two years. And that's begun to present a scenario like you describe in a surprising way, and its taken a lot of the middle people and shifted them over to the disadvantaged group when it comes to their housing. They're basically pushed out of the market. Especially young people who are just getting started and could, through hook or crook, one way or another, find a way to get a home. I'm talking about middle-income young people, clerical support workers, service workers; they could figure something out. And now, almost all of that is going now, because of the price of housing.

So, is that just life in global capitalism?

That's more or less what I heard when we met with Hindi Iserhott, an organizer for the City Repair project in Portland that does all kinds of fun placemaking stuff: intersection conversions, installations, art projects, gardens, community events, straw bale buildings, and lots more. Hindi took us on a tour of the Sunnyside neighborhood where their office is located and they have done much of their work. As we walked around I asked her if she lived nearby. She said, "No, I don't. It's too expensive. None of us really do." It's another twist on gentrification: in making a neighborhood a real community, the people who do all the work get priced out.

And of course it's not just new-school hippies and community organizers who are scattered, it's all working people. People who operate without trust funds, investment portfolios, and padded savings accounts rely on the social capital that dense city neighborhoods foster so easily, but when those same people are pushed to the urban periphery, the capacity to replicate similar dense networks is undermined, and society drifts ironically in exactly the opposite direction that "smart growth" or New Urbanism planning was explicitly focused on creating.

***

The market puts us in a Faustian bargain: almost any attempt to beautify, improve, develop, or embolden a community inevitably means it will price its most vulnerable/valuable citizens out and undermine all that good work. Capitalism values selfishness and self-interest above all. Progressive planning and social policy try to mitigate this, but are always behind the curve and at a pronounced disadvantage. Some Marxist urbanists, maybe most powerfully Manuel Castells circa the mid-1970s, argue that this has been precisely the role of urban governments under capitalism: to ameliorate conditions for the worst market casualties, mitigate crises, and provide enough basic infrastructure for capital to continue to accumulate.

I refuse to believe that there is no alternative to that depressing narrative short of the mythological revolution, and I still have faith in revolutionary possibilities. Cities *can* do something other than smooth the way for capital and/or clean up its messes. It is possible to articulate and develop genuinely democratic and inclusive strategies that are not self-defeating, that don't reduce "community" to a commodity. There have to be ways to imagine sustainable community development that doesn't price people out. I think we can carve huge areas out of this economy for non-market life.

I want to further this argument by considering housing specifically. Not just because there is something rapidly approaching a genuine housing crisis in Vancouver, mirroring many cities in the Western world, but also because I think our approaches to this issue are emblematic of the kind of city that this is becoming. In many ways, housing is Vancouver's signature issue (though hardly exclusively ours) and how we confront it is a bellwether of our urban future. There is a ton of potential here and, rather than cower, we should embrace our current scenario as full of possibilities for remaking the city.

Housing is perhaps the most tangible and consequential symptom, but the real issue is the intentionality of Vancouver's development and planning policies. I am arguing that this city has to be willing to confront the global economy—rather than seeking ways to insert itself into global economic flows and then clean up their worst excesses.

It's a fundamental point. We should be using our privilege and position to create counter alternatives: a different way of understanding city-making that doesn't by definition produce whole classes of winners and losers, rejects the dogma of growth and rethinks "development."

Housing presents the ideal opportunity to resist simplistic market ideologies. The kind of housing a city has is dialectically entwined with its social milieu: a city dominated by a voracious, market-based commodification of shelter will allow itself to be propelled in complex but specific ways. It's an old cliché that two forces drive the market: fear and greed. And it wouldn't be too far off to say those are the two driving forces behind Vancouver's development trajectory. Sticking a fork in that callow ontology means imagining a fundamentally different kind of city.

So, what then? What shape should that resistance take? The two obvious and well-trod responses are largely good and true: the top end of the market has to be restrained aggressively and the bottom end has to be generously supported.

At the top end of the market, every possible avenue has to be explored to restrict the excesses of speculation and profiteering. Non-occupancy of condos downtown has to be reduced. We have to find ways to restrict the ability of investors to purchase property as speculative ventures. Huge disincentives have to be implemented against conversions that displace renters—taking three and four unit houses and turning them into one yuppie abode. In poor neighborhoods, especially, there can be no net-loss of beds just so someone can get rich. There are good ways to restrict the top end of the housing market by cleaning out subsidies for the very rich. For example, Rex Burkholder told me that the biggest housing subsidy in the United States is the home-mortgage-interest tax deduction and suggested that just eliminating that subsidy for second and third homes and moving that revenue to affordable housing could free up billions.

At the same time, social housing of all kinds has to be emboldened in much bigger increments—subsidized housing, rent supplement programs, shelters of all kinds, emergency beds, city-run

Single Room Occupancies, safe houses, CMHC (Canada Mortgage and Housing Corporation) co-ops: every version and rendition of public and social housing needs to be investigated. Much of the city's current arguments around housing point to the collapse of federal (and provincial) social housing funding and that's correct. As local superstar and MLA (Member of the Legislative Assembly) Jenny Kwan put it to me:

> Canada used to have one of the best social housing programs in the world between the early 1970s and the early 1990s. We have a great legacy of affordable housing all around the shores of False Creek from the east side to the west side. By 2001, British Columbia and Quebec were the only two provinces still building affordable social housing in Canada for a range of needs—from supportive housing to co-op housing. We were still building 1,200 units a year in BC until the Campbell government came into office and took a hatchet to it. Since then, we haven't even come close to that number.
>
> Without government intervening in the market and providing affordable options for housing, we will continue to see a crisis in housing affordability. It's terrible for the economy if people have to pay more of their income on housing—it lowers their expendable income and ultimately drives up personal debts. Literally in the last ten years, we have created a society where many families put their groceries on their credit card. That wasn't the case ten years ago. It is economically sound and cheaper to house people rather than to leave them in the streets. If we lift up everybody, as we build our economy, our whole society benefits. These initiatives must be seen as an investment in our communities instead of a cost.

This is all good, of course, and pursuing innovative approaches to subsidize housing is well documented and really just awaits political will and priorities. The argument that I'm after here is additive: it doesn't displace these two conventional approaches (restricting the top end and supporting the bottom end) but supplements them.

•••

I have real suspicions about some of the calls for social housing and the kind of society it suggests. Dubai, for example, builds a huge amount of (grim) government housing for immigrant workers so that they will have a ready supply of available, cheap labor. To some extent, that is what many of our proposals for social housing here suggest: that we need some way to house low-income people so they don't become homeless and an eyesore, don't offend tourist sensibilities, and so that there is a ready supply of workers to pour coffee and clean toilets. As development consultant Mike Geller once said to me:

> Whistler for example, has very specific programs to ensure that housing gets built for employees. Otherwise there won't be anybody there to deliver the pizzas or work in the restaurants, or even to work in the police force or teach in the schools.

So, what kind of city does that suggest? In part, a dual city like Castells, Sassen, and others have described, in which the very poor and very rich live in close proximity, with only the most distant hope of upward mobility for the impoverished. In many respects, I think we need new ways to think about housing that confronts the claim that the market or amelioration are the only routes. I think we need an aggressive approach to rethinking housing that provides everyday people with a huge array of possibilities that do not reduce homeownership to a salvific dream but also don't fetishize it.

There are a number of intertwined assumptions that have turned home ownership into a fixation. The most basic of these is essentially Jeffersonian: the idea that a truly free and democratic society has to be based on independent land-holders, because only property-owners are positioned to make responsible choices due to their liberties and commitments. There are lots of other good reasons to want to own: it offers a measure of stability, keeps you from pouring your earnings into a landlord's pockets, invests you in the neighborhood, makes you accountable to the people around you, and gives you a certain kind of freedom.

Theses values are revered in Vancouver largely beyond any kind of critical eye, except by sore losers like me. Many smart, thoughtful people have given me the same advice: "Get into the market—at any cost. Do whatever you can, move wherever you have to, but *get into the market.*" This advice is usually offered the moment they figure out that I am forty years old and have only ever rented and my parents have never owned a house either. This perceived imperative has ushered in a city where people are desperate to buy even if it means thirty-year leases and 70 percent of their income buried in their rancher.

GIANT

And why not? I hate seeing my money wash down the landlord drain as much as anyone (don't take this personally, John, really!). We have spent a little longer than eleven years in our current house and have paid more than $185,000 in rent over that time.[91] Just writing that made me throw up in my mouth a little. It doesn't take a financial genius to realize that we could have done things a little smarter. Maybe. Or maybe not.

Beyond the personal, financial benefits, I agree that there are some real social benefits to having a base of individual homeowners, but I also think that the edifice of home ownership should be challenged. I think many of the de facto assumptions about the value of home ownership are specious and there are many other ways to ensure stability and commitment with a well-housed citizenry that doesn't reduce housing to commodity and allows for flexibility and autonomy.

There are cities in which renting is not seen as something that only happens when you're too young, broke, or irresponsible to buy. I talked to landscape architect Duncan Cavens recently about this notion and he explained that in Zurich, where he used to live, renting is an extremely common and accepted option across the social spectrum, even in one of the world's richest and oft-cited most-liveable cities. He claimed that the rental stock, while as tight as it is here, is of excellent quality, that all kinds of people tend to rent permanently or semi-permanently and there just isn't the expectation that home ownership should be everyone's ultimate goal. This is true across Switzerland where "at less than 34 percent, Switzerland has the lowest home ownership rate in Western Europe. This may seem odd given the economic strength of the country."[92]

Or maybe not that surprising. I think there is ample reason to rethink the correlation between home ownership and prosperity, and even more reason to rethink our reification of homeowners as necessarily the pillars of a good and generous society. Homeowners, for example, are always among the most conservative and reactionary political factions in any community, in part because they tend to be fixated on their property values. I have a great deal of suspicion about how ownership turns a basic human need into an investment and, at some deeper level, I buy the Digger line that "no man has any right to buy and sell the earth for private gain," but we'll let that slide for now. What I am really after here is creative thinking about what innovative, equitable, and stable housing solutions for our current crisis might look like.

More specifically, I think there is a really good argument to be made for aggressively enriching what might be called a "third tier" or "third sector" of housing that sits outside conventional formulations of the market and social housing dualism. There are huge arrays of possibilities—some driven by creative density, some by financing innovation, some by social scheming, and some by the adjustment of individual expectations, but really we need to be thinking differently about housing.

•••

Very often upping the supply side (and thus density) is posed as the core answer to our current housing issues, and earlier in this book (especially in the Istanbul chapter) I considered some of the constellation of issues around density arguments. It's the simplest of economic arguments—if the supply is bumped up, the advantage will inevitably tilt toward tenants/buyers and by necessity prices will fall.

That's sort of correct, but for a good decade Vancouver has experienced an unprecedented construction boom and yet prices keep rising. Maybe the market will eventually find a threshold where supply outpaces demand, but that is a default answer, and a very poor one. A major flaw in the approach is that people aren't just buying to satisfy shelter needs; they are buying housing as an investment, and very often leaving the units empty, so that while there may be a limited demand for actual shelter, the demand for investment properties is vast.

That said, creative and thoughtful densification *will* help some. Vancouver badly needs a greatly expanded range of housing forms and our current design, planning, zoning, and by-law restrictions all need to abandon many of their current blinders. We need infills, laneways, row houses, secondary and tertiary suites, industrial lofts, garages, and all kinds of alternatives beyond single-family detached and glass-tower condos. As Lance Berelowitz writes:

> We need to explore those other forms of housing that Europe has mastered over the centuries, such as the central courtyard block housing of Barcelona, Paris or Berlin, the mansion block and adaptable row housing of London, the semi-detached narrow lot duplex housing and brownstone housing forms of North America's east coast cities, the side courtyard housing of southern California, the galleria housing forms of South America. And smaller secondary houses inserted into the rear of larger single family lots.

> We also have an opportunity to optimize the physical infrastructure we already have, such as using Vancouver's extensive lane system much more intensively for some of these alternative housing forms. Why can't we have housing that faces onto the lane, above (or instead of) the parking garage? And we need to consider radical changes to Vancouver's parking bylaws to reduce the required amount of parking, which currently helps perpetuate many of the problems we are trying to address.[93]

There is definitely a far-wider range of possibilities than Vancouver has been traditionally willing to consider, but it doesn't solve the basic problem, in fact may exacerbate it. If not supplemented with a similar social commitment, simple densification will give developers a free reign to densify their profits and everyday people will still be stuck with the same problem. Currently formulated, densification is the most facile possible approach, but is being leapt on by those with profit to make because it adds potential to their dwindling supply pool.

Density might well be powerful, but only if it is constructed as counter-hegemonic: as getting in the face of privilege by creating the conditions to alter existing power relations. To my mind, that can be done by countering the urgency, the panic, to get into the market with other options that don't shackle people with some crazy mortgage but also doesn't allow their money to evaporate and make someone else rich. There are several avenues, all of which I think can be described as falling within a third sector or non-market continuum.

Very often third tier solutions are interpreted as "helping people get into the market" with subsidies and incentives, and that's fine, but what about helping people get *out of the market* or sidestep the market as currently constructed?

What if cities started acting like non-profit developers? Why shouldn't cities use their vast resources (including credit availability, land, and by-law powers) to finance affordable housing themselves, while selling units as cheaply as possible with strict resale restrictions to prevent profiteering? And that's not even considering all the creative financing mechanisms that are available and pretty widely understood as means of locking in affordability.

I recently stayed with a pal in Worcester, Massachusetts at the Collective A-Go-Go house, a great place on five acres inside the city limits. The house was purchased a couple of decades ago by an anarchist who received an inheritance that he didn't want. After buying the house, he gave it over to a specially created trust fund, which now administers the property. Residents pay puny rents that cover taxes plus maintenance and the surplus goes into a common fund. At the end of the year the collective takes the cash and donates it to a local non-profit project. Collective members live in a great house on a beautiful property, the house is contractually mandated to be permanently affordable, and the city gets some engaged citizens with the time and inclination to contribute their energy and money to the common good.

What's wrong with this model on a larger, municipalized scale? It doesn't have to be this exact rendition necessarily, and I'm obviously simplifying many of the issues, but I think that it's a micro version of precisely the kind of innovations we need. And those innovations exist and are working, not perfectly and with some bumps, but they have real promise.

•••

Over the past couple of decades both Canadian and American cities have used a variety mechanisms, many of them federally-funded, to get people into the market: down-payment subsidies, sweat equity grants, creative mortgage instruments, adjustable rates, reduced down payments, balloons, and a whole array of other attempts to support low-income people's market entry. Portland is doing what it can to leverage some of this. Burkholder filled me in on a few of their approaches:

> One way is to use urban renewal funds for subsidizing housing development for lower income households. Those funds can be combined with tax credits (as well as some federal transportation dollars if the development is along light rail for TOD) to either build public housing or assist non-profit providers. The other end to work from is to reduce the cost of transportation, currently up to half of the cost of living for lower income households. We are doing this by providing good transit and biking options as well as zoning housing and employment and shopping/services in close proximity. Not there yet, but this is the trajectory we are pursuing. Of course, having an equitable federal housing policy would help immensely.

These approaches are all good, and of course they need to be vigorously pursued from all angles, but I think we can get more creative than that and look to cities like Chicago, Burlington, and even Portland for some real inspiration in challenging the conventional home-ownership wisdom.

There are active and viable third sector models, particularly shared equity ownership models, which are making real impacts and, to my mind, have enormous potential for Vancouver. The baseline of shared equity is permanent affordability by restricting the resale and appreciation value and sharing the equity between homeowner and a stewardship organization, usually a non-profit community society. Maybe better called "common property" or "democratic property," landownership becomes a hybrid that puts individual needs in a social context and allows individuals security of tenure without profiteering.

Maybe the best articulation of shared equity housing is the Community Land Trust (CLT) and it's really not complicated at all. A CLT acquires housing stock and sells the housing units to individual buyers but retains the ground lease: that is to say, the homeowners own the house and the CLT owns the land. Then the agreement builds in some kind of resale formulas where the homeowners can resell when they leave but with limiting restrictions that preserve affordability for the next buyer. Thus, the subsidy is only required once: after the first purchase affordability is locked in permanently.

Homeowners build wealth, have all the rights and responsibilities of ownership, including security and stability, but have access to stock they would have no shot at otherwise. Buyers are making a simple trade: they get a substantial front-end subsidy but take a loss at the back end by giving up their right to (theoretically) unlimited appreciation on the open market. It's not one everyone would accept, but is highly attractive in many ways, not just for the possibilities it opens up for individual homeowners, but also for the kind of city it invokes.

Shared equity models, especially if imagined on a wide-scale, should be viewed as an opportunity to reshape the city. The market currently forces people to think selfishly—to look after their own self-interest, to panic about their housing futures, to profiteer just because they can, to be small-hearted, etc. This kind of world-view turns housing into just another hustle. The market takes people's worst instincts and valorizes them. Shared equity housing turns that on its ass and gives people an opportunity to think differently, not just about their money, but how they spend their lives.

There are of course a number of objections: libertarian-type capitalists (correctly) perceive this as an unfair government intrusion, undermining the "free" market with unwarranted subsidies that create distortions. I agree and think that's necessary and very good. Similarly, developers and realtors will (correctly) view CLT's as undermining their efforts and cutting into both supply and demand. I'd also agree with that and, again, it's still a good thing.

Others claim (incorrectly) that shared equity schemes doom tenants by never letting them build enough wealth to move into the private market. Certainly it's true that owners of resale-restricted homes can't get lucky and cash in for crazy money when the market goes nuts, but it's just not true that they will walk away with no equity. It's also not guaranteed that housing will inevitably and constantly appreciate, but the shared equity agreements are just that, shared, and homeowners do build wealth (typically pegged to inflation plus upgrades made during tenure). All statistical evidence supports the claim that homeowners do leave these arrangements with significant equity, often enough to enter into the market.[94]

Obviously there are a number of factors required to make any third sector or common housing scheme work, and those factors have to be just right for it to have real social impact. First and most fundamentally, funds have to enter into the system to get it going—someone has to buy the housing. That's obviously the biggest issue, and it can come from public or private sources, but that expenditure is a one-time subsidy, and then the units are locked into a permanent-affordability cycle.

The other key factors are mostly organizational and pretty much in place here in Vancouver. You need financial institutions willing and able to deal with innovative models. You need community support and desire. You need flexible and creative resale formulas and agreements. And you need organizations that can steward the process long term in a responsive and responsible fashion. In many ways, Vancouver is the ideal greenhouse to give CLT's a fair and scalable shot, the money is here, the need is here, and the will can't be too tough to generate.

•••

Community Land Trusts are just now emerging in Canada but there is a strong (if short) history in the States of shared-equity, hybrid models. The first American CLT was created in 1967, emerging out of the civil rights movement in rural Georgia as a way to secure tenure for African American farmers, and the first urban rendition was in 1981 in Cincinnati, by a church and community coalition whose goal was to prevent parishioners from being forced out of neighborhoods by "urban renewal" schemes. The first municipally generated CLT was established in 1984 in Burlington, Vermont.

Now there are over two hundred communities across forty-one American states with major CLT projects underway, including Chicago, where the city's Department of Housing has created a non-profit (the CCLT) determined to make the land trust the biggest city-wide initiative in the nation and the Champlain Housing Trust in Burlington, Vermont which is currently the biggest CLT in the United States with more than 2500 members, 410 owner-occupied houses and condos, 100 co-op apartments, 1200 units of rental housing, and fifteen non-residential buildings and condos in a city of only 40,000 people(!).

Having spent quite a bit of time in Burlington over the years and seeing the great work that has been done there, I asked board member John Emmeus Davis to identify the core successes of the Champlain Housing Trust:

> I would say there are three. First, we have expanded access to homeownership for lower-income households who are excluded from the market, while preserving access to that same homeownership opportunity for the next generation of lower-income homebuyers; CHT has enabled its homeowners to build personal wealth, while retaining the public's investment in that home; and CHT has protected security of tenure, with only nine foreclosures and no homes lost over its 25-year history, while enabling its homeowners to resell their homes quickly and to move easily into other homes.
>
> Second, the CHT has seeded and supported a major policy shift in Vermont, where a public commitment to subsidy retention and permanent affordability has been woven into the funding priorities, planning goals, and public laws of both the City of Burlington and the State of Vermont.
>
> Third, we have demonstrated the effectiveness, versatility, and scalability of Community Land Trusts to a national audience—and, with last year's World Habitat Award from the UN—to an international audience. If a CLT in a small city in Vermont can build such a diverse and sizable portfolio, then CLTs in larger cities, having more public resources for affordable housing, can do the same.

I think that right now, especially in a time of economic crisis and flux, is the time to be learning from places like Burlington and aggressively developing the non-market sector of Vancouver's housing stock. John agreed with me:

> The potential is great for rapid and sustained growth of this sector in any city. All that is lacking is the equity investment from public sources to buy the land and close the affordability gap between what the housing costs to build and what a lower-income homebuyer can afford to pay.
>
> Will such public investment be forthcoming? Unfortunately, too many institutions, professions, and individuals have a vested interest in perpetuating the present system of debt-financed, market-priced homeownership to believe that significant resources are going to be diverted into nurturing a new system of shared equity homeownership anytime soon. Even in the face of the mortgage meltdown in the United States, most of the federal money being expended to save failing banks and ailing homeowners is being poured into rescuing the very system that caused the meltdown in the first place. To paraphrase Peter Marcuse, we don't have foreclosures because the system is not working; we have foreclosures because that's the WAY the system works.

Of course, the crux of the problem, which John points to, is that there is an immense amount of vested interest in a system that is designed to keep people in massive debt for most of their adult lives. But perhaps the incredible rate of foreclosures and the dismantling of trust in the banking industry in the United States might change a few minds.

> The CLT carves out a protected space where market forces, political pressures, and speculative incentives are held at bay. It captures land gains created by society and prevents the loss of public subsidies invested by society, so that lower-income people are not excluded—or extruded—from neighborhoods as real estate markets go through periodic cycles of boom and bust.
>
> The impact of these non-market enclaves on the larger city, were they to be brought to scale, is difficult to predict. Certainly they would promote and preserve greater racial and economic diversity. They would provide a more durable, effective, and fiscally prudent

> vehicle for the investment of public dollars in affordable housing and community development. They could also have the political effect of empowering and engaging local residents in planning and guiding the future development of their own neighborhoods.

There are tons of organizational and fiscal variations on the shared-equity theme—which are necessary as the model is adapted to fit local conditions and predilections—but really the core is a fundamentally different approach that both implies and creates a different kind of city, one which isn't defenseless in the face of the market and doesn't curl up and whimper when threatened by the advances of capital accumulation. It suggests an aggressively imaginative social sphere, both public and private, that isn't willing to let the city be reduced to gentrification and profiteering.

The key is to actively expand the non-market sectors of the economy and society—not just in terms of housing but to imagine municipal governance as a cooperative, counter-hegemonic exercise in urbanity. City governments have to position themselves as creating a city of citizens, resisting the inevitability of the market that insists that rich people should always get their way just because they're rich.

Community Land Trusts are one pressure point that has a lot of potential and a history of success, but my argument is not about valorizing that particular model per se but to keep insisting on the city as a shared social space for democratic culture, not just a mechanism for wealth-building. Real choices, real policies, and real politics are possible and housing is right there among the key, available arenas.

If Vancouver and Portland fail to recognize this, all their hard work and progressive innovation will be lost and "sustainable smart growth" will become one more accoutrement of privilege. If we aren't actively confronting privilege we end up with a society that has very little civil about it, the fabric of order has to be maintained with increasing police and security apparatuses, and the way we talk about urban "safety" becomes distorted and weird. There's a reason that all those expensive condo developments come with swipe cards, security cams every three feet, and teams of security guards. If we can't ensure equitable access to the common wealth—and secure housing is a key—our society slips further from ethical legitimacy.

NEW YORK CITY, NEW YORK

PHOTO BY AMANDA MARCHAND

BAIT AND SWITCH

New York City, New York

It's incredible how deeply etched New York is in Western ideas about urbanity. Maybe everyone reflexively thinks of whatever culturally dominant megacity is closest to them—Tokyo or Mumbai or London or whatever—but when I first think of a great city, I think of New York City.

Part of that is just my own experience. I moved to NYC with about a hundred dollars, an internship "job" at the *Nation Magazine* that paid seventy-five bucks a week, a single backpack full of ratty clothes, and a piss-and-vinegar attitude. I didn't know anyone, had nowhere to stay, and really no clue.

I spent the first week sleeping under my desk in the office, totally surreptitiously thanks to the help of a kind staffer. Then I rented a foldout bed in the living room of a one-bedroom apartment in Hell's Kitchen with an obnoxious woman and her two obnoxious kids. Then, after a month, I moved to a cheap room at Eleventh Street and Avenue C, just off Tompkins Square Park. I hustled almost any job I could find after work. I stuffed envelopes, ran errands, painted apartments in the Bronx, moved furniture in Brooklyn, cleaned a library in midtown, begged two-day old bread at bakeries, sold used books at The Strand, bummed subway tokens from editors, and went to dozens of events that offered free food.

After six months, I reluctantly left town. Selena had moved down to stay with me in April and she became pregnant, literally within days,[95] so we moved to Vancouver to have a baby, intending to turn right around and return to NYC as soon as possible. That was a long time ago now: Sadie is seventeen,[96] we're still living in East Van, and I can't really imagine leaving.

But my goodness, I miss New York. I miss it almost everyday and I definitely miss it right now. I can't really think of a particularly articulate way to put it. You know what I'm talking about, though. It's the sheer volume and rush and energy, the inescapable feeling that something is going on. I remember leaving NYC so clearly, thinking that I was going from somewhere to nowhere. When I arrived in Vancouver, I walked around and wondered where all the people were: Were they all inside? Where was everyone?

I was just in love with New York and still am—me, and a couple hundred million others. Sure, part of that is because I last lived there when I was twenty-one and falling in love in a more specific way. If Selena and I had been in Ottawa or Omaha, it still would have been a great time of my life, but that ain't all of it. I have always felt easily at home in New York, and still, maybe voyeuristically, fully intend to live there again. I go back once or twice a year and every time I am still struck by that thing. It's the magnitude, the heft of the place: get on a Q or F train and take it for forty-five minutes out to Coney Island and there's still more urban density in Brighton Beach than most anywhere in Vancouver. You can spend years wandering around the boroughs and still be stumbling into great neighborhoods that you never heard of.

But it's also the sheer density of culture—theaters, libraries, clubs, dance companies, book publishers, magazines, and galleries, etc. From Sesame Street to where Lennon got shot to the Met to Carnegie Hall to CBGB's to ABC No Rio to the Brooklyn Bridge to the Apollo to Yankee Stadium to MSG—iconographic images and places are everywhere you turn. I remember walking through Central Park once and realizing that I was strolling beside the pond where Stuart Little won his yacht race. It was exactly like the drawing in the book, which for some reason really impressed me. For dancers, radicals, writers, bohemians, punk rawkers, hip hoppers, artists, and filmmakers, among others, you just have to go to NYC to measure yourself, to figure out where you stand.

Like Mario Maffi put it, "The moment you decide to go in search of a city is fraught with difficulties. Magical, yes, but also very tricky, because it is precisely in that moment that you determine your relationship with it: where and how to begin. Unlike other cities, New York won't hang about for you to solve these problems."[97] New York might not be gentle, but it has always been very kind to me.

But as great as New York is, it just ain't the same. Where is? Something started in the late 1980s that has changed New York and especially Manhattan in a fundamental way. And that something was/is an ugly storm of Giuliani, Reagan, the War on Drugs, and a civic commitment to militarized law-and-order that went on HGH after September 11, 2001.

There's not really one historical point when that transformation began, but if I had to choose one it might be the 1988 Tompkins Square Police Riot when police attempted to clear the park of the growing numbers of squatting homeless people and punks and then went crazy all through the night of August 6. Four hundred and fifty (!) cops were deployed, stampeding in Cossack charges up and down Avenue A, attacking random bystanders and activists, beating and arresting everyone they got close to, and injuring at least forty-four people. Hardly surprisingly, no cop was convicted of anything, and despite the initial galvanizing effects for radicals and activists ("Whose fucking park? It's our fucking park!"), the city won the war.[98]

The repercussions from that night are still visible today. Immediately following the police riot, near-martial law was imposed on the neighborhood with a truly remarkable number of NYPD officers and vehicles posted at every street corner and a strict park curfew established. Homeless people were episodically run out, and in June 1991 the park was closed for more than a year for "reconstruction," which included the razing of the historic band shell, ostensibly to calm neighborhood tensions and remove the homeless presence permanently.

The closure of the park was really the beginning of the end for the Lower East Side. It was the shock treatment[99] that began the steady displacement of community and flavor from the neighborhood in favor of gentrification, a market mentality, skyrocketing rents, and a distinct loss of vibrancy.

Aside from the loss that radical New York has suffered with the decline of the neighborhood and the increasingly impossible Manhattan rents, the occupation of Tompkins Square represents a key point in the remaking of New York, and Manhattan especially. A central aspect of that transformation, a newly aggressive policing strategy known as the "Broken Windows" approach has had ramifications for municipalities all over North America and is having a direct impact on Vancouver.

•••

There is significant statistical data documenting that New York City has experienced a major and steady drop in crime since the mid-1990s.[100] Rudy Giuliani has been given (and eagerly taken) a huge amount of credit for that decline, as well as numerous others who have made their names off their NYC reps, including Giuliani Police Commissioners William Bratton (now Chief of the LAPD) and the infamous Bernard Kerik (briefly Bush's nominee for Secretary of Homeland Security, then post-occupation and historically-abysmal Interior Secretary of Iraq, and now multiply-indicted felon).

There is also a huge amount of data and analysis suggesting that the NYC crime drop is highly questionable on a number of fronts: crime and homelessness weren't "solved," just pushed further out;

incarcerating huge numbers people is hardly a solution; and gentrification doesn't equal safety.[101] It is also true that many other American cities with divergent crime-fighting strategies experienced very similar statistical drops during the same period and NYC benefited from national trends and circumstances like everyone else. In fact, crime dropped significantly all across the United States throughout the 1990s, pretty much regardless of policing strategies. As Donohue and Levitt first argued in 2001:[102]

> Since 1991, the United States has experienced the sharpest drop in murder rates since the end of Prohibition in 1933. Homicide rates have fallen more than 40 percent. Violent crime and property crime have each declined more than 30 percent. Hundreds of articles discussing this change have appeared in the academic literature and popular press. They have offered an array of explanations: the increasing use of incarceration, growth in the number of police, improved policing strategies such as those adopted in New York, declines in the crack cocaine trade, the strong economy, and increased expenditures on victim precautions such as security guards and alarms. None of these factors, however, can provide an entirely satisfactory explanation for the large, widespread, and persistent drop in crime in the 1990s. Some of these trends, such as the increasing scale of imprisonment, the rise in police, and expenditures on victim precaution, have been ongoing for over two decades, and thus cannot plausibly explain the recent abrupt improvement in crime. Moreover, the widespread nature of the crime drop argues against explanations such as improved policing techniques since many cities that have not improved their police forces (e.g., Los Angeles) have nonetheless seen enormous crime declines.[103]

Donohue and Levitt famously suggested that legalized abortion presents a far stronger correlation with the drop in crime than any other single factor. They posited that "legalized abortion is a primary explanation for the large drops in murder, property crime, and violent crime that our nation has experienced over the last decade,"[104] and that given a twenty-year lag time, legal abortions could account for up to half of the overall crime reduction, with the vast increases in rates of incarceration nation-wide making up most of the other half.

These two were hardly the first to make this correlation and their methodology and rationales have come under steady fire.[105] Clearly there are many other factors to consider, all burdened by ideological assumptions and antagonisms. I don't want to leap into those arguments here, but the point is that decreases in crime and decreases in particular kinds of crime are rarely explained easily and simple "get-tough-on-crime" and "zero-tolerance" policies are not only politically and ethically challenged, but very often highly suspect empirically as well.

But the nuances and contours of those conversations have been pretty much lost in the bombast and bluster of Bush, Ashcroft, Giuliani, and all their conservative law-and-order brethren who are convinced that they have uncovered the route to clean and safe cities. That conversation has of course been complicated after 9/11, which locked in Giuliani's cred and gave him national stature, although his legacy had been cemented long before, first as US attorney for the Southern District of New York in the Reagan administration (1983–89) and then as mayor (1993–2001).

That New York legacy is being felt significantly in Vancouver, not only via the now-defunct Project Civil City (PCC) initiative and the provincial Safe Streets Act, but also through an increasingly shrill desire to "clean-up" the city, propelled by the usual roster of business associations, corporate media, and political hacks, and jet-fuelled by the Olympic hysteria about what the "world will see."

New York City not only has an iconic grip on North American culture, but it also has a tight clench on our understanding of crime and how to deal with it. Mob crime, white-collar Wall Street crime, gritty street crime, ghetto crime, gun crime, police crime: our notions about crime and policing are all bound up with NYC. From noir detective novels to hip hop to *NYPB Blues* to *Do the Right Thing* to Martin Scorsese to Abner Louima to Spider-Man to *American Gangster*—when we think of crime we often think of NYC, and that's part of why Giuliani and Bratton and CompStat and Broken Windows are particularly important to Vancouver—because, in following their lead, Vancouver is actively courting a crime-fighting strategy fixated on clearing out "problems" like homelessness, "cleaning up" blighted areas, and making the city safe for unrestricted capital accumulation and bland touristic placation. It is a strategy that is actively about reshaping Vancouver just as Manhattan is being remade.

•••

Broken Windows analysis ain't complicated and its trajectory is well documented. In 1969, a Stanford psychologist named Phillip Zimbardo took two similar cars and put one in the Bronx and the other in Palo Alto, California. The first he left with its hood up and license plates removed, the second was locked and parked legally. Virtually immediately the Bronx car was systematically stripped, then completely vandalized, while the California car was untouched for more than a week. Then Zimbardo smashed in a window of the Palo Alto car and, again, within hours that one was destroyed and flipped over. In both cases the vandals overwhelmingly appeared to be middle-class, White folks.

One of the key conclusions he reached was that once a certain threshold of carelessness had been breached, then it was a free-for-all. In 1982, James Wilson and George Kelling wrote an article building on this research in the *Atlantic* that expanded the analysis into urban space and policing, arguing that if a building's broken windows were left untended, then soon you'd have kids breaking more windows, then break-ins, and then squatters.[106] In 1996, Kelling and Catherine Coles expanded the analysis in *Fixing Broken Windows: Restoring Order and Reducing Crime in Our Communities*, in which they argued that if cities can attack low-level crime, vandalism, litter, disorder, and general messiness that they will be nipping much larger crimes in the bud.

Kelling was hired by the NYC Transit Authority in 1985, and then became a mentor to Bratton and Giuliani, who made calling for "zero tolerance" of street disorder into a key plank of his campaign and governing strategy. They immediately went after squeegee kids, homeless people, public drinkers, subway fare evasion, loitering, graffiti, welfare mothers, public artists, and anyone else violating any ordinance, real, imagined, or invented. The law-and-order dictates turned into open season on anyone not doing the right thing.

Zero tolerance/Broken Windows-style talk is an easy and spectacularly predictable strategy for certain kinds of politicians, for all the obvious reasons, which is why no one was surprised when Mayor Sam Sullivan introduced his Project Civil City Initiative in 2006 as a means to create "streets that are clean and free from aggressive and disorderly behaviour," to "find long-term and sustainable solutions to homelessness," and "eliminate the open drug market."[107] PCC aimed to put more cops on the streets, bring back auxiliary officers and quasi-cop "Downtown Ambassadors," install CCTV cameras widely, toughen ticketing and by-law procedures, get all over panhandling and street-level drug sales, and institute a wide-variety of similar measures, all directed at "street disorder." Even more creepily, the mayor asked citizens to turn on each other: "Use existing city employees such as parking enforcement and sanitation engineers to become the new eyes and ears on the street … to better work with our police to identify and report criminal activity."[108]

Vancouver's Project Civil City closely echoes so much of Giuliani's New York rhetoric, especially in its fixation on "public disorder": graffiti, misdemeanors, panhandling, noise, jaywalking, public urination, unkempt laneways, binners, people sleeping outside, and "open" drug use. It is also no secret that PCC closely mirrors the long-campaigned-for and very public goals of Vancouver's Board of Trade. On October 30, 2006 the Board sent a letter to Sullivan, Premier Campbell, and Prime Minister Harper "demanding action":

> Vancouver is in the grip of an urban malignancy manifested by an open drug market, rising property crime, aggressive panhandling and a visible, growing population of the homeless," stated an Oct. 30 letter signed by a dozen local business leaders…. "We have not lacked recommended solutions. What we have lacked is a sense of urgency, a will to put solutions into effect."[109]

Project Civil City was announced in November 2006, but the mayor said that it had nothing to do with the Board. The energy to control "public disorder" has hardly relented since, but given PCC's frequently noted anemic performance,[110] the dominant conversation began to shift within a year of Civil City's launch, looking for new rationales to support an increasingly aggressive police pose. Throughout 2007 and in an escalating series of crescendos since, Vancouver's corporate press has remained near hysterical about gang violence.

"Gang War imminent!" "Slaughter in Surrey!" "Gang war grips the Metro!" "Raging turf wars over drug loot leave cops struggling to keep up!" "Gang Mayhem!" "SOMETHING has to be done!!"[111] This stuff is like crack for Vancouver's servile corporate media. If you only read the *Sun*, *Province*, and *24 Hours*, with maybe a little CKNW and BCTV thrown in, you would be certain you were living in a war zone. Unchecked violence. Bullets flying everywhere. Innocent citizens cowering.

There are plenty of good reasons for the corporate media to be incessantly highlighting "gang warfare": it makes for good headlines, converges nicely with the law-and-order agenda, reinforces ideological presumptions, and makes easy work for columnists. I am not minimizing the impact of gangs: it sucks and sucks badly, for example, that seventeen mostly young men were killed in 2007 (a high point in gang activity) in gang-related violence. I agree: needless, violent death is always to be mourned and resisted.

But it's well past time for the local media and the police to get realistic about what and who are really causing violence in the Lower Mainland. Instead of launching an expensive, histrionic "assault" on gangs, why not a sweeping attack on poverty, greed, inequality, and mindless profiteering in which confronting gang violence is one plank?

With that in mind, there are three specific and interrelated points that I'd like to make:

1. In talking about gangs and violent crime, it is impossible to ignore the context.

There is ample reason to "get serious" about gang crime. Losing young men to violence is terrible, and far too many gangs are flourishing in the Lower Mainland, like everywhere else. It's not a "war" and people are not afraid to step outside, but talking about crime in those terms is a very potent and time-honored tradition. And, even more specifically, in a time of gangster economics, to steal a phrase from Cornell West, people should hardly be surprised that a certain percentage of the population will go a little further to get their hands on some loot.[112] The scourge of gangs and violent crime has to be placed in context; otherwise trying to confront them makes no sense at all.

Vancouver spent much of the first years of the millennium in an Olympic profitgasm: on fire with a free-for-all, get-what-you-can economic ethic that is reified and celebrated by our media. There has been so much money to be made and there is always a little collateral damage: it's to be expected in a market economy in hyper-drive. Doing whatever you can to get ahead in the world is the dominant economic ethic and that always means a certain number of losers.

But virtually everyone involved in gang violence is/was involved with gangs. They knew what they were getting into. If a day-trader goes broke, it's part of the deal. If a gangster gets shot, it's also part of the package. There are always victims in a thug economy—sometimes they're victims who tragically get in the way of gang profits, sometimes they are residents who get in the way of other kinds of profiteering. When everyone has to hustle for a buck, that means property speculation and flipping condos for some, while another small percentage make illegal enterprises their sector of choice. The idea is to get over by any means, access and secure markets, and screw morals if they get in the way.

People want in on the action when there is mad profit to be made but, for more and more people, conventional channels are increasingly inaccessible. In March 2009, the Canadian Centre for Policy Alternatives (CCPA) released a report highlighting that real earnings have declined significantly over the past thirty years for 60 percent of families in British Columbia. As Iglika Ivanova, a CCPA economist, put it: "People have been talking for years about finding it hard to get ahead. These figures show it's true."[113] For many families, especially from marginalized sectors, the Canadian mythology that hard (legal) work equals significant economic advancement is mostly a myth. Is it any wonder that some try alternative routes?

Add to that the blindingly obvious possibilities that global capitalism offers for extra-legal networks.[114] British Columbia's economy is deeply dependent on the international drug trade, with just marijuana sales responsible for a major percentage of the province's income. In 2004, Forbes estimated the pot crop value in British Columbia at around $7 billion or more than 6 percent of GDP, although "even that huge number, says Kelly Rainbow, a civilian analyst with the RCMP in Vancouver, is 'conservative, laughably conservative.'"[115] And those numbers don't include other drugs (which are a big deal in a port city) or the rest of the underground economy. For a kid with few options, the choice between an $8 hourly minimum wage[116] (still the lowest in Canada despite having the country's highest rents[117]) and ostensibly flashy, drug-economy work is a real one.

•••

There is a great deal of evidence indicating that not only are there a lot more really poor, homeless, and under-housed people in Vancouver, but also that the situation is out of control. As Miloon Kothari, the UN Special Rapporteur for Housing, said when he visited Vancouver:

> There is a deep homelessness problem here. I must say I was taken aback by the scale of the crisis here in the Downtown Eastside.
>
> It's glaringly apparent in Vancouver that for quite some time … successive governments have failed to create the housing that is

necessary. You have a legacy of misguided government policy that has led to this massive crisis in housing and homelessness.

We didn't hear this in other places. The decrepit nature of SROs, the conditions of the buildings that people are living in, very poor health ... I was repeatedly struck by the contrast that I see because it is such a beautiful city, because there has been so much investment. It is striking that a few blocks from million-dollar condominiums, that there is such immense poverty.

There seems to be a disconnect between the economic policies in Vancouver and the social policies that need to be in place.[118]

Vancouver's homeless population is not just huge, it is also rapidly expanding and entrenching in a time of unbelievable capital accumulation. The GVRD (Greater Vancouver Regional District) homelessness counts showed that homelessness more than doubled from 2002 to 2005 and then went up another 22 percent in 2008[119] and, by every indication, that trajectory is staying sharp. And it is not only homeless people, but also poor, working, and middle-class people who are all feeling extreme pressure. Housing is just one more corollary of the gap between rich and poor that is growing quickly. As a 2009 CCPA study highlighted, more than ever, the rich are getting richer and the poor poorer:

Inequality in British Columbia has grown since the late 1970s, with income increasingly concentrated among the richest families. While the bottom half of families earned over one quarter (29 percent) of total earnings in 1976, their share dropped to less than one fifth (19 percent) by 2006. Gains for the upper half of earners went almost *entirely* to the top 10 percent, whose share of total earnings increased from 22 to 29 percent.

In other words, the gap between the rich and the rest of British Columbians has widened to the point that the top 10 percent of BC families now earn considerably more than the entire bottom half of families.

Compared to other provinces, British Columbia saw a particularly rapid growth in the share of earnings going to the top 10 percent of families with children and a particularly steep decline in the share of earnings for the entire bottom half of families.[120]

TRAFFIC
CALMED
AREA
TRAFFIC
CALMED
AREA

Keep dogs off grass
Children play here

POLICE

As usual, the everyday effects of poverty tend to be felt most keenly by kids. For the fifth-straight-recorded year, British Columbia has the highest child poverty rate in Canada. In 2006 (the last year stats are available for):

- The proportion of children living in poverty in BC in 2006 was 21.9 percent, well above the national poverty rate of 15.8 percent.

- BC's Aboriginal children under the age of 6 living off-reserve had a poverty rate of 40 percent in 2005.

- The poverty rate for BC children living in families headed by lone-parent mothers was 50.3 percent in 2006, while the poverty rate for two-parent families was 16.3 percent.[121]

Are you freaking kidding me? More than a fifth of kids in this rich little corner of the world are living in poverty? More than half of single-parent families? What the hell is that? And the only thing newspapers can fixate on is gangsters shooting gangsters?

I work with teenagers everyday and I want kids to stay out of gangs and find healthy ways to live and make their money as much as anyone. But in this kind of economy, a few folks get rich quick and easy and many more get their asses kicked. It is an ethic, a way of life, and a set of economic rationales that infuse everyday interactions, morals, and decision-making. If we want to undermine gangs, we have to undermine this assumption of inequality if we really want to make an impact.

2. *What and who we call criminal is entirely political.*

Abbie Hoffman once said, typically brilliantly; "There's no such thing as a political prisoner. All prisoners are political prisoners. All trials in America are political trials. And when you go to jail you see that." He also said: "Understand that legal and illegal are political, and often arbitrary, categorizations," and he's exactly right on both counts.

The criminal justice system in North America and specifically in Vancouver is fixated on describing crime as primarily a threat from the urban poor. As Jeffrey Reiman suggests in *The Rich Get Richer and the Poor Get Prison*, the real value of fixating on crime as primarily the work of the poor is "that it deflects the discontent and potential hostility of Middle America away from the classes above them and toward the classes below them."[122] So, despite every bit of evidence and common sense that links poverty and endemic hopelessness to crime, upon whom do we fixate as the real problem in Vancouver? Homeless people, mentally ill, panhandlers, squeegee kids, drug addicts. How cowardly.

I asked community activist Am Johal what he thought about it:

> There is a real tendency amongst political parties to take the easy approach and be "tough on crime." It works within the simplistic centralized messaging campaigns that political parties tend to function under—political parties are no longer places of ideas, but extensions of PR companies or communications consulting firms.
>
> There is a media narrative which rears its ugly head every ten years or so. In the 1970s, it was Operation Dustpan, in the 1980s it was Expo, and in the 1990s they tried to police everything away as well. This tension between law and order obviously contends with health and human rights approaches. It's just that the health and human rights approach is more complicated—it implies a whole different way of approaching law and order. It's also about changing rank-and-file policing culture. The whole series of concepts and positions which limit the right to the city are discriminatory in basis—the police, civic departments, and private security have created a bubble unto themselves that helps them justify this direction in public policy. This is a complex issue and it will require complex interventions despite the populist politics that are being played out.

There's no elite conspiracy here: our criminal justice system has evolved in bits and pieces, fits and starts, but there is ample reason for those who are doing really well to keep everything in place. As Reiman puts it:

> I have not said that criminal justice policy is created to achieve this distribution of benefits and burdens. Instead, my claim is that the criminal justice policy that has emerged piecemeal over time and usually with the best of intentions happens to produce this distribution of benefits and burdens. And because criminal justice policy happens to produce this distribution, there is no inclination to change the criminal justice system among people with the power to do so.[123]

That's why they call it "maintaining order." There is plenty of reason for a certain number of people to keep things exactly as they are right now. As David Eby, Executive Director of the BC Civil Liberties Association, said to me:

> As individual citizens, we all have a role to play in ensuring our communities are welcoming, safe places for everyone. Broken windows fails to recognize the idea that community involvement, that getting people out into their neighborhoods and interacting with neighbors is the best way to break down stereotypes, ensure safety, and prevent crime. The false sense of "safety" created by turning our streets into police states is not only exponentially expensive, but fails to establish the sense of empowerment and belonging that makes people happier.
>
> For Vancouver, however, it's almost impossible to ignore the reality that no matter how many community gardens and public spaces are created, adequate social housing, drug treatment, and the decriminalization and regulation of illicit drugs including marijuana, prescription heroin, and oral cocaine would wipe out the vast majority of street crime and gang violence almost overnight. Until we can admit that our money is best spent on housing, treatment, and health care for people with chronic addictions rather than policing them and their dealers, we will not be able to move forward as a humane, compassionate society.

It is what is called the Pyrrhic defeat theory: the system needs to keep fighting crime in high-profile ways, but just enough so that it is always a problem in the public's eyes, always a virulent threat, but never solved in any substantial way. By maintaining a certain level of failure while never addressing the root causes of crime, public discontent is always focused at a certain end of the spectrum, and outrageous disparities in wealth and privilege remain obscured.

3. *Something is badly out of whack with our perceptions of danger.*

If our local press were really interested in talking about violence, if they were genuinely trying to prompt "drastic action" to help reduce what is killing people in British Columbia, they would be writing a lot more about cars. By any measure, cars are killing people at a relentless rate, kids in particular: motor vehicle accidents are (by far) the leading cause of death in British Columbia—and in Canada—for newborns up to twenty-one-year olds[124] and cars kill far, far more people than guns or gangs.

Interestingly, since 2002, the number of people killed annually in traffic accidents in British Columbia has dropped by roughly 25 percent, from more than 450 a year to around 350.[125] It is a drop that mirrors declines in traffic deaths in many North American jurisdictions, and authorities have no good idea why, except that maybe more people are wearing their seatbelts, people are driving less, and perhaps the price of gas is causing people to take fewer trips in general. In contrast, more people were murdered in British Columbia in 2008—140—than in any other year in its history, according to statistics recently compiled by the RCMP. Of all the murders in British Columbia last year, forty-three are believed to have been gang-related.[126]

So to recap: in 2008 there were exactly 2.5 times as many traffic deaths as murders in British Columbia and more than seven times as many road deaths as gang deaths. And those declines in traffic fatalities are attributable to systemic social changes, while, despite stupendous police and media efforts, gang violence is rising.

And even beyond that, it has always been a criminological truism that the vast majority of murders are committed by someone familiar to the victim: more than 80 percent of murders in British Columbia are committed by someone the victim knows.[127] It is overwhelmingly gangstas who get hurt by gangsta stuff. Targeted hits, drive-bys, fights—if you're not involved in the drug trade or gangster activity, that stuff only very rarely comes near you. In actuality, the vast majority of young men who have been killed as a result of gang violence were involved in some sort of gang activity themselves.

Traffic victims, on the other hand, are overwhelmingly innocent. Pedestrians and bikers—what did they do to deserve getting mown down? I guess you can argue that if people drive aggressively or drunk they are making their own beds, but what about all the passengers and the kids killed by cars? Those are genuinely innocent deaths.

So why aren't columnists getting hysterical about cars? Why aren't there enormous headlines screaming about this? Major car accidents with multiple deaths tend to get fourth-page stories detailing the crash, and that's about it. Single traffic fatalities are too banal and too common to report apparently. There is such a sense of inevitability when someone gets whacked by a car: that's just life. Deal with it. Why don't we feel the same sense of outrage as we do when a thug shoots some poor bystander?

So, to steal a line: *Something has to be done!!* And a lot of the answers are simple and obvious. Not only is there ample evidence that vehicle-related accidents are reduced substantially in denser neighborhoods (obviously) but there's also a huge body of evidence that rethinking urban design to emphasize pedestrian and transit-oriented streets reduces vehicle-related injuries and deaths.

It is a strategy that we know works, will substantively reduce death and injury, and will reduce ancillary violence. In the summer of 2008, the Vancouver police shut down traffic on four blocks of Granville Street for a weekend, a normally rowdy and fight-infested stretch of downtown's "entertainment zone" and confirmed that the area miraculously turned into an almost entirely violence-free zone.

> Const. Tim Fanning said the "test-run" street closure in the entertainment district and an injection of additional officers resulted in just one reported fight and one partier arrested for being drunk in public on Friday night.
>
> Police working the strip Sunday had nothing to report.
>
> "That's unheard of on a long weekend," Fanning said. "The patrons down there loved it. It was like a big love-in."
>
> On the average weekend, police on Granville Street deal with an influx of 25,000 young people, handle 20 street brawls, witness 70 to 100 more fights and arrest approximately twenty people for being drunk in a public place.[128]

If it is true that people are really ready to do "whatever it takes," are ready to take on radical measures, are ready to make genuine, lasting, and effective changes to reduce violence, especially against young people, lets start shutting streets down and doing whatever it takes to get people on transit, on bikes, and on their feet. We know this works, now the police know it works, it is cheap and doable, can begin immediately, and attacks what we know has always been the leading cause of violent death in British Columbia. I'm just saying.

•••

Combating poverty and homelessness, attacking the wealth gap, and doing everything possible to reduce car-culture are all strategies that do not fit within dominant ideological agendas, but if we are really interested in reducing crime and violence it would do us all good to try a little rationality and realism, rather than cheap headlines and clichéd rants about crime. If Vancouver is genuinely interested in liveability, it would do well to start acting to reduce the real causes of public disorder.

Reducing crime and violence to a bare minimum is a really important part of every city: a good city has to be safe and citizens have to be secure both in public and private. Combating inequality, nurturing convivial neighborhoods, emboldening community, and creating vibrant public space and common places are the surest and most lasting routes. Metastasizing polices presences, clinging to prohibition-style drug laws, ratcheting up fear, and inflaming gang paranoia only continue to decontextualize the roots of violence. As Am put it:

> Building community essentially means building relationships. It's when people have their back to the wall, when they are alienated from social life, when public institutions treat them poorly that people act out, predominantly out of desperation. We need every person to be aware of their human rights and civil rights. Canadians are the most passive people I've ever met in my life. Rights don't exist unless they are asserted. Every day, we have an obligation to fight for our rights and make sure every citizen has that right. It's a daily battle. The fight for human rights is not a spectator sport.

Bingo. If we can build a more convivial, less avaricious city we will have a far better base from which to reduce gangs, violent deaths, and thug mentalities. We aren't going to find that city on the global marketplace; we're going to have to build it ourselves.

DIYARBAKIR, KURDISTAN
PHOTO BY SELENA COUTURE

URBAVORE

Diyarbakir, Kurdistan

I was brought to Diyarbakir in the southeast of Turkey to speak at a conference put on by a women's organization named Kamer. It's one of those events that puts your own work into perspective. More specifically, it made it patently clear to me what a cupcake I am.

Stepping out of the plane in Diyarbakir in June was like getting blasted in the face with a powerful hair dryer turned to "wicked hot." It took a second for me to figure out how to breathe. I hadn't even gotten off the tarmac and into the terminal before the first tiny, barefoot kids started hitting me up for money. The rubble all through the city core was a sobering reminder that I was in the epicenter of a simmering war-zone.

Diyarbakir is the historic capital of Kurdistan. Of course, if you look for Kurdistan on your map, it ain't there. But it should be. For centuries, up to the beginning of the 1900s, it was subsumed under the Ottoman Empire as the Province of Kurdistan, but after WWI the Allies promised the Kurds an independent state in the Treaty of Sevres. After heavy lobbying and conquest by Kemal Ataturk, that plan was abandoned and the region was absorbed into the new Turkish Republic, with small parts being carved off and given to Syria, Iran, and Iraq, while the Kurds were left without a homeland.

This failure to create a Kurdish state has had a number of profound implications. The first is that resistance to Turkish rule has been fierce and unrelenting. There have been major rebellions, brutal episodes of repression and martial law, on-going guerilla warfare led in recent decades by the PKK (Kurdistan Workers Party), scores of Kurdish villages razed, the evacuation of huge chunks of the countryside, approximately forty thousand Kurds killed in the 1980s and 1990s, on-going antagonisms and human rights atrocities, and deep, smoldering resentment.

The "Kurdish question" remains perhaps the most tense, virulent issue facing modern Turkey, and racism, violence, and hostility toward Kurds is commonplace, even in styling Mediterranean cities like Istanbul, Izmir, and Antalya, which are hundreds of miles west of the centers of conflict. If you tell people in Istanbul that you are going to Diyarbakir, many will ask "Why? It's backward. And dangerous. What the hell would you do there?"

On top of the actual warfare, there are all kinds of other repressions intended to eviscerate Kurds as a people. Turkish authorities habitually and grossly underestimate the population of Diyarbakir so as to minimize Kurdish influence: it is often reported as a city of a half-million, but it is widely believed to be at least double that. Cops lurk everywhere, heavily armed, ready to crush demonstrations. Until 1991, publishing, broadcasting, or performing in Kurdish was disallowed. Even now the Kurdish language is severely restricted in public—in 2007 the mayor of Diyarbakir was censured for sending municipal New Year's cards out in Kurdish—and there are a whole host of legal and extra-legal suppressions of Kurdish language and culture. The police made little attempt to hide their surveillance of our conference, and it was highly recommended to me that I not mention the phrase "self-determination" at all during my talk, which of course made the impulse damn near irresistible.

We traveled through a number of small communities in the southeast while visiting Kamer projects and the reality that there is a war going on was impossible to escape. Most of the centers are staffed by women whose husbands have been killed in the fighting or have gone "to the mountains"—a euphemism for "joined the rebels." But it's not just the violence of occupation that women face, it is also severe domestic violence, honor killings, fundamentalist repression, and endemic cultural violence.

But I'm painting a grim picture here. Diyarbakir is of course also fantastic and brilliant and awesome. Its history is densely packed with kingdoms and peoples and religions and sects that I had never heard of. Diyarbakir was the capital of the Aramean Bet-Zemani in the thirteenth century BCE. It was once the center of Assyrian and Syriac cultures, was critical to both Roman and Byzantine empires, and has a central importance in Armenian history. There has been a mind-boggling history of sieges and conquests by Hurrians, Urartians, Assyrians, Arabs, Persians, Oghuz, Anatolians, Turkmen, Alexander the Great, Seleucus, and of course Kurds. It's freaking Mesopotamia, the Tigris runs through town, and history is what you breathe.

Diyarbakir is also surprisingly funky. I hadn't been in town long before a couple of local hipsters located me and dragged me into the bowels of the old city for an evening of hitting the nargila pipes filled with tobacco, herbs, and god-knows what else. The next evening the event organizers filled a couple of vans and took us out to a tea garden outside of town. There was a whole hill covered in little stages with bands playing raucous traditional-party music, hundreds of benches, tables, ottomans, and blankets, with people—multi-generational families mostly—eating, drinking, and dancing. I sat and watched a swirling, traditional dance of old guys waving handkerchiefs and, right in the middle, were three young women dancing happily—total hotties with their arms around each other, in skimpy clothes, smoking cigarettes. And wearing headscarves. Of course this whole scene, taking place in a traditional area known for its repression of women, made no sense to me. But in less than a week I could only glimpse how much I don't understand about the place.

There are a ton of stories but that'll tire you [*you sure you don't want to see more slides? I've got lots more of us RVing to Tahoe!*]. I really want to say something specific here, something about the fate of cities in a neo-liberal globalized order, Diyarbakir and Vancouver included.

A couple of days after the conference, I was wandering along beside the old city walls and stopped at a fruit cart. I had eaten a foolish amount of watermelon over the past few days (which the area is known for) so I chose an apple instead. It had a little apple-shaped sticker that said: "Grown in Washington, USA."

Are you kidding me? There I was, way in the Middle East on the banks of the Tigris, in an area historically famous for its fruit, and I'm buying an apple for ten cents that was grown in the Pacific Northwest? I flew 6500 km (4039 mi.) to buy an apple grown maybe 200 km (124 mi.) from where I live? What the fuck? How does that possibly make economic sense? How could that guy with a wooden cart in southeast Turkey possibly turn a profit on those ten cents when surely it cost way more just to fly it there?

•••

That's exactly the dislocation and fracturing of the globalized world. Everything is up for grabs, the entire world is one monster 24/7 market and "place" is a anachronism, entirely subsumed by the flows of capital and goods. Somehow, some way, that apple had made its way to Diyarbakir and landed on that guy's little wooden cart. I had a couple of quick bites—against my best impulses—and it tasted OK. Maybe a little woody, but not so bad. I couldn't really imagine a scenario in which it wasn't totally covered in pesticides and preservatives though and, frankly, it just seemed weird, so I chucked the half-eaten thing to some dogs that hovered over it instantly.

But that's really the conundrum facing cities in the twenty-first century. Globalization has meant the incredible stretching and expansion of social and economic exchanges—both accelerating and intensifying possibilities—so that traditional restrictions on trade, communication, and movement are just quaint. I can walk down my street and buy flowers that came in that morning from Ecuador and they're way the hell cheaper than the flowers beside them on the shelf that were grown in a greenhouse in Abbotsford. And, by some reckonings, they're even more carbon-friendly.

Globalization has also transformed traditional national borders and trade mechanisms: the volume of international commerce is so intense that regulatory bodies can barely keep up. Cities that were once embedded in regional and national economies and largely dependent on national support have become increasingly independent. As the world urbanizes in unprecedented volumes, cities have found themselves burdened with all kinds of new responsibilities and demands, but without sufficient government support—Vancouver's housing and homeless crisis, to give just one example, can be directly traced to the withdrawal of federal funding. We are in a new economic era that is built around the global marketplace, one in which cities are largely left to fend for themselves, and have to find new ways to thrive.

Of course, Vancouver is inserting itself easily and profitably into those flows, positioning and branding itself as a tourist destination, an investment site for high-end real estate buyers, an Olympic host, and an Asian transport hub, while it is still a resource investment locale and is trying hard to find its place in a number of other sectors. Diyarbakir is having all kinds of trouble finding any kind of niches: Who wants to go to Diyarbakir? Who wants to invest there? What role can an isolated, unstable place on the edge of the desert play in the new global economy? At one time, Diyarbakir was at the center of empires, a branch of the silk route, an important stop en route to Constantinople, perched on the Tigris with a direct transportation path down to the Gulf, deeply enmeshed in regional and inter-regional trade. Now? The city has been kind of forgotten.

So, how does a city like Diyarbakir get some cash? It's definitely not coming from the Turkish government. Right now the whole region is a loser in the global marketplace because it doesn't really have anything to sell. In the neo-liberal marketplace cities are just trying to sell themselves to capital, trying to find ways to attract investment, and right now Vancouver is a winner while Diyarbakir is on the losing end of the equation. However, the reality of that ethical and economic logic is not immutable, nor is it necessarily very stable. You're only as good as your last sale.

•••

By very strange and fortunate circumstances, a week after I got back from that trip to Diyarbakir I took one of my grad classes to attend the World Urban Forum (WUF3) that was held in Vancouver where municipal officials and bureaucrats from cities across the globe gathered to discuss their most pressing urban issues. Front and center was the same conundrum facing Vancouver, Diyarbakir and every other city: how cities can find a place in a globalized world.

The forum was titled "Our Future: Sustainable Cities—Turning Ideas Into Action" was billed conspicuously by local media as "15 Days to Save the World."[129] Organizers acknowledged freely that the event had no formal mandate, no capacity to sign anything binding, no real resources, and that it was actually just a schmooze-fest. It became eminently clear from the very first hours of the forum, and much to the vocal dismay of many participants from the Global South that there were simultaneous tendencies operating side-by-side, with little acknowledgement of the fundamental antagonisms between them. As Jockin Arputham, leader of Slum Dwellers International, put it:

> With 10 percent of what this conference cost, we could put on a conference where the poor people of the world would be invited to speak and tell about their experiences in the slums, and the delegates you see here today would not be allowed to speak, but would only be allowed to listen.[130]

It was these kinds of tensions that vibrated throughout the week. Overwhelmingly present, but entirely subsumed was a critical discontinuity between a neo-liberal-globalization agenda articulated by the World Bank, the IMF, and an omnipresent array of private financiers and development companies, and an apparent consensus on the importance of decentralization, local economies, local energy production, local control, and local democracies.

•••

This discontinuity was made evident repeatedly in the literature, both that provided by the conference and that distributed by participants and presenters. At first glance, it would appear that WUF3 was riding a wave of urbanist theory that embraces localism and community while still simultaneously positioning the event as a dating service that helps desperate, capital-hungry municipalities hook up with willing and able international financiers.

After a week of closely observing the WUF3, I could only assume that the bureaucrats, mayors, policy wonks, and others assembled somehow came to the conclusion that while local, sustainable development might be attractive in theory, the money is only going to be found through the market. Every session, every dialogue, worked around the same premise—that local control and participation is central to creating sustainable cities, especially in the face of global warming, climate change, and energy shortages. But the concrete conversations about money were reduced to the same base, neo-liberal rubric: capital markets, bond markets, IMF loans, private financing, and "innovative" private sector relationships are where the money is.

The inherent contradictions between these two perspectives is one of the most obvious and compelling narratives of our time, but at WUF3 the dissonances were overwhelmingly either ignored or forgotten or, maybe as a nod to Canadian politeness, just imagined away.

It all seemed very cozy and consensual at one level but, after a little more focused observation, the boots-on-the-ground reality emerged: economic globalization is driving municipalities into direct competition with one another for capital resources, seeking to attract funding with incentive packages promising juicy profits for investors. Simon Compaore, the mayor of Ougadougou, Burkina Faso who chaired a session titled "Local Public Finances and Decentralization," agreed with this: "We just have to go and get the money where it can be found."[131] For cities bereft of national government support, without infrastructure to support development, and already burdened by debt, the choices are very few. If the solution means selling basic resources and services to corporate transnationals, well, OK. What are we supposed to do?

At that same session Lamine Mbassa, the Director of Financial Affairs of Douala, Cameroon, described the way Douala has entered the bond markets with a vengeance. He said that his city has had to attempt to access private market capital via bonds because "there was no other way.... We have to market ourselves to companies."

And those private investors, banks, international lending organizations, and a myriad of consultants and companies are right ready to step in: USAID, the World Bank, Padco, PriceWaterhouseCoopers, IPF consultants, Evanson Dodge International, Shore Bank International, TCGI International, and seemingly innumerable private sector financiers were constantly visible at WUF3. At the bar, at sessions, at private meetings, in the halls, and in the literature all manner of financial consultants and representatives were willing and able to "talk" with mayors and bureaucrats looking for money. Running a city in the twenty-first century is all about the hustle.

At a Wednesday morning event titled "Municipal Finance: Innovation and Collaboration," Brian Field of the European Investment Bank pointed out that his organization now had three times the lending volume of the World Bank at 52 billion euros. So many hands immediately shot up at that point that the moderator made a suggestion: "Maybe you might want to get together later with Mr. Field?" he said, looking up hopefully, plaintively. "Umm, is your money available anywhere in the world?" he asked. "Why, yes, yes it is."[132]

At an afternoon session sponsored by Industry Canada, Dan Hoornweg, senior municipal engineer for the World Bank, put it more bluntly. "Look, give us enough of the right incentives and we'll be there. There is no shortage of investors. There are hundreds, thousands of investors, of pension funds willing and eager to invest if the incentives are right," he said. And, while speaking of water delivery and sanitation, he continued: "Look, if services are so bad and we can improve things so much, people will be willing to pay fees for basic services. We can't supply service that we can't collect money for, but we will talk with anyone."[133]

Anwar Versi, the Editor of *African Business* magazine, which is appropriately headquartered in London, England (!) opened his session with perfunctory remarks and handed the microphone over to the speakers by saying, "This is a dialogue, we want to talk. We really just want to know how we can raise some money."

Jacqueline Shafer, who spoke as a representative of the Bureau of Economic Growth and Trade, USAID (which had a massive presence at WUF3), responded directly. She said that USAID was looking for municipalities with "corporate-style governance," that they would help cities "partner with the private sector," "structure innovative funding opportunities," and "assist with revolving funds, bond funds, and encourage partners to seek capital-market funding." She also pointed to places like Mexico, where Evanson Dodge established the first bond-bank, and Karnataka, India, where a massive World Bank loan has developed the water system, as examples of the work that they were interested in.[134]

•••

Neo-liberalism wants to leave cities, like people, competing with each other on a globalized stage—each competing for money, investment, jobs, and attention. Thus, rather than ethical collections of citizens democratically pursuing a common good and addressing common challenges, cities are reduced to atomistic economic actors in search of the next buck. It is a future that Jan Sturesson, from PriceWaterhouseCoopers was very comfortable with. In his Monday afternoon presentation, "Cities of the Future—Global Competition, Local Leadership," he said:

> Cities have to start acting like corporations … service as a core business is dead, it is now a requirement to be playing in the premier leagues, people expect top-class service everywhere, and now sustainability will be expected to be in place…. Cities have to be looking for competitive advantages everywhere…. Cites have to find, improve, and define their competitive position by creating their own brand … you have to bring attention, talent and money to your city by creating a corporate identity—a *city brand that burns.*
>
> [Author's note: you have read that last bit with a thick Swedish accent and hold your hands out in front of you, clutching at air]

In a world where national actors are often reduced to bit parts, some folks place their hopes in international governance. It would be a good idea not to have much faith in the United Nations as a defender of sustainable local development, though. The UN has been steadily and unapologetically moving toward closer and closer ties with corporate allies, relying on "partnerships" to raise capital for projects, welcoming high-level executives into inner-circle advisory capacities, and making sweetheart deals with some of the worst polluters on the planet.

This clear new direction for the UN is titled the Global Compact and was unveiled by Kofi Annan in 1999 to encourage transnationals to become UN partners in development. Since then, a mind-boggling array of companies has joined forces with various United Nations projects, which included UNICEF dubbing November 20 "McDonald's World Children's Day" as McDonald's and UNICEF teamed up to "raise money for the world's children"[135] and BP-Amoco and Rio-Tinto sponsoring the World Conservation Monitoring Centre (WCMC). Other prominent Global Compact members include Shell, Nike, Novartis Aventis, Bayer, BASF, DuPont, and DaimlerChrysler.

As Maurice Strong, the godfather of the corporatization of the UN, said just before the Rio Earth Summit in 1992 while answering questions about his and the UN's close relationship with the corporate world: "The environment is not going to be saved by environmentalists. Environmentalists do not hold the levers of economic power."[136]

•••

Those levers of economic power were on promiscuous display at WUF3. What was ostensibly a meeting of the best urbanist minds from around the globe was a veritable slime-fest of cross marketing, convergence, and deal cutting: a living diorama of neo-liberal fantasy. WUF3's Corporate Prospectus, for example, made very clear that anything and everything at the Forum could be had for the right price. And with that price came very valuable and appealing privileges.

> Several levels of corporate sponsorship and support are available and offer unique branding and profile opportunities. With each package comes a valuable range of entitlements commensurate with the nature and level of your investment.
>
> **Contribution Levels**
>
> | | |
> |---|---|
> | $500,000 | DIAMOND |
> | $250,000 | PLATINUM |
> | $100,000 | GOLD |
> | $50,000 | SILVER |
> | $25,000 | BRONZE |
> | under $15,000 | SUPPORTER |
>
> Packages are created to be flexible and mutually beneficial arrangements will be tailored to meet the interests and proposals of select organizations in order to maximize business development opportunities. Sponsor entitlements in all categories may include all or some of the following:
>
> - An invitation for a senior executive to attend a private, high level social function(s)

- Assistance organizing a press conference for the special announcement of your choice
- A complimentary exhibit in the WUF3 Exposition
- Your corporate logo on all signage on site including plenaries, session rooms, networking and social functions, and other prominent display areas throughout the event site
- Reserved seating for all special functions
- Your company's promotional item in conference delegate bags
- Additional signage on or around the sponsored event, area or item
- An opportunity to make a presentation in the Presentation Theatre on the Exposition floor
- An advertisement in the on-site conference program
- Prominent identification on the web site (diamond level sponsors will secure the home page banner) with a hot link to your site
- Assistance with organizing a private networking function during the event
- Opportunity to supply the media center with press releases and other related corporate information.
- Express registration for your delegates
- Use of the WUF3 logo in your promotions and advertising

**Not a comprehensive list; entitlements will be unique to each individual sponsor.*

Achieve maximum impact

Sponsorship can be general in nature, or choose a specific function or item below, or a combination of several to create a powerful and productive vehicle which will best position your company to meet your corporate business development objectives. Properties available for sponsorship include but are not limited to:

$45,000	Internet Café
$50,000	Main Stage
$40,000	Registration
$10,000	Conference Program
$15,000	Media Centre
$30,000	Presentation Theatre

$10,000	Information & Message Centers
$45,000	The Longest Bar
$20,000	Meeting areas (each)
$20,000	Luncheons
$12,500	Coffee breaks
$100,000	Closing Ceremony
$30,000	Audio Visual
$12,500	Networking Breakfasts

I know you think I made this up, but I didn't. It's straight out of the Prospectus, quoted verbatim. Twelve and a half grand and you can sponsor a coffee break. Nice. The Forum would have sold you the potted plants, the rocks on the beach, the sky, and the oxygen inside the convention hall. They would have sold you anything and everything for the right price. There was so much sleaze at the WUF3 it would have made Roger Stone blush. And that is exactly what certain, very vocal, and powerful sectors are claiming as our urban future.

But let's not fuck around here, how 'bout? Our world is currently confronted with challenges of colossal magnitudes and it is this fixation on greed and profit that has got us to this point and it ain't going to get us out. Addressing these challenges both locally and globally will require a genuine commitment to *ethical* solutions and *ethical* discourses. We absolutely have to reject greed as a force for good and remake our cities. Like right now.

If we are going to talk about genuinely sustainable change in cities all over the world, we have to talk about genuine local democracy empowered to make real choices, not bound by market-driven imperatives and debt-fettered discussion of privatization and private-public partnerships. We have to be talking about fundamentally redressing the massive imbalances of power that exist both within and between nations. As one WUF3 participant speaker from the United States said, "In my country, the richest 1 percent now controls a trillion, *a trillion*, more dollars than the bottom 90 percent. Why are we continually talking about outside financing, about attracting investment? Why are we not talking about self-sustaining cities?"[137]

Um, yeah, why not?

•••

Sustainability conversations often include complex and interconnected issues of energy, climate change, finance, transport, governance etc., but really, the fundamental issues around sustainability are not rocket science; the world has too many poor people, too many greedy rich, too much over-consumption of resources, too many cars, too much corporate polluting, and too much lack of restraint. There are solutions all around us. The questions are overwhelmingly one of *will*. People do not starve in this world because there is not enough food. People do not go without houses because we are short of building materials.

I think the most fundamental question facing cities across the globe, whether they are current winners like Vancouver or losers like Diyarbakir is a stark one. Is there the political and ethical will to work toward sustainable cities that are based on local knowledge and local economies or must cities simply roll over and show their belly to the global marketplace?

Let's not be naïve about this. There are endless grey areas, compromises to be made, complex choices, and the paths are rarely that clear, but at heart cities have to make a very fundamental decision that they will aspire to self-reliance and citizenship and not re-imagine themselves as mechanisms for capital accumulation. The global marketplace is by definition unethical and, while it may seem very attractive right now to court the attention of transnational capital, it has all kinds of consequences and is at best a very temporary party. Cities all over the world are discovering what happens when they make huge concessions, lure capital, and then—when the profits dip—capital moves on to the next place. Even once triumphant stories like Dublin are coming to realize whom they have been sleeping with.

Put frankly, cities have to discipline themselves to stop chasing wildly after investment and making massive compromises with capital markets whose basic responsibility is "shareholder responsibility." Instead, all cities, and especially this city, have to aggressively imagine a saner future. The idea of sustainability is not just one more arrow in the branding quiver; it has to be taken seriously, and I mean that in every sense. And that is going to mean a fundamentally different economic path, one where actual choices have to made, choices that mean giving stuff up.

A sane future cannot mean flying Washington State apples to the other side of the world even if it is ostensibly viable economically. The implications of that choice are so profound, and reverberate so far into the society, that its immediate logic has to be resisted. A sane urbanism has to mean an intense commitment to relocalization, specifically to local economies. It means not spending $8 billion dollars to expand highway capacity via the Gateway Project, not fixating on international mega-event investment like the Olympics, building grotesque convention centers to lure corporate swilling, and selling off our rivers to private-public partnerships.

Times are high in Vancouver right now and money is everywhere. Now is the ideal time to make some deep changes, but it'll probably take a crisis before we are actually willing to shift fundamentally. Maybe cities, like all of us, tend to stick with what works until it doesn't, and then hope that there will be enough citizen resilience available. My favorite example of this is Havana, where the collapse of the Soviet Union meant an abrupt and devastating end to the massive food, gas, and supply shipments that had sustained the island for a generation. Over the course of several decades, Cuba, and Havana in particular, had become increasingly dependent on the imports and, accordingly, a very limited capacity to feed itself.

The end of Soviet support plunged the whole country into a food crisis, a "Special Period" that literally saw average weights plummet across the island, staples severely restricted, and a near-national panic. Actual food was not arriving, and the oil to power refrigeration and transport food from rural areas, as well as the pesticides and fertilizers relied upon for agriculture, were largely gone. In response, the city of Havana has seen an explosion of urban gardening, first driven by popular initiatives and now officially supported. Right now, more than 100,000 city residents are directly involved in growing their own food in 20,000 gardens growing in every spare bit of city land: vacant lots, rooftops, parks, front yards, behind hospitals and schools, everywhere.

In the last ten years Havana's food production has gone up fifty times, with more than 90 percent of the vegetables consumed in the city now grown locally and more than a million tons of milk, eggs, and meat being produced within the city limits. There are still some food shortages, but nothing close to the mid-90s and actual food security is within Havana's grasp.[138]

It's a freaking awesome story in all kinds of ways, and I love it not just because I'm a gardener, but because of its hopefulness and attitude in the face of crisis. Is that what it's going to take before Vancouver and North American urbanites will consider relocalization? Worldwide food shortages, climate change, peak oil, biodiversity collapse, species extinction, and alien attack? What's it going to take? Right now we have our collective heads up our ass, pretending that the way we eat and think about food is justified. Like Michael Pollen put it:

> There are so many stories we can tell ourselves to justify doing nothing, but perhaps the most insidious is that, whatever we do manage to do, it will be too little too late. Climate change is upon us, and it has arrived well ahead of schedule. Scientists' projections that seemed dire a decade ago turn out to have been unduly optimistic: the warming and the melting is occurring much faster than the models predicted. Now truly terrifying feedback loops threaten to boost the rate of change exponentially, as the shift from white ice to blue water in the Arctic absorbs more sunlight and warming soils everywhere become more biologically active, causing them to release their vast stores of carbon into the air. Have you looked into the eyes of a climate scientist recently? They look really scared.
>
> So do you still want to talk about planting gardens?
>
> I do.[139]

Hey, me too. I've talked about gardens here and there throughout this book, and the Havana story really concretizes things for me. In the past, I kind of suspected that gardening was more of an aesthetic event—something for yuppie lifestylers and proto-hippies—but with little real political impact. Over the last few years though, I have changed my mind and now think of gardening as potentially deeply radical with serious potential for social change.

In part that's because we have started farming the hell out of our backyard. We're turning every square inch into food production, doing everything all permaculturey, got some chickens, and are eating a ton out of there. It really is a good time in all kinds of ways and intensely satisfying. I know part of that is the trajectory of my own aging, but there is something more there. There are all kinds of good reasons to grow food, but far more than I have previously understood, gardening is a social activity infused with potentiality.

I first started noticing this when I was working in front of our house. Seemingly every third person wanted to stop and chat—old Italian guys with grape-vine advice, hippie couples wanting to share the vibe, aging ladies on their way home from church stopping to talk about pruning, etc. The sheer number of conversations was really noticeable, not just with strangers, but with our neighbors.

同仁
威斯康辛州
煮干いわし
NW 20KG

We had already taken down the fence with the house next to us and installed a fire pit. Then, this spring, we took down the fence with the neighbors on the other side of the house and installed the chicken coop. Now all three houses of people are constantly walking back and forth, visiting, picking greens, and hanging out. And there are always other people coming by too: our pal Mark who is sharing the garden with us, friends coming to talk trash and have a beer in the yard, kids picking berries, etc.

And that's where I think the real heart of gardening is. If it's just a private affair—growing some pretty flowers or a few carrots, that's all good—but really it's almost never like that. You always want to share your food and talk about your plans. It turns the backyard into something very different from enclosed scenery. And that process becomes genuinely important if we can think about the whole city like that. What about modeling the urban agriculture of Havana right here, right now, even if we aren't going hungry? Why don't we start growing food in every nook and cranny, every inch of the city? Why aren't we turning every spare bit of land, every lawn and every ornamental garden into food production?

It's when I start thinking about community gardens that all my theorizing about a common city makes the most sense to me. In many ways it seems that neo-liberalism and our current conceptions of urbanism have boxed us all in. When we all stay in our own houses and our own cars, the city gets small and restrictive and we tend to get miserly about defending our own little turf. But when we think of the city as common space, the city gets bigger, both metaphorically and actually.

Consider the sheer number of trees in Vancouver: just on the boulevards, not in the parks or on other city land, there are more than 130,000 trees. Really: 130,000! If you start looking you'll notice them everywhere. So what would happen if half, or a third, or even ten thousand of those trees were fruit trees? Why do we have all those maples and elms instead of apple and cherry and plum trees? How many people would that feed? How would it change the way we use the city?

The idea got me excited so I went and talked to David Tracey, a local urban agriculture activist and author of *Guerrilla Gardening: A Manualfesto:*

> If I had my way, I'd have 40,000 of those as fruit trees. I can see why there is resistance because people often have a weird block about anything new. But what we have in the city is not a natural forest;

it's an artificial forest that we have to manage. We can all agree that trees are good things that come with a certain amount of hassle: leaves fall and clog drains, they create a slippery mess, the roots crack sidewalks—but we have already decided that trees are worth the effort. So why not make the effort to have fruit trees?

But it's got to be a community thing. Those trees won't be just planted and picked by city workers. Communities have to take care of the trees and harvest them or most of the fruit will go to waste. That's the point of our Tree City project. We want to get more people engaged and lose their timidity around shaping their own environment, including caring for trees. We've brought together all kinds of people with little in common except that we're working to preserve and take care of trees. It's community building via environmental stewardship, and vice versa.

Attitudes around urban agriculture are shifting, but slowly. It's not the kind of speed we're hoping for but if we keep hammering away we'll get somewhere. And if a crisis does come via climate change or food shortages or peak oil—we're trying to build community in advance. Start meeting our neighbors, sharing produce, getting ahead of the curve, and breaking down our isolation.

The trouble is that global capitalism has created a monster that produces really, really cheap food. We spend less on food in North America than anyone ever has—although we don't have that concept because food seems expensive. But there are all kinds of costs that society takes on to make that happen—social, ecological, and financial subsidy costs—that make the way we eat impossible to continue. But I'm optimistic because people can change things quickly if they change their habits, and eating is something we all do every day.

There is of course a rapidly intensifying literature around relocalization, much of which I have referenced throughout this book and much of which you are already very familiar with, but the point I want to make here is that there are choices in front of us that really are not all that obscure. We can embrace a future that is limited and restricted by sustainable localism or a limitless, neo-liberal globalization of unending growth. There is no way that these two worldviews can be made compatible—one will necessarily emerge as hegemonic. The fantasy that events like WUF3 and Vancouver's current development trajectory suggest is that we can have that cake and eat it too—that we can fund a sustainable urbanism with massive doses of international investment and market ethics. It is the great lie of capitalism that there are no limits to growth, and the implications of those lies are only now becoming really clear. The freedom of neo-liberalism turns out to be not much freedom at all.

I'm not a futurist and I'm not particularly interested in projections around peak oil and food shortages. I think those kinds of predictions are likely correct but I am most interested in interrogating the way of life that is based on the plundering of the natural world. A way of life predicated on massive consumption of non-renewable resources is by definition fucked. How else could it be? Maybe we will run out of oil and then will find ways to power our economy with sunflower oil or biodiesel or whatever—but that will just temporarily revive a way of life that has unsustainability at its core. Maybe we can replace oil, but biodiversity? The atmosphere? All the big fish in the ocean? A way of life based on ever-increasing consumption is what has to change; otherwise all we're doing is rearranging the deck chairs on the Titanic.

That imperative has to be understood as antagonistic: we cannot have global capitalism and embrace localization. They run directly in the face of one another no matter what Lululemon or BP or the Body Shop tries to tell and sell us. Our only alternative is to constrict the economy. We cannot have economic growth and ecological sanity. As Conrad Schmidt, the founder of the Work Less Party puts it:

> The only thing that can reduce our ecological footprint is a contracting economy. The question becomes how we adapt our values to a contracting economy. My two favorite ways of how this can be done are a) reducing the workweek, and b) efficiency shifting.
>
> What's causing the upcoming depression is that technological efficiency has made much of us redundant. The more efficient technology is, the less labor is required to produce the same or more goods. So, unless we consume more, we end up in a depression. For various reasons, consumption is having trouble keeping up with production. So the solution is to shift efficiencies. Make some industries extremely inefficient. The best would be agriculture.

There can hardly be any more doubt that an ecological future precludes more economic growth. And despite the hand wringing and panicked whining from certain sectors, it is a future we should be thrilled to embrace. We have to reject the notion that constricting growth will exacerbate poverty and inequity: it is global capitalism that has created this immense disparity of wealth both intra- and internationally. More of the same will not solve the problem. As the 2008 Economic Degrowth For Ecological Sustainability and Social Equity conference in Paris described de-growing the Global North: "(de-growth) is characterized by substantially reduced dependence on economic activity, and an increase in free time, unremunerated activity, conviviality, sense of community and individual and collective health; [and the] encouragement of self-reflection, balance, creativity, flexibility, diversity, good citizenship, generosity and non-materialism." Booya. Bring it on.

Maybe the easiest way to think about contracting the economy is getting your hands dirty and growing some food. There's not much ambiguity there. It's simple and cheap and convivial. But more than that it represents exactly how we need to be de-commodifying our relationship with the natural world and reconfiguring our cities as common ground.

KAUNAKAKAI, MOLOKA'I

POSTCARD IMAGE BY JIM BROCKER

AQUACULTURE

Kaunakakai, Moloka'i, Hawai'i

There's an edge of panic that seeps into me whenever I step into the Honolulu airport. The place is awash with disgorged, septuagenarian cruise shippers, bloated Midwestern families dragging mountainous piles of luggage, predatory package tour operators waving little cards in the air, swarming Japanese holiday groups, and so much obligatory lei and sunglass-buying quasi-euphoria that I immediately start scanning for the emergency exits. The only thing that keeps it from turning into a genuine code-red, wild-eyed experience are the little birds that swoop in and out through the glassless windows, scooping up leftover Mickey D's and greasy stir-fry remnants.

Getting out of there and onto an Aloha Airlines local-hop plane feels like an escape and landing on Moloka'i is a sweet, *that's-what-I'm-talking-about* kind of relief. Moloka'i is the least developed and least tourist-friendly of the five major Hawai'ian Islands. In fact, it really shouldn't be considered major; it is more rightly grouped with secondary islands Lanai, Ni'ihau, and Kahoolawe. The Big Island of Hawai'i, Oahu, Maui, and Kauai are the places where everyone goes: the Hawai'i of resorts, condos, golf courses, vacation packages, Diamondhead, and Waikiki.

There is a reason Moloka'i isn't that popular and it is obvious the first time you fly over. It's actually sort of amazing: the western half of the island looks like a weird cell structure under a microscope, all brown and arid and empty except for a tight, thin ring of deep green membrane all around the edge. The eastern half of the island is pretty green but it is also almost totally uninhabited, inaccessible, volcanic/mountainous wildness. Moloka'i has almost none of the dense lushness that you think of when you think Hawai'i—the palms and coconuts, hibiscus, plumeria, ginger, and orchids—and almost all of its tropicality is concentrated right around the edges.

The inhabited western half is accessible, but almost equally empty. Get much away from the water and you find plenty of huge bushes covered with lethal spikes,[140] dense thickets of brownish grass, the occasional wild pig or deer, and lots of generally arid terrain good for mountain biking or sturdy hiking, but not much for holiday frivolity/lolling around.

There is something like seven-thousand people who live year-round on Moloka'i, the largest group being native Hawai'ians who make up a little more than a third of the population, the largest percentage of any of the major islands. Tourism is widely described as "minimal," with approximately 75,000 folks visiting every year[141] and there just ain't much to do. The only town of any size is Kaunakakai, which is about two blocks long and feels straight out of the fifties. There is really no shopping to be done, there are no flashy resorts, no big buildings, no bars or clubs, not a lot of surfing beaches, and no social scene.

Two things that *are* always present in Hawai'i, and especially in Moloka'i, are the ocean and a sense of isolation. Although maybe less pronounced, these are also two core aspects of the experience of living in Vancouver: ocean and isolation. The Hawai'ian Islands are just hell and gone, maybe further than you realize at first. Don't let the fact that it's a American state fool you, they are *way* out there: close to 2,400 miles (3,860 km) southwest of Los Angeles, 3,700 miles (5,955 km) southeast of Tokyo, and the nearest landfall is 2,000 miles (3,219 km) away. The islands are even isolated from one another; spread over 1,500 miles (2,414 km) of Pacific.

Vancouver is obviously nowhere near as distant as Hawai'i from other population centers, but I remember when we first moved here, coming back to British Columbia from New York, and it just felt so separated: a thousand kilometers and the Rocky Mountains away from Calgary, two hours and a border from Seattle, nothing going on forever to the north or west.

Relative isolation has always been a huge part of Vancouver's identity, pinned between the Pacific and the Coast Mountains, a northwestern arcadia, protected from the roil of American culture. Even more than that, Vancouver is defined by water: the ocean, the bays and inlets, the false creeks, the Fraser River, the streams and rivers pouring off the mountains, the glaciers, the rain, the mists, and the drizzle. Hawai'i is a lot like that too, surrounded by thousands of miles of open water with some of the wettest spots on earth on the windward sides of the Islands.

•••

Living in Vancouver, it's easy to think that all the talk about a growing global water shortage must be a joke. Some days it seems like there is enough water here for the whole world. Sitting in my study this past spring, watching anaconda-thick torrents slide off the roof, it felt incredible that there could be a lack of water anywhere in the world.

But of course there is. And it doesn't take a retro-evening viewing of *Mad Max* to realize that conflicts around water are a sure feature of the future. As Michael Specter catalogued in his 2006 *New Yorker* article, "The Last Drop":

> Nearly half the people in the world don't have the kind of clean water and sanitation services that were available two thousand years ago to the citizens of ancient Rome. More than a billion people lack access to drinking water, and at least half that many have never seen a toilet. Half the hospital beds on earth are occupied by people with an easily preventable waterborne disease. In the past decade more children have died from diarrhea than people have been killed in all armed conflicts since the Second World War.[142]

And it's not just clean, drinkable water that is running dry: freshwater in general is disappearing as cities and industrial agriculture all over the globe drain water tables. Scores of cities worldwide have water deficits that register right on the edge of code-bright-freaking-red, with few viable escape routes. The UN figures that two-thirds of the world's population will be living with "water stress" by 2025. And that's only the quickest and dirtiest recitation of a few of the water issues we face.

Most of the world's great civilizations emerged beside rivers and virtually every major city in the world still lies along a riverbank: the Hudson, Seine, Tigris, Moskva, Thames, Nile, Tiber, Han, Yangtze, Rio de la Plata, Hugli, and so many others.[143] Those few cities that are not right on a river have a serious supply of fresh water nearby and are inevitably an ocean port. That's not only due to the physical requirements for water for drinking and cleaning and cooking: humans have a deep need to be around water, especially huge bodies of it, and not just for transportation purposes. We are all drawn to water: to the beach, to the rivers and lakes. Urban design has always been focused around water, not just the provision of usable and fresh water, but also its social and emotional resonance.

"We come from the water; our bodies are largely water; and water plays a fundamental role in our psychology. We need constant access to water, all around us; and we cannot have it without reverence for water in all its forms."[144] That need for water plays itself out in all kinds of ways in urban planning and design: planners and developers lust after water access, residents are always looking for ocean views, prime parkland is always by the river or lake or ocean, etc. To say you have "waterfront property" means something, and it's usually cold cash.

Lance Berelowitz argues in his book *Dream City* that Vancouverites are drawn to the edges of the city, to the water and especially to views of the water, so completely that the waterfront has become our dominant form of public space:

> Vancouver's true culture of public space is evident on the waterfront. Not only are the apparent populist notions of a public space culture in this city highly codified there and therefore subject to an overwhelming romanticization but it is also true that Vancouver, in its emphasis on public activity at its edges as opposed to the center, illustrates a variant of well-established forms of public life of the waterfront city....
>
> The cultural, social and political functions typically fulfilled by the more traditional public spaces of the Western city are, in Vancouver's case, primarily performed by the spaces associated with the shoreline, waterfront park and seawall promenade. [145]

It's really true, and I think Berelowitz is on to something very important. The water is where we gather here. Think about it: you go for a walk with your honey along the seawall, you go to the beach with the kids, bike around Stanley Park, take the dog to Spanish Banks, go to a festival at Cates Park, etc. People in Vancouver overwhelmingly gather by the water and that has real implications for how we view our public experience because sitting together at the beach or walking around the seawall is very different than having a coffee in a plaza or going to a show. Public spaces are reconceived as vehicles of private desire.

> Preoccupied with the experience of nature, Vancouverites have reduced their public spaces to serving private experience: the public *flaneur* becomes the private voyeur. Of course the transformation of public person from performer to consumer of spectacle (in this case nature) has had a profound effect on the forms of public culture.[146]

Maybe the ocean is prettier than any of us could ever be and maybe swimming is always going to be better than any conversation or show. There are very few cities anywhere that have Vancouver's combination of mountains and river and ocean, and perhaps that's just the way this city is oriented, and will always be. Water is what makes Vancouver great, what makes it a trial some Novembers, what makes this place what it is. Is it possible that a real urbanism can be created beside this much water and natural spectacle? Or will the natural setting always be overwhelming?

This is still a young city struggling to find its feet and there is every reason to think that a cosmopolitan urbanity full of great public and common spaces can develop beside such beauty, but it will require a certain kind of shift. I think a particular element of that shift will have to be around the way we speak of water.

•••

I was thinking about exactly this while sitting on Kaunakakai's dock, looking out at Lanai and blistering the hell out of my nose. The dock is perfect: quiet, fishermen coming and going, the whole place is just minding its own business amid all the sparkle and flash of the sun on the water. The ocean dominates everything about Moloka'i. It is the most basic fact of existence. But interestingly, Kaunakakai is not right on the beach, it is inland a little; maybe a half-mile and you can't see the water from "downtown." The dock is not an obvious part of the town.

I was wondering why the town was set so far away from the beach and asked a guy who was fishing nearby: "The storms, man, the storms. You only need to have your roof torn off once before you build back a bit." We talked some more and I noted that locals don't seem to hang around the beach. I saw people coming to surf or fish, but I didn't really see folks spending a lot of time on the beach in the way, say, I do. They seemed to use it, but not fixate; maybe because of its awesome omnipresence? "Yeah, its there, we don't need to look at it all the time. Tourists do that, probably because they don't get enough of it at home. But we do."

I could easily see what he was talking about. People came to the dock to park their boat, fish, swim, catch a ferry, or buy some fish, but all the hanging out was happening in town: sitting on benches in front of stores, shopping, having coffee, shooting the shit, etc. How people gather in Kaunakakai struck me as essentially different from what happens in Vancouver.

It reminded me of something Chris Alexander, Sara Ishikawa, and Murray Silverstein wrote in *A Pattern Language*. They described a monk living high in the mountains with a beautiful view of the ocean, far in the distance. But you couldn't see the ocean from the house or from the road; it was only when you crossed the courtyard along a path and found a slit in the wall surrounding the yard that, if you were lined up in just the right way, you could catch a glimpse of the water.

> The view of the distant sea is so restrained that it stays alive forever. Who that has ever seen that view can ever forget it?...
>
> This is the essence of the problem with any view. It is a beautiful thing. One wants to enjoy it and drink it in every day. But the more open it is, the more obvious, the more it shouts, the sooner it will fade. Gradually it will become part of the building, like the wallpaper; and the intensity of its beauty will no longer be accessible to the people who live there.
>
> Therefore:
> *If there is a beautiful view, don't spoil it by building huge windows that gape incessantly at it. Instead, put the windows which look onto the view at places of transition—along paths, in hallways, in entryways, on stairs, between rooms.*[147]

In contrast, think about how so much of the new Vancouver has been driven by a fixation with "the view." Vancouverism's signature architecture is the tall, thin, glassy tower: a form designed specifically to give allow every unit their own private, gaping view of the water. The desire to witness nature, even at home, drives condo pricing and footprints, but reveals the depth of the impulse to iconicize, and of course the impulse to sell, the "natural" experience.

Making the view one more standard-issue condo selling point, trumpeted as predictably as granite countertops and stainless steel appliances, instrumentalizes yet another public good. A view of the ocean should be enjoyed in the public realm: get out of your houses, come on down and enjoy it with the rest of us.

And we're all down there. Very fortunately, Vancouver continues to energetically and effectively make the ocean publicly accessible. The Seawall, the beaches, and the piers all flow into one long stretch that, in volume and integrity, are more intact than almost any other city I can think of. Of course that beautiful beach access is only from downtown to the far Westside; there is almost no Eastside access and equally little in South Vancouver where the riverfront is dominated by industry and none of it is anything you'd ever want to swim in. But that's totally predictable in its banal pandering to privilege.

There is also a lovely ribbon of parks all around the waterfront (only the Westside again) that has displaced industry, sanitized the edge, and has in part kept multi-million-dollar homes from crowding right up on the beaches, which is great for joggers and bikers, but as Lance Berelowitz put it:

> I'm not sure we've made the most of the waterfront. We've virtually completed the highly cleansed and sanitized waterfront where nary a dirty industry will be seen again. It's a remarkable transformation from when False Creek was a cesspool of industry. Now it's a beautifully manicured edge.
>
> But the problem is that there isn't much else going on. It has become sacrosanct that the whole waterfront walkway has to be not only continuous but undifferentiated. It's a path for walking combined with cycling or rollerblading, and I think that's a very narrow description of the range of human behavior.
>
> Where are all the restaurants, all the bars that other cities have on the waterfront? We haven't got there yet. We have done the first thing. We made it accessible.

I'm not real certain that I want the Seawall and beaches crowded with bars and restaurants, but then I think of sitting under the Galata Bridge and drinking at a quiet bar, or eating at a fish shack on the beach, or watching whole families fish off the pier in Kaunakakai, and I can imagine a time when the whole Seawall and all of Vancouver's beaches would be used in more complex fashion and retrofitted for common use. I'd like to see a much more complex and variegated range of uses on the waterfront as much as anywhere.

I am thrilled that Vancouver has made real progress in protecting the water's edge: now people need to learn how to inhabit it. The city needs to back off a little and let people figure out how to use the waterfront. I am sure that there are all kinds of regulations prohibiting it, but what's better than watching old guys fish in the sunset along Kits Beach, people canoeing by, or little kids crabbing off of Jericho? That kind of activity needs to be encouraged, just like the folks who live on their boats and float houses should very definitely not be evicted. Like the rest of our public spaces, if the waterfront is choreographed and expertly managed, it becomes sterile and public simulacra. If water is what defines this city, how about we don't package it up as product? Let's let it become part of common life.

•••

Here on Canada's Left Coast we have long marketed ourselves as a destination (and population) that is pure, clean, wholesome, and super natural! Vancouver being "The Best Place on Earth!" Water has always been our best asset and we've rarely been afraid to shake it a little, even in our demure, passive-aggressive kind of way. Come to British Columbia and wash away your sins and cares! Kayak through the sparkling Gulf Islands, hike alongside tumbling mountain streams, swim from our pristine beaches, and drink deeply from our pure, clean glacial water.

Cleanliness has always been at the heart of Vancouver's branding of itself, for visitors, tourists, investors, and residents alike. It's a marketing that is reflected in many of our presumptions about what a city is for and how it should be built. As Berelowitz once wrote:

> What remains different about Vancouver, certainly in the Canadian context and perhaps even in the global one, is the extent to which the surrounding natural landscape, as opposed to the built city, is the source of inspiration in the creation of urban form. There is a strong, almost "moral" sensibility that unsullied nature is superior to human artifact and that the urban construct is an intrusion on, and not a complement to, the landscape.[148]

It's not just nature per se that is so reified here, but water in particular, that is imbued with a morally redemptive character. Vancouver habitually describes itself as a clean, fresh city; it is an urban environment, sure, but viscerally removed from the dirt and filth of typical (read: Eastern or American) cities. It is clear to anyone, visitor or resident, that this city sees its own reflection when constantly staring at the water.

It is an image that becomes clear in the omnipresent howls to "clean up the Downtown Eastside." The crime and the drugs and the immiseration, especially concentrated in Canada's poorest neighborhood, are spoken of as a "stain" on the city, something we have to "wipe away" because the mess is repelling tourists. It's like noticing the cats have shit on the carpet just as guests are about to arrive. Somebody clean that up, quick. Get a mop or some antiseptic wipes or something.

Water's symbolic equation with cleanliness and purity is infused in the branding of Vancouver's populace and our ostensible lack of filth, both metaphoric and real. In locating the ocean as the focus of our public lives and venerating views of nature, we reinforce a dogmatism that constructs this city as something better than a city, something above and beyond, removed from urban grit, a place that takes it cues from nature and water as a place of new life, freshness, and rebirth.

It's not a new strategy. Water has historically been inscribed with symbolic and real value, and cities have used water not just to clean their streets and residents but also to demonstrate virtuousness and health. In *The Conquest of Water*, Jean Pierre Goubert writes about the use of urban fountains to symbolize the vitality and power of towns and cities:

> In the course of the nineteenth century, an increasing number of fountains and wash-houses, symbols of the conquest of water, were installed in public spaces in towns and cities.... In the eighteenth century, every town, however modest, felt obliged to erect a monumental fountain.[149]

You would think that essentially living in a rainforest, right on the ocean, and alongside an enormous river, Vancouver would not feel compelled to integrate much water into its public realm, but if you have a quick look around you'll be surprised at how many faux waterfalls, streams, ponds, and creeks have been built. All of this is pretty ironic because Vancouver has been systematically erasing virtually all vestiges of existing flowing water for the past century.

The city was once riddled with creeks and streams, often salmon bearing, that ran through almost every part of the city. A couple of times I have listened to a friend, Gene Bougie, who grew up near 41 Avenue and Fraser, talk about spear fishing for salmon with wooden poles that he and his buddies made in the "sizable" creek that ran alongside Cambie Street as late as the mid-1940s. Check out the great book *Vancouver: A Visual History* by Bruce McDonald and you'll see major creeks and streams crisscrossing the city right up until the early 1960s. Scores of little waterways ran every which way for millennia, lining the Lower Mainland like veins in a hand. We've carefully and deliberately erased an indescribably complex network of water movement only to turn around and reconstruct water flows in limited and controlled sites.

•••

The idea that water cleanses a city's streets and morals is artifactual and the "perception of the city as a place that must constantly be washed is of recent origin. It appears at the time of the Enlightenment."[150] Water has resonance in urban theory and the popular imagination beyond an everyday concern with sanitation, leaking into an olfactory sensibility that derides messiness. Nowhere more than Vancouver is freshness used so profligately to describe an urban environment. The more water we have, the cleaner we must be, *n'est pas*? Is it possible, however, that the relationship between aqua-aesthetics and civic virtue is more complex than it seems at first glance?

> The popular wisdom which holds that water possesses "natural beauty" and that this beauty has impact on civic morale is not always overtly expressed. However, you only have to poke fun at the belief in the civic magic of a body of water, and people react as if you had made a dirty joke.[151]

Is it possible that in managing, manipulating, and commodifying water that we are stripping it of its symbolic value and undermining the everyday joy of water? In presuming our water to be a scarce resource, we are reconstituting it as a commodified element to be packaged and contested, reduced to just another industrial product that can be bought, sold, and consumed.

I tend to encounter this remaking of water most viscerally in the form of a $1.29 bottle of Dasani, and I am hardly alone. The world is drinking amazing amounts of bottled water. The United States of course consumes more than any other country, the United Arab Emirates buys the most per capita, and China's consumption is growing faster than anywhere else. Americans spent $15 billion on bottled water in 2008 and Canadians about half a billion (CAN) and, despite the fact that Canada has an embarrassment of freshwater supplies, we import about fourteen times as much bottled water as we export. And that's without even mentioning Vitamin Water, "enhanced" water, or carbonated waters.

To get me in the groove, and in the interest of good reporting and general fairness, I really do have a bottle of Fiji Natural Artesian water going. I got so fired up reading about all this water that I walked to the corner store and bought myself a bottle. Can't say it tastes like much, but I'm sure it's doing me good. It was the most expensive thing I could find on my bit of Commercial Drive:

$2.59 for a half liter. Pretty cheap actually, but still five times the price of gas.[152]

Bottled water has sprinted from absurdity to ubiquity in only a couple of decades, but recently there's been a little pushback. Over the past three years, municipalities from Charlottetown to Nelson to San Francisco have banned bottled water in civic buildings and, in many countries around the world, real efforts are being made to limit the pandemic of bottled water buying. In April 2009, Vancouver's city council voted to eliminate bottled water from all staff and council functions, to phase it out of all municipal facilities, and to eventually remove it from all city-owned concession stands.

The arguments against bottled water interlock: at least one-third of the bottles end up in the garbage, and the rest have to be recycled; it's hugely wasteful as one more unnecessary product; bottled-water availability takes pressure off cities to provide clean tap water; half the time bottled water is full of contaminants and bacteria; the omnipresent Coke and Pepsi brands (Dasani and Aquafina, respectively) just use municipal tap water anyway; there is a growing body of evidence to suggest that soft-plastic bottles leach carcinogens; etc. (Now I'm feeling a little guilty about this bottle of Fiji.)

Fighting bottled water isn't just confined to earthly concerns: even God's getting in his shots. In 2006, the National Coalition of American Nuns adopted a resolution asking members to refrain from purchasing bottled water unless necessary. Their position is that water, like air, is a God-given resource that shouldn't be packaged and sold and, therefore, opposing bottled water is a matter of faith and virtue.

At their heart, arguments against bottled water revolve around an objection to commodification. There is just something deeply creepy about companies making money selling us water. But corporations all over the globe are working double overtime at exactly that and largely succeeding. The same core dispute is driving virtually all battles for and about water: Is it just another commodity that can be packaged, bought, and sold? Or is water something else, a part of the commons, that should never be reduced to a product?

But there is just a certain amount of absurdity to everyday post-modern life. Last spring, I was getting a load of soil delivered for my garden. As I was hauling it to the backyard, my neighbor Dan came and watched for a while. He dryly noted that I had paid a couple of hundred bucks for it: "Nice world, where you have to buy dirt. And water. What's next, air?" Um, yeah, that's pretty much where we're headed. There's really nothing that can't be bought and sold.

A growing number of California farmers, for example, have figured out that it is becoming more profitable to sell their subsidized water to other farms and towns than to grow crops. "It just makes dollars and sense right now," says Sacramento Valley farmer Bruce Rolen.[153] California's current water is approaching crisis levels and is responsible for price hikes that are seeing water become more and more valuable and scarce.

These, and many other shortages are also changing the ways farmers and everyone else understand water: it is now a commodity to be hoarded and managed, rather than a fundamental part of the natural world, including our own flesh. This is a new era of the human relationship with water that is re-inscribing and re-describing water as a scarce resource, calling for technical management and professional distribution mechanisms.

•••

In many ways the absurdity that has us buying ever-"purer" bottles of H_2O is reflected in our conflicted imaginings of urban waterfronts. Alexander, Ishikawa, and Silverstein put it nicely when they wrote:

> *People have a fundamental yearning for great bodies of water. But the very movement of people toward the water can also destroy the water.* Either roads, freeways, and industries destroy the water's edge and make it so dirty or so treacherous that it is virtually inaccessible: or when the water's edge is preserved, it falls into private hands….
>
> The problem can be solved only if it is understood that people will build places near the water because it is entirely natural; but the land immediately along the water's edge must be preserved for common use. To this end the roads which can destroy the water's edge must be kept back from it and only allowed near it when they lie at right angles to it.[154]

Most of the literature around urban waterfronts has focused on the relationships between city and port, but new economic forces have recast the waterfronts of most cities as frontiers, available for redevelopment, capital investment, and colonization.[155] What's a better determinant of real estate prices than proximity to the water? What is a quicker indication of privilege? And few cities are quite as nakedly ambitious as Vancouver in iconicizing access, not just physical access but visual too.

As I was writing this I found myself wondering what a common relationship with our water—a relationship that doesn't destroy or demean that water—might look like. I was struggling to imagine what that might look like so I went to talk with a good pal, Dustin Rivers, who is a Skwxwú7mesh-Kwakwaka'wakw activist, artist, writer, and canoeist. I asked him about Coast Salish conceptions of water and the canoe projects that he is involved with:

> The moniker we identify as, Skwxwú7mesh, has been translated into definitions that relate to the water. A loose translation would be, "People of the Sacred Water," specifically drinking water, or water we consume. There was something believed about our waters, creeks, rivers, that carried healing qualities. We we're known for this apparently. In a spiritual context, the glacier waters running from the mountains are akin to breast milk coming from the mother who provides and nurtures. We cleanse ourselves, purify ourselves, and strengthen ourselves by bathing in this water. This is the sacredness of our water.
>
> As ocean-going, salt-water, and fresh-water people, we went by canoe for hunting, gathering, and traveling. Canoes of all sizes and designs were used by our communities. A basic tenant of this custom is acknowledging the sacredness and strength that the ocean carries. We always work with the spirit of the water. With the tide. Not against.
>
> Traveling in our traditional cedar dugout canoes is a sacred and overwhelming task. It connects the power of our ancestors to recent memory, and not just to untangle ways through story or myth. It provides, in a modern context, a way to practice our customs and beliefs, and to carry it within ourselves every day. Since its contemporary revival, it has spurred a cultural growth in leadership, creativity, and rebuilding.
>
> In reviving our tradition, we take what we can to live the lifestyle of our ancestors. In a Canadian context, the "Indian Problem" has always been framed within an issue of "the Indian failing to modernize." In living the tradition, we have a way to learn our traditions, and the old teachings of our ancestors, and really live it as a lifestyle,

> not a hobby. It becomes a community initiative, not a program or service to market to a demographic to meet funder's expectations, but as our people doing what our people have always done. The canoe culture can teach us so much, about life, about community, about leadership, and respect for what we can accomplish, and what has been accomplished.

That strikes me as clearly articulating one route toward understanding our collective connections with the water. Whether it is the view or the beach or the river or the rain, we have to be able to dwell and revel in this place without commodifying it. This has to be a city of public spaces that are not built on staring at the ocean: it should be a city full of common places that are not dominated but enlivened by intersections with the natural world.

In clinging to visions of the city as fresh and pure as sparkling water, we undermine the best qualities of urbanity. Cities, especially great cities, aren't like that; they are messy and impure, full of unexpected interactions and challenges. As soon as we commodify water, and access to water, we reduce it to an industrial product and risk consuming our waterfront much like Waikiki or Maui have consumed their once-spectacular beaches. There has to be a way that a great city full of great public places can emerge, even in such a spectacular location, and I suspect that it has a lot to do with the ways we think about water. Dustin offered this:

> Within Skwxwú7mesh culture, "ownership" and "property rights" are viewed differently from the European tradition. This included things like names, stories, ceremonies, songs, and resource gathering sites (hunting grounds, fishing spots, and harvesting sites).
>
> Things are defined more by "using" and "carrying." You use this tool, you carry this regalia. You use this canoe, you carry this name. All things of property are considered in such regard. In our naming tradition, the ancestral name you hold is something you carry. You don't just own it within an individualistic here-and-now sense, because someone before you carried that name, and someone after you will carry that name.
>
> Thus: your treatment of that name and how you carry yourself.

Industrial capitalism is defined exactly in opposition to these kinds of notions: it is an attempt to commodify everything imaginable, and that includes washing water right along with the rest of the neo-liberal tide. Everything is a product, everything can be priced out, and everything should be bought and sold and owned. It is the imbricated logic that layers dubious rationales on top of callow lifestyles until water bars, $50 bottles of bling, and marketing ocean views are rendered inevitable "market realities."

We need to change our relationship with water. We can adjust managerial jurisdictions, but unless we change how we use water, how we consume it, and how we live with it and the land around us, we won't be changing much. As usual, Kentucky farmer and essayist Wendell Berry said it best in *The Idea of a Local Economy*: "A change of heart or of values without a change in practice is only another pointless luxury of a passively consumptive way of life."

Whether it's water or food or homes, the same essential contentions are being played out here in Vancouver and cities across the globe. If anything, this book is an exhortation for us all to think about cities in ways that don't plunder the natural and cultural richness around us. And fortunately we don't have to look far for ideas. Whether it's Vancouver, Kaunakakai, or anywhere else, we have to start looking to common ground, and know that a better urban world is possible.

VANCOUVER, BC

PHOTO BY SELENA COUTURE

OUTRO

Another City Really Is Possible

OK. So, what then? How's this story going to go? I doubt even God knows, but how about this:

This book rests on the assumption that an ecological future has to be an urban future, and I've been arguing for a particular rendition of urbanism: a vibrantly compact, locally-run, living city. With any luck, you've bought some of that argument. And an urban future isn't necessarily a dense future: to paraphrase Murray Bookchin, we might well end up with a vast, sprawling, amorphous urbanization without cities, Kunstler's geography of nowhere. If we let it, that monster will consume all of our best notions of the city while gobbling up the remnants of small town character and agricultural life. That's a perfectly possible fate, maybe even likely, but we're not without hope or other narratives.

That's part of why nuancing the imperative of density is so crucial. I've spoken often about arguments for dense cities and strategies for making them work, but it's more than strategy: it's a sensibility, a commitment to an ethical economy that bespeaks a different way of allocating resources, a city that doesn't brook massive inequities or greed-based development.

I want to emphasize that what we have is no accident or anomaly. There is a reason, in this insanely rich city with billions to pour into the Olympics and condos, why we have the country's lowest minimum wage, the highest rates of child poverty, a homelessness crisis festering among the glassy towers, and the highest rents and housing costs in Canada, which are forcing working people far out into auto-dependent suburbs. This is what it is *supposed* to be like. This is what a successful—maybe *the ideal*—neo-liberal city looks like.

In part because of that ostensible success and this city's endemic self-congratulation, contesting that logic isn't always going to be pretty. Some of it will be easy because the answers are all around us and ripe for the taking, but other parts of building a different city are going to be a straight-up brawl, and we shouldn't fear that. Nobody likes to lose privilege but it's going to have to happen, and the sooner the better.

There are very real social conflicts of interest in every city and we're not all going to get along. Bill Rees, the co-author of *Our Ecological Footprint*, puts it right when he says that "A planned economic contraction aimed at optimizing outcomes would certainly be more prudent than today's spontaneous financial train-wreck."[156] But it's still virtually anathema for any politician or planner to advocate for a steady-state economy of any kind, which is fine, we can do this ourselves, but any contraction is going to be messy.

It would be great if a radical economic reconfiguration happened symmetrically, with rents and the cost-of-living dropping steadily in concert with consumer spending and a productivity decline. But it ain't going down like that. Some people are going to lose their freaking shirts: people who deserve it, and plenty who don't. Some small (and lots of larger) businesses are going to lose money and staff and maybe the whole deal as spending drops but landlords don't reduce their rent and costs say static. Non-profits and arts organizations are going to see their funding slashed, just like government agencies. Elites of all kinds are going to see their net worth collapse.

We've seen lots of this through 2008 and 2009, as the financial meltdown metastasized and exposed the inherent fragility of global capitalism. We have also seen governments across the world do precisely the wrong thing: panic, pour money into propping up the remnants of the exact systems that created the collapse, and pretend that we can make a few adjustments here and there and all will be well. That "crisis" gave us a sneak preview of what we need to happen, and if we get busy, we can take the lessons learned and get ahead of the curve. Our future is not neo-liberal pillaging capitalism; it will be a lot more local and a lot more sane, but also with a lot less liquid capital floating round.

When people like me start growing our own food, we take money out of the pockets of local grocers. That's reality. I love shopping at Donald's and Norman's. They are great neighborhood businesses, important parts of this community, and I will continue to support them forever. However, this summer my family has eaten part of every meal, and very often the whole meal, out of the backyard. All the food that we grow and all those eggs being produced displace a certain number of economic transactions. And I want to encourage everyone all over the city to do the same thing, but at any mass level, local food production is going to really hurt business, and lots of those people who are going to get hurt are our friends and neighbors. This is not going be a sweet, gentle slide into a happy, smiley eco-future. It's got to happen and there is a lot we can do to mitigate the repercussions, but there will be plenty of real pain.

The same thing happens when lots of us start riding bikes everywhere: we stop buying cars and gas and it hurts business. This also occurs when we start closing streets down or living in co-op housing or planting fruit trees all over the city. All of this is all good and fun and ecological and "green," but really it presents a direct, antagonistic challenge to capitalism. And so it should be. I want planting gardens to be not just an aesthetic activity or an attempt to ameliorate capitalism's worst excesses but the first punch in a street fight.

•••

Riding in a Critical Mass event is a great vantage point for witnessing this collision. The current incarnation of Critical Mass was founded in San Francisco in 1992 and now rides happens in over three hundred cities all over the world on the last Friday of every month. Some of the rides are huge—April 2009 in Budapest saw 80,000 people come out (!)—and all of them are decentralized, horizontal, and participatory—the same potluck-style of organizing that I've been describing throughout the book. They're often called "organized coincidences": they have no leaders, a celebratory vibrancy, people of every possible stripe, and real sense of good times. They're a ton of fun.

They also take over the streets. The holler line is, "We're not blocking traffic, we are traffic," which is true, but also a little cheeky/snarky. The rides do block vehicular traffic: thousands of cyclists rolling through the city core, over the bridges, ignoring the traffic lights and covering all the lanes will do that. The Vancouver rides are now up to three thousand folks and wind back and forth over bridges, all through downtown, and are big enough to genuinely snarl car traffic to a standstill. Of course, this pisses a certain number of people off, and it's hard to blame them: you're sitting in a hot car at the end of a workweek, trying to get out of the city and back home, and then—boom!—you're stuck again while a huge pack of crazies flout the rules and laugh while they do it.

At every ride there is always some antagonism. Some people drive by and yell or give you the finger. I've seen cups of coffee thrown. Sometimes drivers try to force their way through. People have gotten pepper sprayed. And every once in a while someone wants to fight. But, really, and a little surprisingly to me, people are overwhelmingly good-natured. You get a lot smiles, thumbs up, supportive honking, waves, and "way-to-go" shouting. Mostly, though, people just sit and relax, lean back, or get out of their cars and stretch as they watch the spectacle roll by. It's usually only fifteen minutes and it's something fun to watch.

For me, the reactions of people to Critical Mass are what I imagine (hope) radical social change of the sort that I am calling for will look like. The rides really are a direct confrontation—a temporary one, and not hostile—in which one group of people unambiguously impose their will on another. It's surely true that car drivers impose themselves on bikers and pedestrians everyday, but this is a clear-cut case of people collectively resisting the status quo, fighting back, and breaking a bunch of laws while they do it. These encounters are not isolated: they are built on the backs of decades of organizing, proselytizing, and arguing for sustainable transportation. It has become a popular, commonly understood, and hardly radical notion that cities have to restrict vehicle traffic and support bike infrastructure wherever possible, so people have been sensitized and are generally supportive of the issue. But still, in Vancouver and by all accounts most cities, the response to the challenge of Critical Mass is mixed at worst and mostly sincerely positive. Most of the time if you stand up for yourself, the bully chickens out and walks.

•••

And sometimes you gotta throw down. Start talking about money and things will get uglier. It's one thing to force people to sit in their cars for an extra fifteen minutes, its another thing to cut into their paychecks, screw with their ability to make a living, undermine the sources of income that they have come to depend on, and reduce their disposable capital. That's when things will start getting sketchy. There is a whole lot to look forward to in a better urban future, but it is going to require sacrifices that may or not be very welcome, and there is every reason to be prepared for contentious spots, lots of very heated moments, and possibly real ugliness. But maybe not so much. I am not going to argue that a very conscious shift away from global capitalism is likely without a lot of flailing around, but there are lots of reasons to think that it could be viable and welcomed.

Part of my hope rests in people's inherent creativity and flexibility. People can become complacent and insular when the social milieu suggests it, but with very little inducement may become active, engaged, and incredibly agile. Think of the Havana example, or better yet, Argentina. That's a clear example of a fairly well off, sophisticated economy collapsing and people (of all kinds, especially animated with middle-class anger) responding to the challenge creatively, recovering factories, building workers' co-ops, planting gardens, occupying businesses, and remaking the economy. Lots of the *autonomista* movement has lost ground in the face of capital restructuring and I am not posing Argentina as salvific, but it sure is inspiring. There are a ton more examples you know of, in all kinds of places and scenarios, from the Zapatistas in Chiapas to Mondragon in Spain and endless others. There's no great mystery here.

There's one last piece that I want to add about money here. The story that I am telling can't be oblivious to cash. I am in favor of continuous bouts of progressive taxation, of participatory budgeting, and of bleeding the wealth of avaricious accumulation. I think any rendition of thoughtful taxation at the municipal level will help. Vancouver has carefully, assiduously, and shamelessly lured developers, investors, and elites to this city with constellations of inducements, tax breaks, and subsidies. We can just as easily disincentivize economic behavior that encourages greed.

There will be lots of fussing, but for the most part the global rich will do what they always do: leave. Investors, developers, and capital won't sit around while their privilege and profits are undermined, they'll slink off to somewhere else, to anywhere else they can turn a buck, anywhere that they won't be fairly taxed and genuinely confronted. I will welcome capital flight with open arms. It is utter nonsense foisted on us that we need to tolerate greedy leeches and unfettered capital accumulation to develop a prosperous city. I am not interested in any way in passing the jurisdictional buck for dealing with exploitation, and Vancouver cannot isolate itself while other cities get pillaged. But we can only start here, where we live, with our friends and neighbors. If we can do it here in the most neo-liberally saturated and passive of cities it can be done anywhere.

Our tax bases will decline and jobs will be fewer and further between and that will be hard. But we have to be able to think better than that, we can't be looking for different ways to do the same thing. We can do so much more with so much less money. Like my friend Geoff Mann said last night: capitalism has distorted the value of everything, including our definitions of what constitutes "value" and "valuable." Our current economic logic suggests that apples and stereos and derivative bundles are all commensurable, that anything can be costed and traded and everything has potentially equal "value," all that matters is how the market prices them.

But we can re-imbed value into things that matter, and remake them as ethical. Saying we don't have enough money to thrive in this city is like saying we have all the knowledge, lumber, tools, nails, wiring, plumbing, and supplies to build a house, but not the inches. Money is just one (imaginary) way to measure things: we can choose to use lots of other ways to describe what it means to thrive.

And the money we do have and can generate locally needs to be kept working in the community. The corporate banking system remains a true enigma to me: I cannot imagine why people continue to support it. Banks explicitly exist to bleed people of their money and they make no attempt to hide this. Then they use those vast pools of money to dominate and manipulate markets, control the flow of credit, and turn global profits. It takes only the most cursory view of the 2008 financial meltdowns to recognize the scurrilous role world banks continue to play in crippling working people while reaping truly massive profits.

Credit unions on the other hand offer nearly all the same options as banks, typically with far better service, lower rates on loans, and higher returns on deposits. More than that, credit unions are member-owned, democratically controlled, and explicitly designed to keep money working in the community by supporting small business, social enterprises, and non-profits. Vancity Savings has emerged as a major force in this city and is now the country's biggest credit union with $14.5 billion in assets, more than 410,000 members, and sixty-one branches.

An even better option in my neighborhood is Community Congress for Economic Change, which operates just likes a credit union but is really a community economic development project that was formed in 1974 by activists from daycare, consumer, and housing co-operatives in order to pool local money. It is an overtly politicized and progressive use of existing resources and, without it, I can't tell you how different this place would be: so many projects, including many of my own, would never have got off the ground without their support. It's not reinventing the wheel and it doesn't require millions of investment dollars; just requires a little cooperative collaboration and persistent hard work.

•••

I don't think remaking the city is going to happen neatly; it's not going to follow a cute Hegelian dialectic with a tidy resolution and historical synthesis. It's going to be asymmetrical, asystematic, occasionally awkward, sometimes ugly, and other times lovely; some initiatives will suck, others will be brilliant. But ride in a Critical Mass sometime: no one is the designated leader, whoever is at the front makes the decisions, people talk and debate, others roll ahead and cork the side streets, and no one knows exactly where it's going. But the rides are always tightly organized, incredibly collaborative and effective, cost no money, and just work. It's the same principle that drives potluck dinners, credit unions, co-ops of all kinds, community gardens, participatory budgeting, land trusts, and so many other renditions. And they all rest on the same principles of horizontality, collective action, shared work, responsibility, and vision—the same potluck style of organizing that has threaded through this book. None of these projects are salvific, especially on their own, but start putting them together in networks, see them collaborate, and there is every reason to think that a social movement to remake this city is really possible.

POWER

BIOS OF PEOPLE I INTERVIEWED

(in order of appearance)

Joan Seidl is the director of Collections and Exhibits at the Vancouver Museum and the curator of the exhibit called The Unnatural History of Stanley Park, which was open from September 2008 until February 2009. She has worked in museums and history houses since she was fourteen-years old, was curator of History at the Vancouver Museum for the previous fifteen years, and now looks after all the collections.

Susan A. Point is a Coast Salish artist who lives and works on the Musqueam Reserve in Vancouver, British Columbia. Her late mother (Edna Grant Point) and late uncle (Dominic Point) taught her the importance of Salish values, traditions, and stories. Susan has been a key figure in re-establishing the prominence of the Salish art form, drawing inspiration from the designs of her ancestors and exploring the use of non-traditional materials. Possibly the most rewarding aspect of her career has been the opportunity to meet elders and teachers from other Salish communities, and to see the current renaissance in Salish culture.

T'Uy'Tanat / Cease Wyss is a Skwxwú7mesh ethnobotanist, media artist, educator, activist, and the mother of Senaqwila. She runs CeaseFire Productions, Senaqwila's Herbal Teas, and conducts teachings around Indigenous medicines, gathering, and preparation. The focus in her arts practice has been community, health, and healing practices and she is currently working with the Vancouver Native Health Society in two urban, Native food-security projects.

Renisa Mawani is assistant professor of sociology at the University of British Columbia. She is a socio-legal historian who works on histories of imperialism and colonialism. She has published widely on law and (post)coloniality and law and geography, and her articles have appeared in many journals. She has just completed her first book, *Colonial Proximities: Crossracial Contacts and Juridical Truths in British Columbia, 1871–1921*.

Frances Bula has been writing about urban issues and city politics in Vancouver since 1994, first for the *Vancouver Sun* and recently for *Vancouver Magazine*, the *Globe and Mail*, and *BC Business*. She lives in central Vancouver and is both delighted and exasperated by her city. She has won numerous awards, including the Atkinson Fellowship in Public Policy, Canada's most prestigious journalism award, for a project on housing and homelessness.

Larry Beasley is the retired director of Planning for the City of Vancouver and now the distinguished practice professor of Planning at the University of British Columbia and the founding principal of Beasley and Associates, an international planning consultancy through which he teaches and advises the private sector and governments around the world. He is the vice president for planning of a major Canadian development company, Aquilini Development and is a member of the Order of Canada.

David Beers is founding editor of the *Tyee*. He has won national awards for his journalism in Canada and the United States, writing for the *Globe and Mail*, *Vancouver Magazine*, the *New York Times Magazine*, *Harper's*, *National Geographic*, and many other publications. He is the author of *Blue Sky Dream*, a memoir of growing up in Cold-War, suburban California. He is a founding member of IMPACS, a Vancouver non-profit firm providing media help to non-profit groups, former vice chair of the Vancouver City Planning Commission, and a lecturer at the UBC School of Journalism.

Witold Rybczynski is the Meyerson professor of Urbanism at the University of Pennsylvania. He is the author of numerous books, including an award-winning biography of Frederick Law Olmsted. He received the Vincent Scully Prize in 2008.

Erick Villagomez is one of the founding editors of *re:place Magazine*. He is also an educator, independent researcher, and designer with academic and professional interests in the human settlements at all scales. His private practice—Metis Design|Build—is an innovative practice dedicated to a collaborative and ecologically responsible approach to the design and construction of places.

Lance Berelowitz graduated in architecture and is a professional urban planner based in Vancouver, where he provides consulting services to the private and public sectors. Lance is also an accomplished communicator, writer, and public consultation expert. His book, *Dream City: Vancouver and the Global Imagination*, won the 2005 City of Vancouver Book Award.

Marcus Youssef is a writer, director, and actor, and is currently artistic producer of Neworld Theatre in Vancouver. His plays have been produced across North America, Europe, and in Australia. They include: *A Line in the Sand*, *Adrift*, *Ali and Ali and the aXes of Evil*, and the *Bobsledder of Baghdad*.

Francisco Ibanez-Carrasco, Canadian Chilean, is a writer, teacher, and AIDS activist, who has lived on the Drive in Vancouver since 1986. He works as a community-based researcher in Vancouver and in the individualized bachelor of fine arts program at Goddard College.

Harsha Walia is a South Asian activist and writer based in Vancouver, Coast Salish Territories. Over the past decade she has been active in a variety of movements: migrant justice, anti-racist, feminist, Indigenous sovereignty, Palestine solidarity, anti-capitalist, South Asian community organizing, and anti-poverty struggles. She is currently involved in No One Is Illegal, Boycott Israeli Apartheid Campaign, South Asian Network for Secularism and Democracy, Olympics Resistance Network, and works at the DTES Women Centre.

Wayde Compton's books include *49th Parallel Psalm*, *Performance Bond*, and *Bluesprint: Black British Columbian Literature and Orature*. He lives in Vancouver, where he is working on a new book called *Liquidities: Essays on Race, Writing and Region*.

Carmen Mills is a co-founder of Car Free Vancouver and the Car-Free Commercial Drive Festival, and of *Momentum: The Magazine for Self-propelled People*. She is a graphic designer and event organizer, currently working with the Be The Change Earth Alliance. Carmen is dedicated to bringing down the insane Gateway Project via her website www.gatewaysucks.org and is a vocal proponent of reclaiming public space and Fun for Free.

Rex Burkholder first joined the Portland Metro Council in 2001, hoping to use his energy, skills, and the knowledge that he gained as a community activist to help create a sustainable region. Now in his third term representing District 5, he is proud of the progress made toward this goal. For example, he sponsored and now leads Metro's Regional Climate Action Strategy, working with regional businesses, governments, and residents to combat climate change.

Gordon Price is the director of the City Program at Simon Fraser University. In 2002, he finished his sixth term as a City Councilor in Vancouver and also served on the Board of the Greater Vancouver Regional District and was appointed to the first Board of the Greater Vancouver Transportation Authority (TransLink) in 1999. Mr. Price is a regular lecturer on transportation and land use for the City of Portland (Oregon) and the Portland State University. He sits on the boards of the Sightline Institute and the International Centre for Sustainable Cities.

Jenny Wai Ching Kwan is the member of the legislative assembly for Vancouver–Mount Pleasant. She was first elected in 1996 and two years later became British Columbia's first Chinese-Canadian cabinet minister to serve as Minister of Municipal affairs. Jenny also served as minister of Women's Equality and minister of Community Development, Cooperatives and Volunteers and was the provincial government's lead person in developing the Vancouver Agreement. Prior to that, Jenny was elected to the Vancouver City Council in 1993, becoming the youngest councilor in Vancouver's history.

Michael Geller is a Vancouver-based architect, planner, real estate consultant, and developer with four decades of experience in the public, institutional, and private sectors. Notable projects include UniverCity at Simon Fraser University, Bayshore in Coal Harbour, and the early phases of the redevelopment of the South Shore of False Creek.

John Emmeus Davis is a partner and co-founder of Burlington Associates in Community Development LLC, a national consulting cooperative. Davis served for ten years as Burlington, Vermont's Housing Director. Prior to that he worked for the Institute for Community Economics in Cincinnati and Boston and spent five years working as a community organizer in the Appalachian region of east Tennessee. Davis holds a PhD from Cornell University and has taught and written widely.

Am Johal is a social activist and founding board member of the Impact on Communities Coalition, initiator of the 2010

Homelessness Hunger Strike Relay, and an organizer with Vancouver Flying University. He has a masters of economics from the Institute for Social and European Studies in Hungary.

David Eby is the Executive Director of the B.C. Civil Liberties Association and an adjunct professor of law at the University of British Columbia. He is also the President of the Canadian HIV/AIDS Legal Network, a research associate with the Canadian Centre for Policy Alternatives, and a regular commentator on CBC, CTV, and Global national news.

David Tracey is a journalist and environmental designer who owns and operates EcoUrbanist, an environmental design and media company. He is the author of *Guerrilla Gardening: A Manualfesto*, is the executive director of Tree City, an ecological engagement group "helping people and trees grow together" and coordinates the Vancouver Community Agriculture Network to create more community gardens, especially among people lacking access to healthy, affordable food.

Conrad Schmidt is the founder of the Work Less Party. He is the author of *Workers of the World Relax: The Simple Economics of Less Work* and the director of *Five Ring Circus: The True Costs of the 2010 Olympics*.

Dustin Rivers is a Skwxwú7mesh-Kwakwaka'wakw activist, artist, writer, and blogger who lives on the Capilano Indian Reserve 5 on the North Shore. Among his current projects is a podcast that will help young people from the Squamish Nation learn the Skwxwú7mesh language.

* These are just the folks I sat down and conducted sustained interviews with. You will note that there are many other people whom I talked with more briefly, consulted, or asked specific questions of. Those people I did not include biographies for, but I am sure that you can find them if you want to talk with them and learn more about their work.

Photo Credits:

(All unattributed photos throughout the chapters taken in Vancouver, British Columbia by the photographers listed below.)

Page 4: Keith Lennig
Page 13: Matt Hern, Diana Hart, Diana Hart
Page 14: Diana Hart, Diana Hart, Matt Hern
Page 19: Matt Hern
Page 29: All images by Diana Hart
Page 30: All images by Diana Hart
Page 47: Diana Hart, Diana Hart, Matt Hern
Page 48: All images by Diana Hart
Page 61: Keith Lennig
Page 71: Diana Hart, Matt Hern, Matt Hern
Page 72: All images by Diana Hart
Page 95: All images by Diana Hart
Page 96: Matt Hern, Diana Hart, Diana Hart
Page 115: Diana Hart, Matt Hern
Page 116: Diana Hart, Diana Hart, Matt Hern
Page 135: All images by Diana Hart
Page 136: All images by Diana Hart
Page 157: All images by Diana Hart
Page 158: All images by Diana Hart
Page 165: Diana Hart
Page 181: Matt Hern, Diana Hart, Diana Hart
Page 182: Diana Hart, Keith Lennig
Page 187: Diana Hart
Page 197: All images by Diana Hart
Page 198: Diana Hart, Diana Hart, Matt Hern
Page 214: Matt Hern

Notes

1. E
VAN
S
T
2. For example, an October 2008 Organization for Economic Co-Operation and Development report found that "Canada's poverty and income inequality rates spiked between 1995 and 2005 until they both exceeded the 30-member organization's average.... While the report found only six percent of seniors were impoverished, it said 15 percent of Canada's children were living below the poverty line." From Michelle McQuigge, "Rich-Poor Gap Widens in Canada," *Globe and Mail*, National Online, March 31, 2009, http://www.theglobeandmail.com/news/national/article717822.ece.
3. Canadian Council on Social Development, "Census Shows Growing Polarization of Income in Canada." http://www.ccsd.ca/pr/2003/censusincome.htm.
4. Statistics Canada, "Income Trends in Canada," http://www.statcan.ca/bsolc/english/bsolc?catno=13F0022X&CHROPG=1.
5. Mark Mazower, *Salonica: City of Ghosts* (New York: Knopf, 2005), 5.
6. Ibid, 11.
7. Cole Harris, *The Resettlement of British Columbia* (Vancouver: UBC Press, 1997), xi–xii.
8. Randy Shore, "Damage to Stanley Park will take years to set right," *Vancouver Sun*, December 20, 2006.
9. *The News Herald*, October 30, 1939.
10. City of Vancouver, *Stanley Park Master Plan, Draft Report*, Board of Parks and Recreation document, 1985, 2–14.
11. Jean Barman, *Stanley Park's Secret* (Madeira Park, BC: Harbour Publishing, 2005), 43–44.
12. Ibid., 92.
13. Randy Shore, "Before Stanley Park: First nations sites lie scattered throughout the area," *Vancouver Sun*, March 17, 2007.
14. Vancouver Board of Park and Recreation, "Stanley Park Landmarks: Totem Poles," http://www.city.vancouver.bc.ca/Parks/parks/stanley/landmarks.htm.
15. Vickie Jensen, *The Totem Poles of Stanley Park* (Vancouver: West Coast Words, 2004), 68.
16. Barman, *Stanley Park's Secret*, 235.

17. Kevin Griffin, "Coast Salish Welcome Visitors to Stanley Park Totem Pole Site," *Vancouver Sun*, June 10, 2008. http://www.canada.com/vancouversun/news/westcoastnews/story.html?id=821c75e8-424a-4e05-9f0f-50d2739bb3be.
18. Orhan Pamuk, *Istanbul: Memories and the City* (New York: Knopf, 2005), 91.
19. Ibid., 41–42.
20. Eighteenth and nineteenth century waterfront mansion of Pashas.
21. Gross.
22. Charles Montgomery, "Futureville," *Canadian Geographic*, May/June 2006, 44.
23. Alan Ehrenhalt, "Extreme Makeover," *Governing*, July 2006, http://www.governing.com/archive/archive/2006/jul/downtown.txt.
24. Lance Berelowitz, "The Myth of Dense Vancouver," *The Tyee*, June 21, 2006.
25. Ehrenhalt, "Extreme Makeover."
26. Montgomery, "Futureville," 51.
27. Something like one hundred thousand people.
28. That stat is deceiving, though, because that's 20 percent just of the core city—the City of Vancouver which has a population under 600,000—but the larger Vancouver, the Metro, is 2.2 million. So, that percentage is really contingent on how you count.
29. Trevor Boddy, "Insight: Downtown Vancouver's Last Resort: How Did 'Living First' Become 'Condos Only'?," *ArchNewsNow*, August 11, 2005.
30. Quoted in Ehrenhalt, "Extreme Makeover."
31. David Owen, "Green Manhattan," *New Yorker*, October 18, 2004, 111.
32. These acronyms stand for: "Not in my back yard" and "build absolutely nothing anywhere near anything."
33. And surely, *surely* I would never resort to such gratuitously juvenile name-calling (except possibly in the sanctity of my own home).
34. David Beers, "A Clear View of Vancouver," *The Tyee*, May 25, 2005.
35. See for example, Manuel Castells, *The Urban Question* (Cambridge, Massachusetts: MIT Press, 1977) or Michael Dear and Allen Scott, *Urbanization and Urban Planning in Capitalist Society* (New York: Methuen, 1981).
36. Lance Berelowitz, *Dream City* (Vancouver: Douglas and McIntyre, 2005), 245.
37. You can find them at: http://www.city.vancouver.bc.ca/parks/info/regs/parkscontrolbylaw.pdf.
38. Chantal Eustace, "Park Bylaws," *Vancouver Sun*, September 08, 2007.

39. Look, I am not going to make any claims of even being a passable dresser. I've been wearing essentially the same clothes since I was fifteen. But if anything is going to make me start dressing better it's coming back from Montreal and seeing an entire city wearing MEC fleece, logo-laden Lycra bike gear, and hiking boots.
40. Even calling it a "vibe" feels a little embarrassingly Left-Coastish.
41. See, for example, *Home: A History of An Idea*, *The Most Beautiful House in the World*, *City Life* and *Waiting for the Weekend*, among many others.
42. Chris Alexander, *The Nature of Order: Book Two—The Process of Creating Life* (Berkeley, CA: The Center for Environmental Structure, 2002).
43. Ibid., 204.
44. Ibid., 12.
45. See Bruce Macdonald's beautiful *Vancouver: A Visual History* (Vancouver: Talonbooks, 1992) for more on the transformation of Vancouver's geography.
46. Visit www.strathconagardens.ca for more information.
47. Canadian Mortgage and Housing Corporation, *Housing Facts*, September 2004, http://dsp-psd.pwgsc.gc.ca/Collection-R/CMHC/NH12-13E/NH12-13-2004-9E.pdf.
48. Canwest News Service, "Montreal Rent the Most Affordable of Major Cities," November 1, 2007. http://www.canada.com/topics/news/national/story.html?id=a9ffa463-5a15-4f9e-b555-11bc18dd1879&k=5335.
49. The youth arts and activism center that I direct.
50. Statistics Canada, "Community Profiles," 2006.
51. Statistics Canada, 2007.
52. See the Canadian Criminal Justice Association website (http://www.ccja-acjp.ca/en/abori2.html).
53. Statistics Canada, "Community Profiles," 2006.
54. One of my favorite examples of this, and one I use often in classes, is Aesop's fable, *The Town Mouse and the Country Mouse*. Check it out sometime. It has exactly the kind of underlying cynicism and hostility that genteel Western culture has always articulated about the city, often with a very real xenophobia and mistrust of the immigrants that have always come to cities. And, in many retellings, there is a barely-suppressed racism.
55. Winona LaDuke, *"Honor the Earth: Our Native American Legacy,"* in Winona LaDuke, *The Winona LaDuke Reader* (Penticton, BC: Theytus Books, 2002), 180.
56. Michael Woolcock and Deepa Narayan, quoted in *Democracies in Flux*, ed. Robert Putnam (New York: Oxford University Press, 2002), 6.

57. No comment.
58. I'm not going to keep putting quotes around diversity, but let it stand that I think it a highly problematic term.
59. John Lloyd, "Study paints bleak picture of ethnic diversity," *London Financial Times*, October 8, 2006.
60. Robert Putnam, "E Pluribus Unum: Diversity and Community in the Twenty-first Century," *Scandinavian Political Studies* 2 (2007): 137–299.
61. International Organization for Migration, "Global Estimates and Trends," http://www.iom.int/jahia/Jahia/about-migration/facts-and-figures/global-estimates-and-trends.
62. City of Vancouver, *Social Indicators and Trends Report*, March 2009.
63. Those places aren't communities, they're something else. Not something trivial, but I think it is really important to keep insisting that community has to be about *place* if it is going to retain political impact. That's a lot longer argument—maybe check out my book *Watch Yourself* (Vancouver: New Star Books, 2007) for a further explanation of why I think this is so important. Or better yet, read any Wendell Berry that you can get your hands on.
64. I don't know why this seems relevant here exactly, but it keeps coming to mind as I'm writing this, maybe just for reference: the City of Vancouver's total 2009 budgeted revenues are projected at $902 million (CAN). A single B-2 Stealth bomber, of which the United States Air Force currently has twenty-one, costs $2.1 billion (US) per aircraft (in 1997 dollars). The 2010 Olympics are publishing an operating budget of $1.76 billion (CAN) for the two-week event.
65. Jane Jacobs, *The Death and Life of Great American Cities* (New York: Vintage, 1992), 114–117.
66. Ibid.
67. Iris Young, "The Ideal of Community and the Politics of Difference," in *The Blackwell City Reader*, ed. Gary Bridge and Sophie Watson (Malden, Massachusetts: Blackwell Publishers, 2002), 431–38.
68. Ivan Illich, interviewed by Jerry Brown, *We the People*, KPFA, March 22, 1996.
69. I'm getting a little cute here and referencing *Learning from Las Vegas*, the seminal, 1972 book by Venturi, Brown, and Izenour which caused a huge stir in architecture, design, and planning by demanding that Vegas be considered seriously. The authors contended that there was a lot of value in neon signs, gaudy iconography, urban

sprawl, and cheap design. Loosely speaking, it was an attack on elitist architecture and a call to reinvigorate thinking about buildings and space from a mass-appeal perspective: that is, everyday people liked Vegas for good reasons and the rest our cities should start figuring that out and replicating it to a certain extent. More on this later.

70. In a survey by Forbes. Zack O'Malley Greenburg, *Forbes*, "America's Most Dangerous Cities," April 23, 2009, http://www.forbes.com/2009/04/23/most-dangerous-cities-lifestyle-real-estate-dangerous-american-cities.html. The first three in order were Detroit, Memphis, and Miami.
71. Marc Cooper, *The Last Honest Place in America* (New York: Nation Books, 2004), 60, 64.
72. The largest gambling company in the world.
73. Which kind of begs the question: Is vice really vice if its legal, encouraged, sanctioned, expected, and commonplace?
74. Place Brands: Places With Purpose, "Place Branding," http://www.placebrands.net/placebranding/placebranding.html.
75. This last item will be turned into high-end condos after the Olympics and includes a beautiful, swanky new community center.
76. The most recently available, comprehensive data.
77. All data from Metro Vancouver, "2006 Census Bulletin #11: Jobs in Metro Vancouver," http://www.metrovancouver.org/about/publications/Publications/2006_Census_Bulletin_11_Jobs.pdf.
78. Sorry about that. It was just sitting there.
79. Cy Ryan, "Jobless Rate Leaps to 13% in Las Vegas," *Las Vegas Sun*, August 21, 2009. http://www.lasvegassun.com/news/2009/aug/21/jobless-rate-leaps-131-percent-las-vegas/.
80. Data from Wells Fargo, "2009 *Nevada Wells Fargo Economics Regional Analysis,*" https://www.wellsfargo.com/downloads/pdf/com/research/reg_reports/rr_lasvegas022009.pdf.
81. And I mean that very literally. It's hard to believe how many glassy tower condos just keep springing up here. That's how we get that crazy concentration of high-rises.
82. The brochure for the development reads: "This is living in the village. It is said the Spanish have the greatest capacity to enjoy life. You can too at España. Olé!"
83. Michael Sorkin, "See You in Disneyland," in *Variations on a Theme Park*, ed. Michael Sorkin (New York: Noonday Press, 1992), 232.
84. A provincially-driven massive expansion of bridges and highways that will facilitate a huge increase in car and truck traffic through our and many other neighborhoods that is (haltingly) underway.
85. Not all that hard to do when we don't pay anyone!

86. For a good example, see: Connie Ozawa, *The Portland Edge* (Portland: Portland State University, 2004).
87. Statistics all from the cities' websites (www.portlandonline.com and www.vancouver.ca). For some good comparative data, see City of Vancouver Planning Department, "West Coast CityFacts 2003," http://vancouver.ca/commsvcs/cityplans/4CitiesFacts03.pdf.
88. Ibid.
89. All numbers from the Real Estate Board of Greater Vancouver, "Housing Price Index for Greater Vancouver," http://www.rebgv.org/housing-price-index?region=all&type=all&date=2009-04-01.
90. Carlito Pablo, "Vancouver Has the Highest Rents In Canada," *Georgia Straight*, June 11, 2009. http://www.straight.com/article-229579/metro-vancouver-has-highest-rent-canada.
91. If you're scoring along at home, that's a very reasonable $1400 per month average.
92. S.C. Bourassa and M. Hoesli, "Why Do the Swiss Rent?" *Journal of Real Estate Finance and Economics*, August 5, 2008.
93. Lance Berelowitz, "The Myth of Dense Vancouver," *The Tyee,* June 21, 2006, http://thetyee.ca/Views/2006/06/21/DenseVancouver/.
94. For example, see this study: Burlington Associates, "Permanently Affordable Homeownership," http://www.burlingtonassociates.net/resources/archives/resale%20complete.pdf.
95. (!)
96. (!)
97. Mario Maffi, *New York City: An Outsider's Inside View* (Columbus: Ohio State University, 2004), 13.
98. For a more complete story, see: Neil Smith, "New City, New Frontier: The Lower East Side as Wild, Wild West," in ed. Michael Sorkin, *Variations on a Theme Park* (New York: Noonday Press, 1992).
99. To steal a line from Naomi Klein.
100. For example, see Franklin Zimring, *The Great American Crime Decline* (New York: Oxford University Press, 2006). But really there is an avalanche of journal articles, books, websites, and position papers documenting this decline. Two avalanches. You won't have to look hard for information and data.
101. Here too. The debate about crime declines in the United States and New York City has been exhaustively documented. There are endless resources on these arguments.
102. Levitt more famously posed the same argument again with Stephen Dubner in *Freakonomics: A Rouge Economist Explores the Hidden Side of Everything* (New York: HarperCollins, 2005).

103. John J., Donohue and Stephen Levitt, “The Impact of Legalized Abortion on Crime,” *The Quarterly Journal of Economics* CXVI, 2 (2001): 379–380.
104. Ibid., 414.
105. Among others, see: Ted Joyce, “Did Legalized Abortion Lower Crime?” *Journal of Human Resources* 39, 1 (2004): 1–28.
106. George Kelling and James Wilson, “Broken Windows,” *Atlantic Magazine*, March 1982, 29.
107. City of Vancouver, Office of the Mayor, *Project Civil City Main Report,* November 2006.
108. Ibid.
109. Monte Paulson, “Mayor Sullivan's Big Ambitions,” *The Tyee*, December 21, 2006.
110. For example, see: Rob Annandale, “City Progress Questioned,” *The Tyee,* November 14, 2007.
111. Various *Sun*, *Province*, and *24 Hour* headlines. Exclamation points mine.
112. Cornell West, interview by Henry Louis Gates, Jr., *Frontline*, *PBS*, http://www.pbs.org/wgbh/pages/frontline/shows/race/interviews/west.html.
113. Doug Ward, “Past Thirty Years Not Kind to Families,” *Vancouver Sun*, March 10, 2009.
114. I haven't said nearly as much as I could or should about the impact and scope of criminal networks in Vancouver and their relationship to the urban future. Perhaps the best and most thoughtful writing on this subject is by Manual Castells, whom I can't recommend highly enough, especially his *The Information Age: Economy, Society, and Culture* (Malden, Massachusetts: Blackwell Publishers), published as a trilogy: *The Rise of the Network Society* (1996), *The Power of Identity* (1997), and *End of Millennium* (1998).
115. Don Cayo, “The Bottom Line of Crime,” *www.canada.com,* June 10, 2005, http://www.canada.com/vancouver/vancouversun/features/nna/story.html?id=3d4c6098-8c72-4852-ac3b-540a91831d97.
116. That actually is six dollars an hour for the first five hundred hours of your first job before it bumps up to the lofty eight bucks an hour.
117. Can you believe that? The richest city in Canada by most every measure, and the province has the lowest minimum wage. Even really have-not provinces like New Brunswick, where the cost of living is vastly lower, have higher minimum wages. Quebec's is $9. Ontario's is $9.50 etc. Stay classy, BC.
118. Am Johal, “UN Observer: ‘Massive Crisis’ in Vancouver,” *The Tyee,* October 31, 2007.

119. Metro Vancouver, *2008 Homeless Count Final Report,* December 2008.
120. Canadian Centre for Policy Alternatives, "BC's Growing Gap: Family Income Inequality 1976–2006," http://www.growinggap.ca/files/CCPA_growing_gap_full_report.pdf.
121. First Call, "Child Poverty Report Card," http://www.firstcallbc.org/economicEquality-whatsNew.html.
122. Jeffrey Reiman, *The Rich Get Richer and the Poor Get Prison* (Boston: Allyn and Bacon, 2007), 4.
123. Ibid., 171.
124. BC Injury Research and Prevention Unit, "Injury Facts," http://www.injuryresearch.bc.ca/categorypages.aspx?catid=1&subcatid=44.
125. Chad Skelton, "Traffic Fatalities Drop to a Six-Year low," *Vancouver Sun*, February 23, 2009, http://www.vancouversun.com/news/traffic+fatalities+drop+year/1320484/story.html.
126. Chad Skelton, "2008 A Record Year for Murders in BC," *Vancouver Sun*, March 5, 2009, http://www2.canada.com/2008+record+year+murders/1358228/story.html?id=1358228.
127. Chad Skelton, "How Much Risk Do You Live With?," *Vancouver Sun*, March 9, 2007, http://www.canada.com/vancouversun/story.html?id=d5262c0c-ebd3-479a-a700-954dfa7d063d&k=24437.
128. Matthew Ramsey, "Granville Strip Closures Curb Violence," *The Province*, August 07, 2007, http://www.canada.com/theprovince/news/story.html?id=f1368d0a-3006-4910-a704-8b78d8a9d288&k=28051.
129. Gross.
130. Pete McMartin, "The poor struggle to be heard in a sea of affluent 'experts,'" *Vancouver Sun*, June 22, 2006.
131. Simon Compaore, "Local Public Finances and Decentralization" (presentation, World Urban Forum, Vancouver, BC, June 20, 2006).
132. Brian Field, "Municipal Finance: Innovation and Collaboration," (presentation, World Urban Forum, Vancouver, BC, June 21, 2006).
133. Dan Hoornweg, "Engaging the Private Sector in Sustainable Urban Development: Frameworks for Sustainable Partnerships" (presentation, World Urban Forum, Vancouver, BC, June 21, 2006).
134. Jacqueline Shafer, "Municipal Finance: Innovation and Collaboration," (presentation, World Urban Forum, Vancouver, BC, June 21, 2006). The total cost of the Karnataka project, for example, will be "$310 million. The share of World Bank, State Government and ULBs [urban local bodies] is 74 percent, 16 percent and 10 percent respectively. The duration of the project is five years and it will be executed from the coming financial year. The rate of interest on bank

loan is six percent." "World Bank clears $216-million loan for State project," *The Hindu: India's National Newspaper*, March 16, 2006. http://www.hindu.com/2006/03/16/stories/2006031615990500.htm.

135. Really. I didn't make that up. Look it up.
136. Kenny Bruno and Joshua Karliner, *Earthsummit.biz: The Corporate Takeover of Sustainable Development* (Oakland, CA: Food First Books, 2002), 22.
137. Unidentified participant, speaking during "Energy, Local Action, Global Impact" (World Urban Forum, Vancouver, BC, June 22, 2006).
138. Some of these numbers are up for debate, but the basic narrative is really not. The best telling of this story that I know is the widely available movie, *Seeds in the City: the Greening of Havana*, DVD, produced by Knowledge in Action (Ottawa, Sound Development Communications Media, 2003).
139. Michael Pollen, "Why Bother?" *New York Times Magazine*, April 20, 2008.
140. The first full day that we were there, I attempted to cut cross-country from one beach to the next, failing to heed warnings about these bushes. Within about thirty steps, one of the thorns had pierced straight through the sole of my new sandals and impaled my foot. It took me about ten minutes, sweating, bleeding profusely, and cussing to get the damn thing out, after which I retreated, chastened, back to the sand. I am not sure what they are called, but I highly advise you not to fuck with them.
141. That seems like a lot to me, but it is true that there just isn't much of a tourist presence anywhere.
142. Michael Specter, "The Last Drop," *New Yorker*, October 23, 2006.
143. That's New York, Paris, Baghdad, Moscow, London, Cairo, Rome, Seoul, Shanghai, Buenos Aires, and Kolkata respectively, if you're scoring along at home.
144. Chris Alexander, Sara Ishikawa, and Murray Silverstein, *A Pattern Language* (New York: Oxford, 1977), 323.
145. Lance Berelowitz, *Dream City* (Vancouver: Douglas and McIntyre, 2005), 244, 246.
146. Ibid., 163.
147. Alexander et al, *A Pattern Language,* 643 (emphasis in original).
148. Berelowitz, *Dream City*, 163.
149. J.P. Goubert, *The Conquest of Water* (Princeton, NJ: Princeton University Press, 1986), 69–70.
150. Ivan Illich, *H2O and the Waters of Forgetfulness* (London: Marion Boyers, 1986), 47.

151. Ibid., 1.
152. Our friend Madonna has, of course, taken high-end hydration one step further. She reportedly spent $10,000 (US) per month on blessed, bottled Kabbalah Water in 2008. Maybe she needs that kind of quality to wash the smell of A-Rod off. The product's site says: "The Kabbalistic blessings and meditations that are used to create Kabbalah Water bring about elegant and balanced crystalline structures in water, while negative consciousness has an opposite effect." Totally. See www.kabbalahwater.com.
153. Garance Burke, "As Supplies Dry Up, Growers Pass on Farming and Sell Water," *SFGate.com,* January 23, 2008, http://www.sfgate.com/cgi-bin/article.cgi?f=/n/a/2008/01/23/financial/f133811S29.DTL.
154. Alexander et al, *A Pattern Language*, 136. (emphasis in original).
155. For example, see: Patrick Malone, *City, Capital, and Water* (New York: Routledge, 1996).
156. William Rees, "What if…," *Alternatives Journal*, June 18, 2009, http://www.alternativesjournal.ca/articles/what-if.

About the Author: Matt Hern

Matt lives and works in East Vancouver with his partner and daughters. He founded, and for nine years has directed the Purple Thistle Centre, an all-ages youth-run community center for arts and activism. Among his other projects is a youth exchange program with an isolated town in northern Canada designed to bring native and non-native kids together to live, work, and travel.

Matt also founded Car-Free Vancouver Day in 2005 which has blossomed into an annual event with sites across the city that sees 150,000 people in the streets.

His books and writing have been published on all six continents and translated into ten languages. He writes features and articles for a wide variety of publications, and continues to lecture globally.

He is the author of *Field Day* (New Star, 2003) and *Watch Yourself: Why Safer Isn't Always Better* (New Star, 2007), and the editor of *Deschooling Our Lives* (New Society, 1996), and *Everywhere, All the Time* (AK Press, 2008).

Matt holds a PhD in Urban Studies and lectures at SFU and UBC in Urban Studies and Education departments and is on faculty at the Institute for Social Ecology and Prescott College in Arizona. He remains active in a number of movements in Vancouver, is a food security activist, avid gardener and unrepentant sports fan. For more info, be sure to visit his website: www.mightymatthern.com.

Support AK Press!

AK Press is one of the world's largest and most productive anarchist publishing houses. We're entirely worker-run and democratically managed. We operate without a corporate structure—no boss, no managers, no bullshit. We publish close to twenty books every year, and distribute thousands of other titles published by other like-minded independent presses from around the globe.

The Friends of AK program is a way that you can directly contribute to the continued existence of AK Press, and ensure that we're able to keep publishing great books just like this one! Friends pay a minimum of $25 per month, for a minimum three month period, into our publishing account. In return, Friends automatically receive (for the duration of their membership), as they appear, one free copy of every new AK Press title. They're also entitled to a 20% discount on everything featured in the AK Press Distribution catalog and on the website, on any and every order. You or your organization can even sponsor an entire book if you should so choose!

There's great stuff in the works—so sign up now to become a Friend of AK Press, and let the presses roll!

Won't you be our friend? Email friendsofak@akpress.org for more info, or visit the Friends of AK Press website:
http://www.akpress.org/programs/friendsofak